It's Hardly
Sportin'

It's Hardly Sportin'

Stadiums, Neighborhoods, and the New Chicago

COSTAS SPIROU and

LARRY BENNETT

NORTHERN ILLINOIS UNIVERSITY PRESS

© 2003 by Northern Illinois University Press
Published by the Northern Illinois University Press,
DeKalb, Illinois 60115
Manufactured in the United States using
acid-free paper
All Rights Reserved
Design by Julia Fauci

Library of Congress Cataloging-in-Publication Data
Spirou, Costas.
It's hardly sportin': stadiums, neighborhoods,
and the new Chicago / Costas Spirou and
Larry Bennett.
        p.   cm.
Includes bibliographical references and index.
ISBN 0-87580-305-9 (alk. paper)
1. Stadiums—Economic aspects—Illinois—
Chicago. 2. City planning—Illinois—Chicago.
I. Bennett, Larry, 1950–. II. Title.
GV415.S65 2003
725'.827—dc21
2002141421

Portions of chapters 5 and 6 are adapted from
Spirou and Bennett's "Revamped Stadium" Urban
Affairs Review (37/5), pp. 675–702, copyright 2002
by Sage Publications. Repinted by Permission of
Sage Publications.

To Patrice and Gwyn for their enduring support and commitment

Contents

Illustrations and Maps   ix

Acknowledgments   xi

Introduction   3

1   **Sports-Driven Urban Redevelopment in Chicago and Beyond**   11

2   **From Urban Renewal to the City of Leisure**   37

3   **The New Comiskey Park**   *Economics, Politics, and Professional Sports Franchise Retention*   59

4   **Rebuilding Comiskey Park**   *The Elusive Link between Stadium Construction and Community Development*   83

5   **Bringing Light to Wrigley Field**   108

6   **Lake View**   *From Complete City to Port of Entry for All the Young People*   126

7   **Redeveloping the Near West Side**   *From Conflict to Collaboration*   142

8   **Stadium Development, Three Neighborhoods, and Urban Revitalization**   165

Appendix   187

Bibliography   193

Index   209

Illustrations and Maps

Illustrations

1   Old Comiskey Park   61

2   New and Old Comiskey Park   62

3   New Comiskey Park   76

4   Morrie O'Malley's   77

5   Philip Bess's Imagined Armour Field   95

6   Wrigley Field   109

7   The View from Wrigley Field   110

8   The United Center   143

9   United Center Replacement Housing   156

10 A Randolph Street Cafe   157

Maps

Chicago's Professional Sports Stadiums   6

The Comiskey Park Area   63

The Wrigley Field Area   111

The United Center and the Near West Side   144

Acknowledgments

Our work on *It's Hardly Sportin'* has been assisted by various friends, colleagues, and loved ones. Portions of the manuscript were read by Bob Beauregard and Terry Nichols Clark. We tip our hats to Adolph Reed and Pat Wright, who read entire drafts of the book. Each of these individuals offered useful suggestions, which we have turned to the benefit of the final version of the book. We would also like to acknowledge Susan Stall and Pat Wright (once more). Susan and Pat very kindly passed on to us research materials that were of great importance to our presentation of the full range of perspectives on the new Comiskey Park development. In regard to the Comiskey Park chapters we also thank Philip Bess for his good-spirited cooperation and, in particular, for providing us with illustrations of his proposed Armour Field project. Marsha McLaughlin and Jill Donovan at Jade Creative Services prepared our maps. At Northern Illinois University Press, Martin Johnson has been an author's editor, patient and supportive. On a personal level, we would like to thank Ploutarchos-Stylianos and Yvonni Spirou, Anthony and Mary Dades, and Stacy Popovich. Their support and commitment to education have proved critical. Finally, our wives, Patrice and Gwyn, lived with this project for several years. Their tolerance and support deserve special consideration. We think we might take them out to a ballgame next season—and leave our notepads at home.

Chicago, 2001

It's Hardly Sportin'

Introduction

As autumn approaches and the first signs of cooler weather appear in the Chicago metropolitan area, residents turn with great anticipation to the city's various professional sports teams. This is an important time for Chicago. Over the years, the city has earned the reputation as a sports-minded metropolis, the site of a unique sports culture that was exported around the world during Michael Jordan's heyday in the 1990s and has been lampooned across America courtesy of "Da Bears" fans on *Saturday Night Live*. Though at this moment many Chicagoans are girding themselves for the professional football season, hopeful that the Bears will once again ascend to the levels of success they enjoyed in the 1980s, football is by no means the only game in town. On the city's North and South Sides, the Cubs and the White Sox are concluding their regular seasons, and depending on their performance, they might still produce an epidemic of playoff fever. The Blackhawks and Bulls are also preparing for their upcoming seasons, trimming their rosters and seeking the right combinations of talent that might promote them to the ranks of their leagues' elite competitors.

Our book, by focusing on several recent stadium development projects in Chicago, demonstrates the increased social, political, and economic importance of sports in American culture and underlines the growing role sports are playing in urban economic development processes. The emergence of sports as a centerpiece of local development activity has followed in the wake of the broad restructuring of North American urban economies in the 1970s and 1980s. Since the 1980s, as many local economies have shifted from a manufacturing toward a service-sector base, and as national urban policy has pushed municipalities to scramble for locally derived revenues, cities have sought to identify alternative means to stimulate local job growth and enterprise development, as well as to pry loose greater and greater flows of consumer spending.

It is within this larger context that the promotion of cultural institutions, entertainment venues, and professional sports has moved to the center of local economic development agendas, often with the goal of attracting tourists (Judd and Fainstein 1999). Typifying contemporary cities' promotion of consumer-borne economic development are the following kinds of projects: conference and convention centers that cater to business and trade shows; stadiums for professional sports franchises; and museums, performing arts complexes, and entertainment districts seeking to tap the discretionary spending of out-of-town visitors. Tourism has come to be viewed as an economic diversifier, offering local governments a broader range of economic development alternatives and more varied revenue streams (Beauregard 1998).

The emergence of professional sports as a key entertainment sector and the increased dependence on sports as an economic growth engine pose a number of questions for observers concerned with the emerging social and physical form of American cities. During the past two decades American cities have experienced an unparalleled boom in stadium construction. Analysts of specific stadium development projects recognize soon enough that two types of issues come to the fore of the public debate—and, in some cases, the outright conflict—accompanying proposals to erect new sports arenas or substantially modify existing facilities. The first group of issues pertains to the broad contours of how these projects are promoted and executed. Specifically, what are the factors that advance sports franchises and facilities to the top of the local development checklist, and what role do they play in reinforcing the social fabric of their cities? On the ground, questions of the overall importance of sports franchises often become debates concerning what level of public funding is appropriate in support of these initiatives. The advancement of such projects also reveals crucial insights about the distribution of political influence in a city, as stadium advocates and opponents jockey to define in expansive or narrow terms who are likely to be the beneficiaries of completed stadium developments.

The second category of questions turns on the local effects of stadium projects. Although in the minds of their advocates stadium development projects always promise to sustain or even regenerate adjoining communities, local neighborhood residents routinely object to them. These conflicts open up various avenues of inquiry. Are stadium projects, as some opponents claim, typically visited upon racial and ethnic minority or low-income areas where the powers of resistance are limited? Do stadiums pay off for local neighborhoods in the way their proponents anticipate? Finally, how well do the ubiquitous new and refurbished stadiums fit within their adjoining cityscapes?

It's Hardly Sportin' addresses the political and economic context that gave shape to three major stadium projects in Chicago and examines those projects' neighborhood impact. The projects are the development of the new Comiskey Park in the tiny South Side enclave of South Armour Square (1991), the installation of lights at Wrigley Field in Lake View on the North Side (1988), and the construction of the United Center on the Near West Side (1994). In each instance, corporate, government, and civic supporters contended that the project would enhance its local environment and at the same time boost Chicago's entertainment, culture, and sports infrastructure. Nevertheless, residents of the neighborhoods adjoining the projects voiced significant opposition. We will identify the forces shaping each project, look at the process of defining each as a physical scheme, review the negotiations between project supporters and opponents, and offer a preliminary assessment of the long-term local consequences of these developments.

Chicago's stadium wars have not come to an end. As summer turned to autumn in 2001, substantial debate persisted over the plan of the City of Chicago, the State of Illinois, and the Chicago Bears to renovate Soldier Field on the lakefront just to the southeast of the Loop, Chicago's downtown business core. Moreover, in the summer of 2001 the Chicago Cubs released plans to expand Wrigley Field and construct a new multipurpose structure to the west of the ballpark. Predictably, neighborhood response in Lake View has been highly, if not uniformly, critical.

The current debates surrounding Soldier Field renovation and Wrigley Field expansion, respectively, illustrate the broader and more local issues associated with urban stadium construction. The Chicago Bears professional football franchise has sought a new stadium arrangement for more than fifteen years. A tenant of the Chicago Park District since the early 1970s, the Bears have long complained about playing-field maintenance and the obsolete infrastructure at Soldier Field. Over the last fifteen years the football franchise has blundered from one prospective stadium deal to another in suburban Chicago, in northwest Indiana, and in several city locations. In the summer of 2000 Bears officials and Chicago mayor Richard M. Daley settled old differences and jointly began to promote an ambitious renovation of Soldier Field and its surroundings. This most recent proposal to renovate Soldier Field promises to deliver to the football franchise a state-of-the-art sports facility wrapped in a historic stadium shell, while Mayor Daley will take another step in his campaign "to restore the Lakefront," a central piece of his administration's ongoing effort to improve Chicago's downtown and near-downtown public spaces (Osnos and Pearson 2000).

The cost of the Soldier Field renovation has fluctuated around the $600 million mark, with the Bears contributing $200 million, half of that coming from a loan from the National Football League, and the remaining $400 million financed by Chicago's 2 percent hotel-motel tax. The Illinois Sports Facilities Authority (ISFA), an agency created to oversee construction of the new Comiskey Park in the late 1980s, will issue bonds to cover the City's share of stadium construction costs. The physical plan specifies the construction of what amounts to a new football stadium set within, though also rising substantially above, the classical colonnades crowning

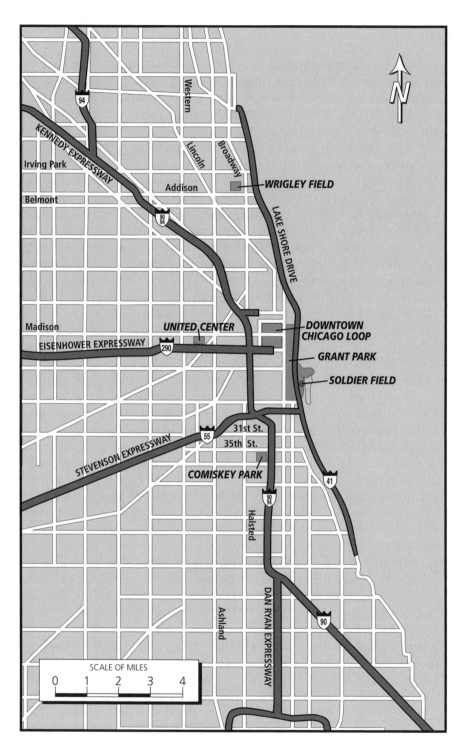

Chicago's Professional Sports Stadiums

Soldier Field's east and west facades. Extensive underground parking will be added, and current surface parking areas to the south of the stadium will be landscaped, adding more than fifteen acres of green space to the lakefront. A new main entrance will be built, with the aim of reducing traffic just north of the football stadium in the vicinity of the Field Museum and Shedd Aquarium (Washburn and Long 2000).

After many years of the Bears casting about for a new home stadium, once the franchise and Mayor Daley agreed to the current renovation scheme, state legislative approval for the renovation project's funding package, following Governor George Ryan's expression of support for the deal, was achieved with breathtaking speed in late 2000. Nonetheless, the approving votes of 33–24 in the Illinois Senate and 64–51 in the House of Representatives indicate that a substantial number of lawmakers were displeased either by the cost of the plan, or possibly by the haste with which it was pushed through their chambers (Long and Holt 2000). By early 2001, the only significant governmental hurdle that remained for the Soldier Field renovation was approval by the Chicago Plan Commission, the local agency that must review and affirm major development schemes along Chicago's Lake Michigan shoreline.

Yet over the next several months the plan to transform Soldier Field generated substantial opposition. The first group to take aim at the plan was a prominent public-space advocacy organization, the Friends of the Parks, which charged that the proposal violated the city's Lakefront Protection Ordinance. According to Erma Tranter, executive director of the group, "the planned seating bowl and steel upper deck would tower above the stadium, blocking lakefront views and conflicting with a part of the city's ordinance designed to enhance the character of the parks" (Challos 2001).

Soon enough the architectural and design features of the stadium renovation also came under fire. The firm of Lohan and Associates, in charge of the reconfiguration of Soldier Field, had indeed proposed a bold plan. Although their redesign sought to retain the classical facade elements of the original facility, their addition would tower above Soldier Field's exterior walls and colonnades. *Chicago Tribune* architecture critic Blair Kamin, who emerged as a vigorous critic of the Lohan design, referred to the proposed structure as a "monumental eyesore" (Kamin 2001b). Responding to Lohan and Associates' submission of a revised, slightly scaled-down design, Kamin commented: "If the team's original proposal for renovating the historic lakefront stadium resembled an enormous spaceship hovering over Soldier Field, then this latest version is that very same spaceship dressed up in a glass skirt" (Kamin 2001a).

The third front of resistance came from an unexpected source, local veterans groups. Following state approval of the Soldier Field financing package, representatives of the Bears had suggested that a portion of the franchise's contribution to the project could be raised by selling naming rights to a corporation, which could promote itself by associating its name with a beautifully refurbished sporting palace. To the Bears' surprise, local veterans took offense at the proposed commercialization of a facility that was dedicated in 1924 to the memory of those who had served in World War I. According to Patrick Quinn, an opponent of the renovation plan who is in touch with local veterans groups, "Every veteran I've talked to feels very strongly about this—they do not want Soldier Field renamed. That would desecrate the memory of the veterans for whom it was named" (Joravsky 2001, 5).

The various opponents of the Soldier Field renovation have also underlined the costliness of the project, typically contrasting the huge scale of the project to the limited uses to which Soldier Field will be devoted. In late August 2001, a *Chicago Tribune* editorial observed that an alternative stadium plan would be approximately $200 million cheaper than the approved renovation. Months earlier, Erma Tranter of the Friends of the Parks had observed that Soldier Field "will be used primarily 10 days—50 hours a year . . . all for the sole purpose of the Chicago Bears" (Challos 2001).

In March 2001 the Chicago Plan Commission and City Council approved the renovation, and by the summer ISFA had begun to sign contracts initiating the project (Ford 2001b). The Friends of the Parks, in turn, filed two lawsuits aiming to derail the project. One charged that the Chicago Plan Commission had failed to review in a responsible fashion the physical effects of the proposed renovation, thus leaving the lakefront unprotected; the second suit claimed that the issuing of no-bid contracts for the project, as mandated by the state enabling legislation, violated the Illinois constitution (Ford 2001a). By the summer of 2001, opponents of the renovation had enlisted the support of the Landmarks Preservation Council of Illinois (a nongovernmental group), which advanced an intriguing alternative proposal to site a new football stadium just north of Comiskey Park, thus permitting a more modest restoration of Soldier Field (Mendell 2001). In the wake of the series of Blair Kamin articles attacking the Soldier Field project, on August 22 the *Chicago Tribune* printed a long editorial praising the plan to build a new football stadium across 35th Street from Comiskey Park. The growing opposition to the Soldier Field renovation yielded some movement by the project's proponents: Lohan and Associates produced a slightly smaller bowl-within-the-colonnades plan, and the Bears backed away from selling naming rights to the rehabilitated stadium.

Another potential hurdle for the Soldier Field renovation was produced by the accelerated national economic downturn following the September 11, 2001, attacks on the Pentagon and World Trade Center, which threatens to reduce the hotel-motel tax revenues pledged to underwrite ISFA construction bonds (Washburn and Long 2001). Moreover, as we write this introduction, the Friends of the Parks' two lawsuits are still pending in Cook County Circuit Court. Nevertheless, the commitment of City of Chicago, ISFA, and Bears officials to the Soldier Field renovation seems undiminished, and it is our guess that some near variant of the present Soldier Field plan will be carried out. This will be in spite of mounting criticism of the overall cost of the project and its potential to degrade a prominent site in Chicago's highly prized Lake Michigan front yard.

Meanwhile, on Chicago's North Side a new Chicago Cubs plan to expand Wrigley Field emerged in the summer of 2001. Months before the Cubs unveiled their proposal on June 18, the press had reported discussions between the Cubs and the City of Chicago regarding the future of the Cubs' ballpark. The City, in turn, was considering whether to designate Wrigley Field a historic landmark (Washburn 2001a). The main features of the Wrigley Field expansion proposal include the addition of 2,100 right and left field bleacher spaces and 215 premium-priced seats behind home plate. West of Wrigley Field a new structure will house a parking garage, a restaurant, and the Cubs Hall of Fame. Most provocatively, the Cubs seek to increase the number of home night games from eighteen (the annual ceiling since 1988) to thirty. To the surprise of many, at the press conference to announce the Wrigley Field expansion plan, Mark McGuire, the team's executive vice president for baseball operations, claimed that the Cubs' finances were increasingly tenuous and that the expansion was necessary if the ball club were to "compete and stay in Wrigley Field" (Spielman 2001).

Many residents of the Lake View neighborhood adjoining Wrigley Field expressed anger and frustration in response to the Cubs' plans. Though Cubs representatives sought to win community support at various hearings in late summer 2001, local indignation at the prospect of additional night games was unyielding. Indeed, the local residents' concerns with traffic and litter control, parking enforcement, and general public safety, reflected stress points between the ballpark and the neighborhood dating to the initiation of night baseball in the late 1980s (Donato 2001).

The current debate over Wrigley Field modification features one new party, the owners of roof-deck facilities along Waveland and Sheffield Avenues who charge as much as one hundred dollars for a birds-eye view of a Cubs game across the street. The bleacher additions to Wrigley Field will elevate the ballpark's left and right field walls approximately twenty-five feet higher than they are at present, which is likely to diminish roof-deck views substantially (Hirsley and Washburn 2001). In early September 2001, even as negotiations between the Cubs and Lake View interests proceeded, representatives of Mayor Daley explained that Chicago zoning administrator Paul Woznicki had "resigned voluntarily after he realized he made a mistake." Woznicki's mistake was having assisted 44th Ward Alderman Bernard Hansen, whose City Council district includes the Wrigley Field area, in preparing a city ordinance that would have granted a zoning exception to building owners modifying their structures to accommodate "rooftop businesses" (Washburn 2001b).

By the early fall of 2001, Cubs president Andy MacPhail had adopted a revealing tone in describing his ball club's situation: "We're getting blockaded at every step. We've been voiceless for too long. It's time for someone to be an advocate, and I am trying to do it in the most straightforward fashion." News reports suggested that the Cubs were willing to accept an increase in night games that would fall short of their desired thirty, and with careful negotiation and some design modifications the additions to Wrigley Field were likely to be implemented (Greenstein 2001).

The current Soldier Field and Wrigley Field controversies illustrate the large-scale and neighborhood-level issues that are typically associated with sports development schemes. In the remainder of our book, as we explore these matters in greater detail, we will make the case that sports-related physical projects have become a keystone development strategy in contemporary cities and that they should be assessed accordingly. It is also our wish to advance the long-standing, though often implicit, project joined by so many other journalists and social scientists who have devoted their careers to documenting Chicago's fascinating local politics and neighborhood life, as well as the city's broader patterns of physical expansion, social conflict, and economic evolution.

1

Sports-Driven
Urban Redevelopment in
Chicago and Beyond

In the spring of 1995 the Colorado Rockies of Major League Baseball's National League moved into their new stadium. Coors Field, at the intersection of 20th and Blake Streets in Denver's Lower Downtown (LoDo) district, anchors an ambitious neighborhood redevelopment effort. The LoDo area initially achieved prominence at the end of the nineteenth century when it served as Denver's principal rail terminus. However, in recent decades LoDo's rail yards and warehouses had fallen into disuse and ill-repair. Coors Field, designed by the HOK Sports Facilities architectural firm of Kansas City, Missouri, is one of baseball's new breed, self-consciously old-style stadiums. The ballpark's seating capacity is a relatively modest 50,000, and its exterior, an exuberant mingling of brick facades, steel structural elements, and turn-of-the-century ornamentation, is intended to evoke older sporting palaces such as Boston's Fenway Park, Chicago's Wrigley Field, or the long-gone home of the Brooklyn Dodgers, Ebbets Field.

In defiance of the conventional wisdom regarding Americans' dependence on the automobile, only five thousand parking spaces have been provided in the vicinity of Coors Field. As a result, many of the sports fans who do drive to the ballpark must park at some distance from their destination and complete their pilgrimage on foot. This forced routing of foot traffic through the LoDo neighborhood has not held down attendance at Rockies games. During Coors Field's first year, the Rockies set eleven baseball attendance records, and more than eight million fans visited Coors Field during the 1996 and 1997 seasons (Ribadeneira 1997). The blocks adjoining Coors Field have similarly thrived. In the words of one observer, they are "awash in gentrified versions of old saloons" (Muschamp 1995). Approximately forty art galleries and numerous other shops also dot the LoDo neighborhood. Since the first ball was tossed at Coors Field, nearly one hundred bars and restaurants have opened in its environs.

Nor have the neighborhood's newly arrived crowds dampened enthusiasm for residential development. Before the Rockies' first game in Coors Field, there were approximately one thousand residential units in LoDo. By 1996, another two thousand units of housing had been added, with sixteen hundred more apartments and condominiums under construction. Most of this new housing has been carved out of the numerous lofts and warehouses in LoDo, whose industrial-era charms seem to have been underscored by the historicist flavor of the new ballpark. Investment has been so extensive that the Downtown Denver Partnership estimates the direct and indirect impact on the downtown at $200 million during Coors Field's first two years (McCartney 1996).

From a fiscal standpoint, the development of Coors Field represents a typical public-private partnership. In 1990, Denver residents approved a one-tenth of one percent sales tax increase in the six-county metropolitan area. The Rockies baseball franchise contributed $30 million, and the Coors Brewing Company paid $15 million in exchange for stadium naming rights. The stadium's total cost was $215.5 million, but given the Rockies' outstanding attendance record and the prevailing low interest rates, the publicly issued bonds may be retired in little more than a decade (Associated Press 1995a).

In spite of Coors Field's evident economic success, it is not universally admired. *New York Times* architecture critic Herbert Muschamp has dismissed the ballpark's willfully playful design as "arrested development in the innocent guise of nostalgia" (Muschamp 1998). From a practical standpoint, the explosion of development around Coors Field has posed some problems for local merchants. When the Rockies are on the road, parking lots near Coors Field charge $5, but when the baseball team plays at home, parking spaces can carry a fee of $15 to $20. At this level, many prospective visitors to LoDo who are not planning to attend a ball game are, in all likelihood, discouraged from making the excursion. Some estimates suggest that, at best, game days are "revenue neutral" for local retailers that are not sports oriented (Vasquez 1997).

Denver officials also insist that the redevelopment of LoDo is not solely attributable to the construction of Coors Field. Even before the Rockies moved into the neighborhood, LoDo was sprouting art galleries, coffee shops, and restaurants. The construction of the ballpark came at the right time and under the right conditions to fuel further redevelopment (McCartney 1996). Nevertheless, the development of Coors Field is an integral part of Denver's effort to upgrade its status as a tourist destination and promote itself as the cultural center of the Rocky Mountain region. The city's $64 million public library includes an impressive Western history collection. Denver is also home to the Tattered Cover Bookstore, the largest independent bookseller in the country. The city is equally proud of its recreational amenities, which include 200 parks, 70 golf courses, and 130 miles of paved biking roads. The recently opened Denver Performing Arts Complex boasts nine theaters with a combined seating capacity of 9,000 (Ribadeneira 1997). Moreover, in its quest to emphasize its cultural and recreational virtues Denver is unabashed in linking local amenities and consumer culture. Coors Field, for example, includes a professional sports first: a microbrewery located within the stadium complex. Nor is the Sandlot Brewing Company's principal product haphazardly named. To ensure that tippling sports fans remember where they are, Sandlot Brewing serves a lager by the name of "Squeeze Play."

Denver's fusion of professional sports, neighborhood development, and downtown restoration is unusual only in the quick payoff it has earned from the Rockies and Coors Field. Most of America's older industrial metropolises are presently attempting to redevelop their physical spaces and redefine their national and international identities through sports- and culture-driven growth initiatives. These strategies include the development of new (or expansion of existing) convention centers, the importation of gambling casinos, the revitalization of entertainment and shopping districts, the establishment and expansion of museums, and of course, the construction of up-to-date sports arenas.

The turn to sports, culture, and entertainment as growth poles for urban redevelopment presents a number of public policy issues. For example, what role do state and local governments play in these projects, and how is the interaction of government units and private enterprise structured? In a broad sense, how do these multi-million dollar investments affect particular cities, and more specifically, how advantageous is the neighborhood impact of such projects? Do these projects provide economic or other benefits for the most distressed of inner-city residents? As a form of cultural investment, how effective is sports-anchored urban development in reshaping the identity of older, formerly industrial cities?

In this book we take research on sports and urban development in a new direction. Though numerous studies have examined the interactions of politics, economics, and sports facility development (Baade 1987; Baim 1990, 1994; Euchner 1993; Johnson and Frey 1986; Johnson 1993; Rosentraub 1997; Scully 1989; Quirk and Fort 1992; Noll and Zimbalist 1997), this literature has devoted only secondary attention to the question of how sports facilities coexist with their surrounding neighborhoods and, more broadly, of how sports, as an increasingly prominent part of the entertainment economy, contribute to the redefinition of urban culture.

Like other U.S. cities, Chicago came to view professional sports as a catalyst in the reinvention of its civic identity. The result was a series of stadium development projects undertaken within a few years in the late

1980s and early 1990s. The first of these projects involved the Chicago Cubs National League baseball franchise, which at last installed lights at the fabled Wrigley Field. Across town on the city's mid–South Side, the owners of the Chicago White Sox shortly thereafter collaborated with the State of Illinois and the City of Chicago in the construction of the new Comiskey Park. Quick on the heels of these significant ballpark initiatives, the owners of the world-famous Chicago Bulls and the somewhat less renowned Chicago Blackhawks of the National Hockey League, with considerable local government support, built the United Center in the city's Near West Side.

Each of these development projects occurred in a complex neighborhood environment. The new Comiskey Park's site straddles a long-standing racial divide between the Douglas area to the east and the South Armour Square and Bridgeport communities to the south and west. Wrigley Field is a much-cherished landmark of the demographically diverse Lake View neighborhood. The construction of the United Center is but one part of an ambitious redevelopment campaign on Chicago's Near West Side. In each of these cases, neighborhood residents criticized stadium plans, and at times came into sharp conflict with government bodies and the stadium developers.

By exploring the economic logic driving these projects, the debates that shaped their implementation within the contexts of their particular neighborhoods, and the ways in which these facilities have transformed their local environments, we aim to articulate in very concrete terms how the emerging forces influencing contemporary urban redevelopment are reshaping the social and physical environment of American cities. In particular, we emphasize the frequently contradictory visions animating the actions of developers, governmental officials, and local residents. In the end, we hope to contribute to ongoing debates regarding how new-style urban redevelopment is redefining American cities, and indeed, whether the new shape of urban redevelopment is likely to produce desirable neighborhoods and more hospitable cities.

Culture as a Strategy for Urban Growth and Regeneration

As cities search for innovative ways to reshape their core areas, "culture industries" have become an integral part of urban redevelopment (Lash and Urry 1994; Zukin 1995). In recent years, entertainment and gaming districts in Baltimore, New Orleans, and San Diego have been spruced up with the aim of capturing the discretionary spending of local residents and tourists. Waterfront areas and their associated recreational facilities have received great attention in the revitalization efforts of Baltimore, New Orleans, New York City, and Philadelphia. In Atlanta, Chicago, Milwaukee,

Minneapolis, Pasadena, and Philadelphia, enclosed shopping malls have anchored downtown redevelopment plans. Finally, new or expanded convention centers in Chicago, New York, Kansas City, and Orlando seek to tap the wellspring of large-scale trade shows and conventions. These projects, in turn, count on spin-off hotel, restaurant, and entertainment expenditures to stimulate their cities' economies (Frieden and Sagalyn 1989; Sorkin 1992; Tabak 1994; Judd and Swanstrom 1998, 365–85).

Along Philadelphia's Delaware River waterfront, the Penn's Landing development exemplifies these trends. Among the historically themed attractions at Penn's Landing are an aerial tram, a 4,000-seat amphitheatre, a twenty-screen AMC cinema complex, a two-hundred-thousand-square-foot "public festivalspace," and a Hyatt Regency Hotel, as well as a variety of national merchants, including Borders Books, Pottery Barn, and FAO Schwarz—indeed, the third largest FAO Schwarz in the world! ("Welcome to Penn's Landing Online" 2001). In Baltimore, the tourism-directed revitalization of the Inner Harbor, complete with museums, historical exhibits, and an aquarium, has filled the void left by the closing of dozens of manufacturing and shipping concerns. As a result, the tourism industry has been credited by some with the overall revitalization of central Baltimore (Levine 1987).

Theme parks, casinos, and the convention trade are other conduits for tourist spending. According to the Chicago Convention and Tourism Bureau, the 1995 International Manufacturing Technology convention at McCormick Place pumped $165.8 million into the local economy (Smith 1995). In 1996, the Associated Press reported that events as specialized as military veteran reunions have become desirable prizes for some cities. For example, the Montgomery, Alabama, area Chamber of Commerce has estimated that veteran reunions contribute $10 million annually to the local economy.

Municipal support for the fine arts is another avenue for economic development. Sociologist J. Allen Whitt (1987) contends that support for the arts contributes to urban economic development in a variety of ways. Investment in physical facilities and well-publicized arts organizations allows cities to vie with communities that depend on natural amenities, such as hospitable climates or seaside locations, in the competition to attract private investment. The presence of museums and historic sites can be a major boost for downtown areas. The audiences for the performing arts tend to have above-average incomes, making them good customers for restaurants and retailers. The enticement of performing arts groups may also be linked to the renovation of historic structures, thus contributing to physical revitalization. Finally, the emergence of vital performing arts can attract allied business activities and have a positive spillover effect on adjoining residential areas.

Some observers argue that beyond the utility of entertainment facilities and the fine arts as tools for improving downtowns, culturally directed development initiatives signal a new stage in both urban development and capitalist production. For example, sociologist Sharon Zukin (1995) argues that the rise of a "symbolic economy" based on tourism and entertainment districts within cities demonstrates the emergence of culture as a crucial form of capital:

> Culture is intertwined with capital and identity in the city's production systems. From that point of view, cultural institutions establish a competitive advantage over other cities for attracting new businesses and corporate elites. But in American and European cities during the 1970s, culture became more of an instrument in the entrepreneurial stages of local government and business alliances. In the shift to a post-war economy, who could build the biggest modern art museum suggested the vitality of the financial sector. Who could turn the waterfront from docklands rubble to parks and marinas suggested the possibilities for expansion of the managerial and professional corps. (12)

Zukin's interpretation of the place of culture within contemporary urban redevelopment reflects Henri Lefebvre's longer view of arts production as a feature of capitalist development:

> Only relatively recently and through institutions has the theater become "cultural," while play has lost its place and value in society. Would culture not be the accommodation of the *oeuvre* and style to exchange value, thus allowing for its commercialization, its production and consumption as specific product? (1995, 171)

The promotion of culture industries within particular cities cannot be effected without the active support of government and leading political figures. J. Allen Whitt and John Lammers's (1991) study of Louisville, Kentucky, arts organizations and their boards of directors, "The Art of Growth: Ties between Development Organizations and the Performing Arts," offers a concrete illustration of these connections. After investigating the ties linking development interests, arts organizations, and their board members, Whitt and Lammers contend that

> (1) . . . growth is the fundamental basis of urban politics; (2) . . . there is a local inner circle of businessmen who provide structural bridges among large corporations, arts organizations, and the leading groups devoted to urban growth policies; (3) the arts are, at least in some cities, governed at the top levels by powerful people (primarily men) who appear to be active participants in the local growth machine; (4) the major arts and cultural organiza-

tions of downtowns may have become essential components of urban growth machines, implying an increasing mutual dependency between corporations and cultural institutions. (388)

The implications of this perspective transcend the fine arts in that a variety of other cultural activities can be directly or indirectly connected to business interests and economic growth. In short, the revitalization of urban centers through the promotion of culturally grounded organizations, facilities, and activities has emerged as a key survival tool for cities across the United States. The rise of a postindustrial, service-oriented economy has brought to center stage forms of investment and modes of human activity that were once viewed as peripheral or merely playful.

Sports as a Culture Industry

In the United States, as in many other parts of the world, sports have become a core culture industry. Professional sports franchises have assumed a central role in expressing civic achievement, and sports arenas are the locales in which these cultural symbols are observed, packaged, marketed, and purchased. Like museums, performing arts complexes, and theme parks, professional sports facilities are social spaces that promote communal consciousness. Thus, the production of capital and the expression of civic identity converge.

Telecommunications technologies that serve to disseminate cultural symbols also produce highly commercialized sports environments. This is not unlike Disneyland, where Mickey and Minnie Mouse do double duty as consumption objects and cultural symbols and, highlighted by their evocative spatial setting, become elements of a powerful commodification process. Like Disney's animated characters, sporting figures such as Michael Jordan have come to anchor multibillion-dollar global culture industries.

This ascendance of sports as a central culture industry occurs in conjunction with the larger economic shift from an industrial to a postindustrial economy. Scott Lash and John Urry, in *Economies of Signs and Space* (1994), explore these new postindustrial economic processes, which they term "economies of signs." These economies derive profit from symbols, images, and desires. Lash and Urry argue:

> The old Fordist, organized capitalist core was characterized by a set of producer networks clustered around a heavy industrialized hub of the motor, chemicals, electrical and steel industries. . . . This old order has been significantly undermined by two processes. The first is the disintegration of the core with finance, distribution, property, service, and knowledge and R&D functions each taking their own autonomy. The second is the formation of a

new core, one in which "the postindustrial tail of the old order begins effectively to wag the Fordist and industrial dog." The new core is clustered
around information, communications and the advanced producer services, as
well as other services, such as telecommunications, airlines and important
parts of tourism and leisure.(17)

Franchise ownership patterns reveal with stark clarity the importance of
professional sports within this new postindustrial economy. Corporate
ownership has become the norm in three of the four major professional
sports in the United States, that is, in the National Basketball Association
(NBA), Major League Baseball (MLB), and the National Hockey League
(NHL). (National Football League regulations prohibit corporate ownership
of franchises.) Consequently, the economics of professional sports has
been dramatically transformed. Currently, more than fifty public companies own at least a portion of the 89 franchises in these three leagues, and
the future is likely to bring complete corporate control of those teams
(Johnson 1997). Ownership of sports teams by corporations, especially by
the telecommunications giants, has accelerated in the last few years (see
table 1 in the appendix).

Sports franchises have become key assets for communications corporations, fundamentally because these media conglomerates can utilize "in-
house" communications outlets to present their product to the public. In
the words of Isiah Thomas, a former NBA star and a founding owner of the
Toronto Raptors (NBA), "I don't see the Raptors as just a basketball team. I
see them as one day being the centerpiece of an entertainment entity. Our
intention is to make this a $1 billion company. Even now our corporate
culture is to create an environment in every division similar to what Disney has done" (Johnson 1997, 46).

The trend toward corporate and, in particular, media ownership of
sports franchises has made professional sports a more potent cultural commodity, and in corporate hands the new marketing aim is to expand prof-
its far beyond ticket sales and parking revenues. Television agreements and
national and international broadcasting arrangements assume greater significance because United States–based teams and leagues can generate
global revenues from TV contracts, advertising, and the sale of merchandise. In 1996, the NBA sold $500 million in licensed products abroad, and
TV rights to NBA programming were marketed to countries as far afield as
Namibia, Mongolia, and Kuwait (Gunther 1997).

The Political Economy of Stadium Development

In the last generation, cities across the United States have devoted huge
sums of public money to finance the construction of sports arenas. Supporters of these projects have used economic impact studies and multiplier

calculations, which purport to measure positive direct and indirect economic outcomes, and have cited various noneconomic benefits, notably the community-building and cultural identification functions of sporting events, to justify these public expenditures. Yet even with the emerging corporatization of sports, as well as the maturation of professional sports as a culture industry, there remains considerable uncertainty concerning the utility of sports construction projects as tools for economic development and urban regeneration.

From 1970 to 1990 the proportion of professional sports teams' facilities that were publicly owned increased from 70 to 80 percent (Quirk and Fort 1992). Driven by intense intermunicipal competition, huge public investments have aimed to retain or attract professional sports franchises. More recently, from 1993 to 1996, $7 billion dollars was spent on the construction and renovation of major league facilities across the country. The public sector provided 80 percent of these funds (Wayne 1996). Analogous pressures are felt by smaller cities—the typical homes of minor league sports franchises—which recognize that if they do not pay for the upgrading of local arenas, other cities will accommodate franchises in their hunt for more commodious "home fields" (Mahtesian 1994; Johnson 1993).

Massive expenditures for the construction of sports facilities in the United States are driven by the profit motivation of team owners and the shifting economics of professional sports. By the 1970s, television broadcasts had become the primary revenue source for major league teams. Stadium revenues from ticket sales became an auxiliary source of profit. As a result, the owners of sports franchises supported the construction of multipurpose facilities with high seating capacities. The outcome of this trend was a clutch of mammoth sports complexes, both domed stadiums and bowl-like structures, including Three Rivers Stadium in Pittsburgh, Riverfront Stadium in Cincinnati, and Veterans Stadium in Philadelphia. In the last decade, the prospect of boosting on-site revenues through the sale of luxury seating and the provision of associated luxury services has led to the physical reconfiguration of many such structures. Luxury seating has become an extremely attractive profit center. For example, the New York Islanders rent luxury suites for as much as $260,000 per season (Noll and Zimbalist 1997).

The economics of upscale viewing has produced a new type of sports arena. The expectation of private viewing environments and the infrastructure requirements for delivering an array of foods, beverages, and other commodities have dictated various design innovations. The current trend in stadium design favors single-purpose facilities that make room for restaurants and taverns, gift shops, and, in some cases, overnight accommodations. One such state-of-the-art facility is the recently opened Fleet-Center in Boston. Among its marvels are portable computers providing "In-Seat Wait Service." Patrons of the Club Seat section of the arena can use this handheld device to order food and beverages from a full-range menu. The arena's management guarantees that food will be delivered within five minutes of the time of the order.

Due to these revenue and design trends, franchise owners increasingly have turned to cities and public coffers to underwrite new facilities. Given the presumed economic and civic benefits derived from the hosting of sports franchises, municipal sponsorship of stadium projects is routinely rationalized as a powerful economic development tool. The drive to attract franchises is consistent with, indeed integral to, the municipal growth ideology. Cities thus compete with each other to attract existing franchises or to win the honor of hosting an expansion team.

Coalitions of city officials, civic boosters, and team owners are at the heart of the construction boom in sports facilities. Economists James Quirk and Rodney Fort (1992) have estimated the annual volume of subsidies provided by local governments to users of publicly owned stadiums and arenas at $500 million. The justification for these subsidies to often profitable professional teams grows from the perception that public funding constitutes a form of capital investment and, as such, is akin to other urban redevelopment investments.

As an inducement to the appropriation of public funds for stadium development, team owners frequently threaten to relocate their franchises, playing one city against another. From 1982 to 1997, seven NFL teams relocated, all driven by the prospect of increased team profitability as a result of stadium replacement or upgrading (see table 2 in the appendix). In the same league, during the ten-year period from 1992 through 2001, twelve new stadiums were constructed and three major renovations completed (see table 3 in the appendix). Across the United States, many additional stadium projects are currently under discussion.

The revenues underwriting the construction of sports arenas come primarily from taxes and bonds. Property taxes, sales taxes (Cincinnati and Tampa), sports lottery revenues (Maryland for the Baltimore Ravens), hotel-motel taxes (Chicago, Detroit, Nashville, and St. Louis), rental car surcharges (Chicago, Detroit, and Houston), team merchandise and ticket taxes (Nashville), stadium parking surcharges (Seattle), alcohol and cigarette taxes (Cleveland), and restaurant-meal taxes (Detroit) are all used to fund stadium building (Noll and Zimbalist, 1997). Sales tax revenues are the most common contributor to the sports-facility financial stream. However, some observers have objected to the use of this financing method. The economically regressive impact of sales taxes means that poor people pay more than their fair share of the costs of stadium development.

A new wrinkle in the financing of sports facilities is the development of stadiums within entertainment districts, the latter providing a revenue base to fund facility construction and upkeep. California has been the pioneer in refining this revenue-raising tactic. Efforts have been afoot to underwrite a refurbished Los Angeles Memorial Coliseum and return the NFL to that city, as well as to rebuild San Diego's Qualcomm Stadium (formerly Jack Murphy Stadium) and finance a new baseball park for the Padres (Williams 1997).

Direct, Indirect, and Intangible Economic Benefits

There is no question that public support of stadium development assists franchise owners in their quest for profitability. For cities the benefits are less evident. Stadium proponents tend to identify three forms of benefits attributable to sports facility investments: direct, indirect, and intangible.

Direct and indirect economic benefits derive from ticket sales, parking fees, and franchise employees' salaries, as well as employee taxes, ticket and parking taxes, food and souvenir purchases, overnight hotel stays, and pregame and postgame entertainment spending. Spending at the stadium or the arena and the revenue generated by service industries supporting the sports events constitute the direct and indirect economic benefits. Advocates of sports-centered economic development claim that this mix of consumer spending further contributes to the local economy by generating tax revenues for municipalities and promoting broader private-sector economic growth.

The logic of this form of economic impact analysis is illustrated by a Coopers and Lybrand report (1995) for Austin, Texas, that estimated the benefits produced by a local minor league (AAA-level) baseball franchise. According to the Coopers and Lybrand study, three different multipliers expressed the ball club's overall economic contribution. One was a measure of total output, representing the total direct, indirect, and induced spending attributable to the franchise's operations. The second measured total earnings, that is, wages and salaries, as well as earnings of associated proprietorships, partnerships, corporations, and other entities. The third multiplier tracked employment, the number of jobs generated by the franchise. The study concluded that over 450 jobs would be created and a total of over $37 million would be generated by a minor league franchise in the city. Stadium construction costs were set at $18 million.

Similarly, a 1985 report by Edward B. Shils of the University of Pennsylvania estimated that the total direct and indirect economic impact of professional teams on the city of Philadelphia during 1983 was $343 million. Shils reached these figures first by determining direct revenues, composed of (1) spending on tickets, television and radio payments, and concessions; (2) spending on food, entertainment, public and private (i.e., taxi and shuttles) transportation, and lodging; and (3) revenue paid by advertisers to television and radio stations during sports broadcasts. He concluded that these three sources of revenue generated $202 million. To identify the overall economic impact on the city of Philadelphia, he used a 1.7 multiplier that estimated the indirect economic impact yielded by direct spending. Thus, the overall economic benefit for the city was $343 million. Shils then used a multiplier of 2.6 to estimate professional sports' metropolitan-wide economic impact (George 1989).

Intangible effects, the economic benefits that result from the attention cities receive because of their professional sports teams, may also be estimated. Specifically, sports development proponents claim that nationally and regionally broadcast events, in addition to team coverage, expose viewers to the host city's attractions. In this view, the presence of a city's name in the box scores of daily newspapers across the country can be a lever for economic growth.

For a large metropolis such as Chicago, these intangible economic benefits are presumed to be substantial. According to a report by the City's Department of Economic Development (1986):

> These "intangibles" make a very real contribution to the economy of Chicago, for any exposure of the team to outsiders—whether potential tourists or businessmen—also indirectly promotes the city of Chicago. . . . The Department estimated that a Chicago baseball franchise produces about three million dollars worth of intangible benefits in an average year, and that a team in a peak year could generate up to eleven million dollars. Throughout these calculations, the Department was . . . conservative as possible. Just how conservative becomes clear when we compare these calculated intangibles with other estimates of the impact of sports publicity. Local advertising executives hypothesize, for example, that the championship-winning 1985–1986 Chicago Bears football team produced publicity for Chicago equivalent to a $30 to $40 million promotion campaign. (5–6)

Nevertheless, a variety of technical questions cloud the estimation of sports-derived economic benefits. It is also clear that due to the convergence of their agendas, profit-generating private interests and public officials in pursuit of economic growth may be tempted to exaggerate the benefits derived from stadium investments. For example, one of the most problematic assumptions made by economic impact analyses is the specification of the sports facility as a spending venue capable of increasing total expenditures within a city or regional economy. Expenditures at the stadium or the arena are assumed to expand total consumption, that is, to extract more disposable income and actually increase the scale of the local economy. An equally plausible assumption views sporting events as just another entertainment choice. It proposes that other venues may experience a decline in revenue due to the transfer of funds expended on leisure activities. Increasing the number of entertainment possibilities expands consumer choice without increasing disposable income. This point has been addressed by sports economist Robert Baade, who analyzed the effect of professional sports teams on metropolitan economies using a sample of forty-eight cities and tracking their economies over a thirty-year period. Baade's conclusion:

> In general the results of this study do not support a positive correlation between professional sports and job creation. This finding, coupled with the absence of a positive correlation between professional sports and city real per capita income, suggests that professional sports realign economic activity within a city's leisure industry rather than adding to it. (1996a, 16)

Economic impact studies, through the use of multiplier techniques, also presume that the larger the project to be completed, the greater the positive outcome it will have on the community. However, as William J. Hunter notes in his cómparison of the economic impact of the construction versus the repair of a bridge:

> The use of the new multiplier in the comparison between old bridge repair and new bridge construction makes the bias of the analysis clear. By increasing public expenditures, even greater increases in community income can be effected through the multiplier's ripple effect. Why then stop with just a new bridge? Why not build an even larger bridge, or perhaps several bridges? Why not build new highways connected to the new bridge? Certainly if one bridge can generate far more community income than additional community cost, several bridges connected by new highways will bring even more income. Can this analysis be correct? (1989, 12)

Not only does multiplier analysis suppose that larger, more capital-intensive projects must produce greater economic benefits than smaller investments, it also groundlessly assumes that increasing the scale of a project increases the likelihood of a return in excess of the initial public investment. In reality, such thinking turns logic on its head. If spending more invariably resulted in increased economic growth, local governments across America would be irresponsible if they did not simply spend themselves into affluence.

The other side of the coin in assessing the reliability of economic impact studies is the matter of vested interests. Who benefits from the inflated figures that sometimes appear in such studies? And who conducts the studies? Consultants who produce these economic impact analyses occupy a substantial economic niche. Although any reputable economist will concede that the methods of input-output investigation are extremely fluid, the firms hired by city governments or sports franchises to produce these analyses, without exception, understand in advance which research findings will constitute "correct" results. Moreover, because the public lacks the training and access to information necessary for properly reviewing the firms' work, what these consultants "find" is, for all practical purposes, indisputable.

A phalanx of academic researchers has challenged the conventional wisdom regarding stadiums and sports franchises and their economic impact. Studies have shown that the local and regional economic impact of stadium construction has been minimal (Baade 1996a, 1996b; Baade and Dye 1990; Baim 1990, 1994; Rosentraub 1988; Colclough, Daellenbach, and Sherony 1994). The work of economists Robert Baade and Richard Dye (1990) is especially provocative. Applying regression analysis to census data from nine metropolitan areas (Cincinnati, Denver, Detroit, Kansas City, New Orleans, Pittsburgh, San Diego, Seattle, and Tampa Bay), Baade and Dye concluded that the effects of stadiums and professional teams on area development were not as great as proclaimed by local officials and franchise representatives. In particular, Baade and Dye noted that the multiplier assumptions of typical economic impact analyses should be viewed with suspicion. Stadium investments were not associated with increases in personal income, and in some cases they may have had a negative effect on local development. Relying on the same research, Baade observed in an earlier report published by the Heartland Institute in Chicago:

> The construction or renovation of a stadium, or the presence of a professional sports franchise, might well have a positive effect on the economy in the stadium's immediate neighborhood. But at what cost to the rest of the city or to the region as a whole? Perhaps a new restaurant will open up in the vicinity of a new sports stadium; it is however, just as likely that an established restaurant fifteen blocks away will close its doors as a result. Is this what stadium proponents consider economic growth?

Furthermore,

> The results of this third regression confirm the thesis that stadiums and professional sports induce a reduction in SMSA income as a percent of regional income. In five of the nine cities, stadiums and professional sports had a significant *negative* impact; in the remaining four cities, the stadium and professional sports variables failed to exert a significant impact, positive or negative, on city incomes. In no instance did a positive, significant correlation surface among stadiums, professional sports, and city income as a fraction of regional income. (1987, 15, emphasis in original)

A study analyzing the impact of the sports-driven downtown development strategy in Indianapolis notes: "Without minimizing the success and publicity Indianapolis has enjoyed, outcomes of this magnitude are so small that it is plausible to consider that, had the city focused on other factors, a larger economic impact would have been possible" (Rosentraub, Swindell, Przybylski and Mullins 1994, 237). Apart from the question of dubious economic assumptions, a city's commitment of resources to stadium projects does involve opportunity costs. What benefits might have been produced by alternative investments? The annual operating budget of a professional sports team approximates the annual expenditures of a single department store, and the majority of employees working for that sports franchise hold seasonal jobs paying an hourly rate near the minimum wage. When considering in concrete terms the place of sports franchises in a metropolitan economy, it helps to bear in mind this comparison.

Sports Franchises and Community Building

City officials and team supporters likewise propose that, in addition to economically grounded benefits, sports enterprises contribute to communal sentiments. Sports franchises, it is so argued, place cities on the national map. Professional teams become municipal icons, ornaments that enhance social cohesion and advance a community's reputation.

In 1995, leaders in St. Louis, Missouri, having determined that the presence of a professional football team was a sure means of restoring their city's national reputation, mobilized a huge financial package with the aim of returning the NFL to the banks of the Mississippi. According to former Missouri senator Thomas Eagleton, the Rams' resulting move to St. Louis was a signal of civic rebirth that justified every effort and dollar committed: "Whether one agrees with it or not, some people measure the caliber of a city in terms of having a professional baseball team and a professional football team. When St. Louis lost football, it became a second-class city. With football back, St. Louis is once again a first class city" (Kramer 1995).

Eagleton's perspective is shared by William Hudnut, former mayor of Indianapolis:

> In Indianapolis, we fought to keep the Indiana Pacers from moving to Sacramento because we realized it would be devastating to our image as an emerging American city if the team relocated. We fought for the Colts against Baltimore, San Antonio, Phoenix, Birmingham, Jacksonville, and Memphis because the potential benefits were equally as dramatic. . . . They transformed us from "India-no-place" into a destination city, "a Cornbelt city with Sunbelt sizzle." (Hudnut 1995)

In addition to offering visible evidence that a city is holding its own in the intermunicipal contest for recognition by the media and the national public, sports franchises, in this view, also serve community-building purposes. Hudnut (1995) asserts that the Colts have served an integrating function for his city: "The team can supply some of the glue that holds a community together. The Colts galvanized the spirit of Indianapolis."

St. Louis and Indianapolis are not alone in looking to professional sports as a source of civic pride. When the NFL's Buccaneers, complaining that their stadium was not up to the league standard, threatened to leave Tampa, social cohesion and community-building arguments quickly emerged in tandem with proposals to meet the Bucs' stadium demands. According to Edwin Roberts Jr., columnist for the *Tampa Tribune,* economic benefits, though critical, were not the most important reasons for holding on to the franchise. Rather it was a matter of "civic worth":

> The economic benefits accruing to the citizenry as a whole from the presence of a professional football team are probably smaller than advertised. Nevertheless, the civic worth of a sports franchise has less to do with expanding local wealth than with expanding local pride, and that's not easy to evaluate. . . . When the Skins won their first Super Bowl, there was so much hugging among strangers in Washington and its suburbs that the celebration put one in mind of V-J Day. Nothing, absolutely nothing can bring to a diverse community so much shared rapture. . . . The Bucs' great gift to us is the unity they inspire among so many different sorts of people, and it is a unity that thrives on the team's success but doesn't entirely dissipate when the team fails. (1995)

Similarly, in Chicago, when the Bears of the NFL threatened to find a new home, a *Chicago Tribune* commentary responded: "The Bears have long been a unifying element for a city where North Side, South Side, West Side, and the Loop all distrust one another, where the Sox and the Cubs split the baseball community and where racial divisions run below the surface like so many fault lines" (Papajohn 1995).

As described in a *Los Angeles Times* article by columnist Kenneth Reich (1989), public officials and community leaders are quite attuned to the social effects that a professional team has on a city. Alameda County Supervisor Don Pareda discussed why his county's drive to return the NFL Los Angeles Raiders to Oakland was important for building city morale and social cohesion:

> It really provides a galvanizing effect for the community. It fuses an identity. It provides the community a separate and distinct interest which people share in common, and for us, in Oakland, that is very important because we have such a diverse community, socially, economically and ethnically. It provides a common reference for us and we know that that's very valuable.

At the other end of the state, California state senator Bill Campbell, hoping that the Raiders would not move north, observed:

> I think there is an extreme value, even to Los Angeles, in these teams. You have the community pride, the cohesiveness that a sports franchise brings . . . In the office, everyone is talking about the game the day before or the night before. It brings an esprit de corps to a community that otherwise is not there.

And labor leader Bill Robertson, who had been instrumental in bringing the Raiders to Los Angeles years before, expressed a particularly interesting variant of the community-identification argument in reference to the neighborhoods adjoining the Los Angeles Memorial Coliseum: "It's very important for the morale of the people living in that community to keep it busy." Without directly saying it, Robertson seems to find another function of professional sports, that is, to divert the attention of marginal social groups.

In the past, cities have also viewed the construction of sports facilities as a way to showcase their progressive leadership or to underline their comeback from natural disasters or other catastrophes. The construction of a stadium, especially a modernistic domed facility, has frequently marked a city's sense of municipal ascendancy. For example, the Astrodome in Houston, the Superdome in New Orleans, the Metrodome in Minneapolis, the Kingdome in Seattle, the Silverdome in Detroit, and the RCA Dome (formerly Hoosier Dome) in Indianapolis have all been the focus of local pride and have served to demonstrate that their metropolitan regions are "up and coming" places (Gershman 1993). As the Superdome was rising in central New Orleans, Mayor Moon Landrieu exuded: "The Superdome is an exercise of optimism. A statement of faith. It is the very building of it that is important, not how much it is used or its economics" (Reed 1974, 80).

Conversely, the loss of a sports franchise can signal municipal decline, as demonstrated by San Francisco's efforts to retain the baseball Giants, whose management was long dissatisfied with Candlestick Park. In November 1989, an earthquake interrupted the World Series and surely directed the attention of San Francisco's residents to more fundamental issues than either the on-the-field tussle between the A's and the Giants or the bargaining-table conflict between the City and the Giants. Mayor Art Agnos, nonetheless, attempted to frame the City's stadium development proposal as a municipal morale-booster in the wake of the natural disaster: "It's our last and final shot to keep the team in San Francisco. It's now or never." He pointed to the construction of a new stadium as a civic response to those who questioned San Francisco's grit in the face of the earthquake. In a letter to the residents of San Francisco, Agnos argued, "Building the ballpark will be a signal that says to the rest of the world that we believe in our future" (Buursma 1989).

These perceived social benefits are fundamental reasons for the municipal wooing of professional franchises and the construction of stadiums and arenas. With sports franchises routinely viewed as prime objects of local resident identification and as key elements in the community building process, municipal officials rush to support team owners with their most powerful elixirs: funding power and the ability to build magnificent, profit-generating sports palaces. In the end, social benefit arguments cement public support for such projects.

Although many critics have questioned the presumed economic benefits of sports-centered development initiatives, the assumption that sports serve as a crucial civic adhesive eludes serious scrutiny. Consider this commentary by *Chicago Tribune* columnist George Papajohn:

> The Bears, more than any other Chicago franchise, represent every cherished character trait and every tour-bus cliché that gives the city its identity. Thinking of big shoulders? Think Dick Butkus. The ethnic success story? Think Bears founder George Halas, the son of Bohemian immigrants. Personalities as unforgiving as steel? Think "Iron Mike" Ditka. Tough but graceful architecture? Think of Walter Payton's bruising and balletic build. The beautiful lakefront? Think Soldier Field. The brutal Chicago weather? Think Bear weather. The Bears are the only reason Chicagoans can take pride in our miserable winter. (1995)

Though Papajohn's allusions are exaggerated, professional sports teams do, in some fashion, underscore civic identity and infuse residents with a sense of local pride. Of course, there are no means available to quantify the worth of these invisible social values, which, from the standpoint of franchise and stadium boosters, may be just as well.

The Other Side of the Coin: The Trials of the Pontiac Silverdome

Denver's amazing good fortune in conjunction with the building of Coors Field is but one example of stadium-centered urban regeneration. Another, possibly more characteristic, tale of sports arena development, economics, and local politics derives from the experience of Pontiac, Michigan, a Detroit suburb that, like many other American municipalities, imagined that sports-related physical development would bring riches.

Thirty years ago, the Lions of the NFL played in downtown Detroit, but, like other sports franchises, were on the lookout for a new home ground. The Ford family, owners of the Lions, turned to the City of Pontiac in Detroit's northern suburbs, whose municipal leadership, eager to lure the professional football team from the central city, offered to build a domed stadium. The Pontiac Silverdome was completed in 1975 and became the home of the Detroit Lions. The Silverdome is one of the most imposing domed sports facilities in the world, and its seating capacity of 80,368 led the NFL. The arena's air-supported, cable-restrained roof is of a fiberglass fabric and is the largest such roof in the world. The cost of the Silverdome was $55.7 million. Owned and operated by the City of Pontiac, the Silverdome complex covers 150 acres and includes 13,000 parking spaces.

For a number of years the Detroit Pistons of the NBA also played their home games in the Silverdome, but in 1988 the Pistons moved to a new basketball arena, humbly known as the Palace, in Auburn Hills, Michigan, approximately four miles from Pontiac. In 1982 the Silverdome hosted professional football's Super Bowl, the first held in a northern city. Twelve years later, several World Cup soccer matches were played in the Silverdome. The facility has also been used for road races and music concerts. However, the City of Pontiac's finances have been most directly linked to the fortunes of the Lions, which generate 50 percent of the revenues earned by the Silverdome (Associated Press 1995b).

The City of Pontiac built the Silverdome for precisely the reasons that other municipalities have supported large-scale sports facility projects. A modest-sized city with a declining industrial base, Pontiac imagined that professional sports and other entertainment events would be the engine for its economic recovery. However, unlike Denver's experience with Coors Field, Pontiac has never earned the kind of return that it expected from the Silverdome. Located at the intersection of two major highways and surrounded by acres of surface parking, the Silverdome has produced little spillover consumer activity in downtown Pontiac. According to Jeffrey Kaczmarek, director of the Department of Community and Economic Development in Oakland County, "The expectations were too high. In the grand scheme of things, the economic benefit is a pittance. The gain is much more about image and status. [There is] nothing around the Silverdome to allow it to be developed as an entertainment complex" (Jones 1996). Kaczmarek's view is echoed by Bill Johnson, *Detroit News* editorial writer:

> What happened to all the retail and commercial development and jobs that were to accompany the 1975 move of the Lions from Detroit to the Silverdome? If nothing else the Pontiac experience showed that a new stadium is capable of providing infusions of people on Sunday afternoons, but cannot guarantee clientele for commercial activities in the stadium neighborhood. (1996)

The economic bust is more graphically described by Naki Christopher, owner of a downtown deli located just a mile from the Silverdome: "After the game, the fans run out of Pontiac like the devil is chasing them" (Jones 1996).

Amplifying the geographic isolation of the Silverdome is the seasonal character of the Lions' economic presence. As noted by Eram Hayes, spokesperson for Pontiac mayor Walter Moore, the Lions are hardly an integral feature of Pontiac life: "I think that Pontiac has been more of a benefit to the Silverdome." This is due, in particular, to the stadium's location along two major highways, which "makes it very convenient for people who don't want to come into our city. Go around and ask business people how much business comes here? They are only here for, what, nine or 10 games a year? How much spinoff comes from that?" (Harmon and Heinlein 1996).

Oakland County executive L. Brooks Patterson has pointed to another downside of Pontiac's ownership of the Silverdome: "The dome has not been a cash cow for the city of Pontiac. In the long run, they could be better off without it. The dome is going to become more expensive to maintain every year" (Harmon and Heinlein 1996). Since its opening in 1975, the Silverdome has not produced dramatic changes in Pontiac. The city has lost residents, housing units, and jobs (see table 4 in the appendix).

Given the Silverdome's limited contribution to Pontiac's economic well-being, local leaders began to question the stadium's worth. Pontiac mayor Walter Moore has described the Silverdome site as "one of the most desirable properties in the entire region," adding that "GM and Chrysler are the type of stabilizing businesses that are real economic opportunities" (Jones 1996). Over the years, the Lions' ownership, in turn, grew dissatisfied with the stadium lease agreement. The Lions did not receive revenues from concession sales or luxury suite rentals, which are typical arrangements between NFL franchises and their stadium landlords. Their lease extended to 2004, but the Lions began to search for an alternative home field as early as 1995. The football franchise was serious enough in its pursuit of a new home field to risk $22 million in penalties should it break its lease on the Silverdome (Puls 1998).

As one might expect, the Lions' disaffection with the Silverdome has been welcomed by the City of Detroit, which did not hesitate to pull together its own stadium proposal as a lure to the football franchise. Pontiac officials, recognizing the indifferent economic performance of the Silverdome, did not rush to match Detroit's proposal. Instead, Pontiac is considering the redevelopment of the Silverdome site as an industrial complex. According to a Southeast Michigan Council of Governments report, in the long run the City of Pontiac might benefit considerably from a new land use on the Silverdome site. The city currently receives $1.2 million in annual property taxes for the site; an industrial park could produce property tax collections in excess of $2.6 million. Merchants in downtown Pontiac, anticipating a higher volume of daily customer traffic, also support the conversion (Jones 1996).

By not seeking to renegotiate the Lions' lease for the Silverdome, the City of Pontiac has likely committed itself to demolishing its once-prized stadium. According to Timothy Kozub, the Pontiac Stadium Authority's general counsel: "We reviewed and re-reviewed and re-hashed and felt that the [deal] would take us back to a zero position. There would be no income for this asset and nothing to give back to the taxpayers. In the long run, we felt that when the lease expired, the property was a valuable asset" (Pepper 1996).

In 1996, Wayne County voters approved a tax increase of 1 percent on hotels and 2 percent on rental cars to underwrite a new Lions stadium in downtown Detroit. At a projected cost of $225 million, this domed stadium joins the Fox Town entertainment district, becoming the Lions' new home field in the fall of 2002. The complex includes the Fox Theater, as well as the Detroit Tigers' new $240 million stadium (Heinlein 1996). These stadium projects and the "re-winning" of the Lions landed former Mayor Dennis Archer on *Newsweek* magazine's list of "25 mayors to watch": "Archer seems to have resurrected Detroit overnight" (Kaplan and King 1996, 32).

The sorry case of Pontiac and its Silverdome underlines with unusual clarity the uncertainties associated with sports-driven economic development. Location, physical design, patterns of use, and tenancy arrangements all play roles in determining economic outcomes. Unless sports facility projects are coherently situated within broader redevelopment plans, substantial positive impact may prove elusive. Building a ballpark and waiting for the people and their dollars to come is not a recipe for successful economic development.

Recent Stadium Projects in Chicago: Three Arenas, Three Neighborhoods

At the very least, Chicago's rush to upgrade several of its principal athletic arenas at the turn of the 1990s offers a preliminary indication of how the city's political and economic elites view sports as an element within the city's broader economy. From an analytical standpoint, the short span of time during which lights were installed at Wrigley Field (1988) and the new Comiskey Park (1991) and United Center (1994) were completed also means that in our study a variety of political economic factors may be held constant. That is, the city's objective economic circumstances, local politicians' perceptions of the city's economic fortunes, and the media's stance on the city's reputation—to note a few such variables—represent more or less fixed contextual elements contributing to the specific decision-making processes associated with each stadium project. On the other hand, the contrasting situations of the three neighborhoods most directly affected by these projects offer a rich ground for comparative analysis. Not only do geography and demographic features distinguish South Armour Square, Lake View, and the Near West Side, each neighborhood also possesses a distinctive political and organizational profile. Our discussion of the particular cases, then, will permit us to analyze why some neighborhood interests are more effective than others in negotiating with municipal and sports-franchise representatives. The variety of neighborhood experience represented by South Armour Square, Lake View, and the Near West Side also allows us to underscore another of our unifying themes: the degree to which sports as a culture industry has come to be a powerful force redefining various elements of Chicago's civic and everyday culture, from local neighborhood life to the city's national image.

South Armour Square

Since 1910, a Comiskey Park has been located at the northern end of South Armour Square, a small enclave approximately four miles south of Chicago's Loop. Early settlers in the neighborhood included Irish, German, and Swedish immigrants. By the time the original Comiskey Park was built at the intersection of 35th Street and Shields Avenue, the neighborhood was a dense, mixed-use settlement just a mile northeast of the huge Union Stockyards complex. During the 1940s, South Armour Square's population increased substantially, in large part due to the influx of southern African Americans taking jobs in the city's booming wartime industries. By the 1960s, the stadium and an adjoining municipal park to its north formed a racial boundary between whites to the north and blacks to the south. South Armour Square was further isolated by an expressway running along its eastern edge and by railroad tracks to the west.

Like many other Chicago neighborhoods, South Armour Square was affected by the movement of employers from surrounding areas. From 1970 to the mid-1980s, the zip code area encompassing Comiskey Park lost half its jobs (Strahler 1986). In the mid-1980s, a journalist described South Armour Square in this fashion: "a working-class enclave of about 2,000 black residents, 85 old homes, and 420 low-rise CHA units, cut off from the rest of the city by the Dan Ryan Expressway to the east and train tracks to the west" (Joravsky 1987, 15). In 1989, the neighborhood's median family income was $7,000, and the majority of the households were headed by women (82%). Most of the households received public aid or Social Security. The population was also aged: 43 percent were more than fifty-five years old (Voorhees Neighborhood Center 1995).

U.S. Census figures suggest that the 1980s represented hard times for South Armour Square residents, with the poverty level increasing from 45.4 percent in 1980 to 88.3 percent in 1990. Nevertheless, residents of the neighborhood perceived their community to be stable and supportive. At one community meeting devoted to discussing the impact of the new ballpark, a local resident observed: "A lot of money has gone into improving conditions here. These people, mostly lower-income families, have sunk a lot of money into restoring their property." A fellow resident described the community as "an old, established neighborhood" (Jamison 1987). Though South Armour Square's population was small and very far from affluent, local residents did not relish a multimillion dollar stadium project that would transform their community.

Lake View

Lake View is another established Chicago neighborhood, situated about three miles north of the Loop along the shore of Lake Michigan. Originally settled by German immigrants, Lake View was annexed by the City of Chicago in the 1890s and experienced decennial population increases until 1950, when the area's population reached 125,000. By 1990 Lake View's population had dropped to 91,000. Concurrently, due to residential high-rise construction and numerous apartment-to-condominium conversions, the eastern fringe of the neighborhood, adjoining Lake Michigan, became a decidedly affluent enclave. Though largely white, Lake View is a racially and ethnically mixed area. It is also the Chicago neighborhood with the most visible gay population (Chicago Fact Book Consortium 1995, 50–53).

Although Lake View has never housed major manufacturers, it does include a number of busy retail areas, notably at its southwest corner, radiating from the intersection of Ashland, Belmont, and Lincoln Avenues. Nearer the lakefront, Broadway, Clark, and Halsted Streets are also important commercial corridors. Wrigley Field is located at the north end of Lake View, just east of Clark Street, west of Broadway and Halsted Streets, and within a block of a Chicago Transit Authority elevated-train station. Originally called Weeghman Park, Wrigley Field opened in 1916 and won its permanent name following the ball club's purchase by the Wrigley family in the 1920s. The presence of the major-league baseball park has not held down residential property values in Lake View. In the Wrigleyville area adjoining the ballpark (the quadrant formed by Ashland Avenue and Byron, Halsted, and Roscoe Streets), average home prices increased from $129,966 in 1985 to $308,003 in 1996 ("Living in Greater Chicago," 1997). Wrigley Field is the most famous physical landmark in an affluent, highly cosmopolitan neighborhood.

The Near West Side

Of the three areas we discuss in this volume, Chicago's Near West Side has experienced the most characteristic pattern of neighborhood decline.

Lying just west of Chicago's Loop, and on its eastern end a complicated tangle of entertainment establishments, wholesalers, light manufacturers, warehouses, and surface parking, the Near West Side has lost population since the 1930s. During its long period of population loss, the majority of Near West Side's residents came to be African American, with a substantial share living in public housing complexes such as the Henry Horner Homes west of Ashland Avenue.

If the Great Depression represented the beginning of the Near West Side's decline, the rioting following the assassination of Martin Luther King Jr. in April 1968 seemed to seal the fate of the neighborhood. Not only did the unrest leave Madison Street, a major commercial corridor, in ruins, but in the years following this disaster two major local employers, International Harvester and Sears Roebuck, closed their large West Side facilities. Throughout the 1960s and early 1970s, the Near West Side was additionally scarred by large-scale, generally maladroit redevelopment projects. These included the construction of the University of Illinois at Chicago campus and the expansion of the nearby University of Illinois Medical Center. The development of the university campus displaced thousands of residents and hundreds of businesses (Rosen 1980). More recently, the southward expansion of the University of Illinois campus has closed down the historic Maxwell Street outdoor market to the south of Roosevelt Road (Longworth 1994).

In the early 1990s, the Interfaith Organizing Project, a local community organization, described the Near West Side in this fashion:

> Like many inner-city neighborhoods, it's short on resources, but long on talent and potential. . . . Chicago's West Side experienced a massive flight of capital and resources in the late 1960s and 1970s; the main shopping district had been torched in the 1968 uprisings following the death of Dr. Martin Luther King, Jr., and high-paying factory jobs soon relocated to the suburbs or Sun Belt. (Interfaith Organizing Project 1992, 1)

The same publication adds: "Much of the surrounding areas suffered from chronic dis-investment—banks refused to lend money, insurers stopped underwriting properties and 'slumlords' were more common than not" (20).

Even as the Near West Side lost residents, and as its small manufacturers and warehouses gave way to rubble and weeds, the area remained an appealing target for corporate-sponsored redevelopment plans. On the one hand, from the 1920s the Near West Side had housed one of the city's venerable sporting palaces, the Chicago Stadium, longtime home of the Chicago Blackhawks and by the 1980s the launching pad for Michael Jordan's amazing dunks. On the other hand, one needed only to look east to

observe the remarkable and very nearby magnificence of Chicago's downtown core. By the mid-1980s government officials, franchise owners, development interests, and many community representatives agreed that the
revitalization of the Near West Side was imminent, though just how new
projects would be implemented, and how some part of their economic re-
ward could be reserved for local residents, were the subjects of considerable contention.

The Proposals

The roots of the New Comiskey Park, Wrigley Field, and United Center
projects run back to the early 1980s. The driving force for these projects
was the franchise owners' profit motivation, yet in each case, the complex-
ities of financing, legal obstacles, and community consultation necessitated the involvement of state and municipal officials. Thus, private interests and governmental agendas converged, increasing the likelihood that
these projects would move from the drafting table to three dimensions.

In the early 1980s, the new owners of the White Sox, disaffected with
Comiskey Park, which had opened in 1910 and was the country's oldest
baseball stadium, began casting about for a new home field. Following
well-publicized dalliances with officials of, first, a western suburb and,
later, St. Petersburg, Florida, the team owners twice negotiated stadium development agreements with officials in Illinois. Ultimately, the State of Illinois and the City of Chicago financed, at a cost of approximately $150
million, the new Comiskey Park, which was erected across the street from
the original ballpark.

On Chicago's North Side, the ownership of the Cubs also changed
hands in early 1980s—passing from its long-standing owners, the Wrigley
family, to the Tribune Company. The latter not only controls the city's
leading daily newspaper, the *Chicago Tribune,* but also the powerful cable
TV outlet, WGN. The Tribune Company quickly enlisted Cubs games as
one of WGN-TV's staple entertainment offerings. By 1984, when the long-
suffering Cubs qualified for postseason competition for the first time since
1945, Major League Baseball began to pressure the Tribune Company to
modernize Wrigley Field, that is, to add stadium lights that would permit
evening play. This pressure happened to be directly compatible with the
Tribune Company's economic interest, which was to increase the number
of Cubs games played, and thus broadcast, during the evening hours.

However, in order to reengineer Wrigley Field, the Tribune Company
had to work its way through a legal and political thicket. For many years,
residents of the Lake View blocks adjoining Wrigley Field had sought to
forestall the modernization of the ballpark, including the addition of lighting. To this end, in the early 1980s local activists won passage of both city

and state laws prohibiting the conversion of Wrigley Field. The Tribune Company pressed for repeal of the statutes, and Wrigleyville activists sought to sustain the status quo. In the end, the Tribune Company won a compromise agreement allowing the illumination of its ball field but limiting the number of night games during each baseball season. The Cubs selected the portentous date of August 8, 1988, for the first night game in the history of Wrigley Field.

The Near West Side was the object of multiple stadium proposals in the 1980s and 1990s. Just a few years before the owners of the Chicago Bulls and Blackhawks won the right to build a new sporting complex across the street from the old Chicago Stadium, the Chicago Bears had sought to assemble a West Side site for a new football complex. Unlike the new Comiskey Park, the United Center was privately financed, though the City of Chicago contributed substantial infrastructure improvements and, possibly of greater importance, encouraged the stadium developers to win the approval of neighborhood residents. For their part, residents of the Near West Side were able to mobilize themselves and define their interests most effectively—and indeed, to win substantial concessions from the sponsors of the United Center project.

The Book to Come

Sports-driven urban redevelopment is an important part—but only a part—of the broader restructuring of American cities. In chapter 2 we explore the analytical perspectives, practical techniques, and local political economic dynamics that give shape to the new modes of urban redevelopment. We also begin the process of examining how these attributes of urban redevelopment contribute to a new type of urban culture, what we call the "city of leisure." In chapters 3 through 7 we provide the detailed empirical discussion that is the heart of the book—first looking at the development of the new Comiskey Park, following with the Wrigley Field and United Center case studies. In chapter 8 we bring our analysis to a close: first, by describing the political economic context that brought three major sports development projects to Chicago in little more than a half-decade; second, by examining how these sports stadiums seem to coexist with their on-the-ground city neighborhoods, and also, summing up what we can generalize regarding the relative ability of different neighborhoods and neighborhood organizing approaches to "face off" with corporations and government; and third, by moving to the more subtle question of how well Chicago's clutch of new and upgraded sporting facilities has contributed to the strengthening of local civic allegiances.

2

From Urban Renewal to
the City of Leisure

Writing in the early 1960s, *Fortune* magazine editor Walter McQuade offered the following characterization of the Boston encountered a few years before by newly elected mayor John Collins:

> Boston . . . was intensely old-fashioned, if not outworn. . . . If the new mayor had drawn a balance sheet for Boston in early 1960, the list of debits would have been long. Perhaps the most obvious minus was Boston's waterfront, the original manufacturer of so many of its fortunes in the rum trade, silk trade, tea trade, and the export of ice to the tropics. It was dead. Business had moved out; the big ships were no longer putting in. Boston was now considered an edge of a market, not a center. . . . Also facing the new mayor in 1960 was the fact that the central retail district of Boston appeared to be on its last legs. Ancient in its buildings, in its growth lagging sadly behind the suburbs, downtown boasted only two notably smug department stores. (McQuade 1973, 261)

Though the particulars of decline varied city by city, such descriptions were a staple of urban affairs journalism in the early postwar United States. Like Boston, other major cities were portrayed as economically obsolete, as boneyards occupied by "ancient" buildings, transportation infrastructure, and other public facilities and, possibly worst of all, headed by insular, backward-thinking civic elites.

For many of these cities, the way out from obsolescence was provided by the federal urban renewal program. Between 1950 and 1970 the U.S. Congress appropriated more than $10 billion to support urban renewal, and by the latter year cities across the United States had initiated the planning of, begun to implement, or completed over two thousand urban renewal projects (Weicher 1974, 2). Many years ago housing advocate Catherine Bauer noted that supporters of the 1949 Housing Act, "like the blind men feeling the elephant, made entirely different assumptions as to the essential nature and purpose of this legislation" (Gelfand 1975, 153).

For some of its congressional supporters, and certainly for the preponderance of activists seeking to expand federal government support for affordable housing, the urban renewal program was a housing measure. It meant using federal funds to enable local redevelopment authorities to designate and clear slums. In turn, it permitted these authorities to release cleared areas to private developers committed to building well-planned, reasonably priced residential projects. Yet for many mayors, city planners, and private real estate figures, urban renewal's purpose was decidedly different. Confronted by middle class flight to the suburbs, eroding municipal tax bases, and the nearly universal perception that over the last generation or so central cities had become old-fashioned, these local elites pressed to use urban renewal to arrest urban decline and shape a new kind of city. To borrow from a mid-1940s New York pamphlet describing upcoming projects in that city, their aim was to create "a new kind of city—more beautiful, healthful, and convenient; a more comfortable place in which to live, work, and play" (Teaford 1990, 37). Amendments to the urban renewal legislation, which increased the scope of nonresidential redevelopment, lent congressional imprimatur to this other view of urban renewal, and by the time the program was terminated in 1974, possibly the majority of government officials and private developers who had had some contact with this initiative assumed that central business district preservation was its principal aim.

After 1974, new federal urban programs such as Community Development Block Grants (CBDG) and Urban Development Action Grants (UDAG) sustained the national government's seemingly parallel, yet ambiguously articulated, commitments to the residential improvement and economic revitalization of central cities. And indeed, until the end of the 1970s federal aid to cities continued to rise (Chernick and Reschovsky 1997, 141–43). However, as the policy priorities first of President Ronald Reagan and then of his successor, George Bush, worked their way through the congressional appropriations process, federal government aid to cities declined dramatically. In a 1992 summary of the previous decade's trends in urban policy, political scientist Demetrios Caraley observed that "the cuts in grant programs that benefited city governments were drastic: from 1980 to 1990 a cut of 46 percent or some $26 billion in constant 1990 dollars" (Caraley 1992, 8).

Washington's abandonment of the cities is surely the most evident source of the new modes of urban redevelopment we describe in this chapter. In an era that several observers have dubbed "postfederal," municipal officials have had to invent new strategies for financing conventional redevelopment projects, as well as rethink the underlying premises of local redevelopment. However, as we trace the shifting policy terrain that links urban renewal and today's city of leisure, another causal element will be revealed: the emerging American cityscape, and in particular the incorporation of all manner of sports, leisure, and cultural facilities within new development projects, is also the result of a fundamental recasting of the analytical metaphor that governs the perceptions of public officials, civic leaders, developers, and investors.

Robert Beauregard, in *Voices of Decline* (1993), offers countless examples of how the perception of urban decline has structured the analysis of American cities in the postwar period. In its most expansive usage, the metaphor of decline connotes "weakness in the fabric of civilization, a threat to society, or a breakdown in social norms." For cities, urban decline has been associated with the end of the life cycle, the withering away of once vital metropolises. Just such apocalyptic concerns animate Walter McQuade's snapshot of Boston on the eve of the Collins mayoralty: that city had become "less desirable as a place of residence and less attractive as a location for capital investment in commercial and industrial activities" (Beauregard 1993, 36), that, in short, it might be just years away from economic obsolescence. The need to stave off otherwise inexorable forces of decline seems to have set in motion much of the postwar redevelopment planning in the United States.

Since approximately the mid-1970s the restructuring metaphor has replaced the classic life cycle/urban decline scenario, in response first to reports of the Frostbelt-to-Sunbelt regional economic shift, and later to accounts of global economic transformation. Municipal leaders whose redevelopment program is conditioned by the restructuring metaphor seek to identify economic niches that suit their cities and promise to drive investment, job growth, and tax-base expansion (Pagano and Bowman 1995; Clarke and Gaile 1998). The restructuring metaphor often induces municipal leaders to search for investment in the growth areas of entertainment, sports, tourism, and other leisure-centered activities. Whereas a generation ago smokestack chasing was a principal obsession of mayors and economic development officials, these days the endowing of a new museum or the awarding of a professional sports franchise are just as likely to drive municipal ambition. In a global economy whose cutting edge is defined by the discretionary spending of its professional, managerial, and technical classes, urban uniqueness is marked by a city's portfolio of arts, entertainment, and sporting institutions.

Managing Decline the Old-Fashioned Way

In *Roger and Me*, Michael Moore's documentary film examining the economic collapse of Flint, Michigan, Moore at one point discusses the city's redevelopment efforts with the president of the local convention and tourism board. The tourism official is pleased to describe Flint's new Hyatt

Regency Hotel: "a luxury hotel in the heart of our city, just like other cities with their luxury hotels . . . what you would find in Chicago or Atlanta or San Francisco." On the one hand, the comment reveals a sense that postindustrial Flint must compete with other cities for the interest and dollars of out-of-town visitors. On the other hand, this local promoter appears to be blissfully unaware that Flint's having a Hyatt Regency "just like other cities" is not, of itself, likely to be a major drawing card for his city. The opening of the new hotel—not a successful venture, as Moore then informs the viewer—represents just another element of Flint's desperate campaign to confirm that it is still some kind of city.

Much the same attitude animated urban renewal planning in cities across the United States. Here is historian Jon Teaford's description of "trailblazing" downtown redevelopment projects in Boston, Detroit, Minneapolis, and Philadelphia during the late 1950s and early 1960s:

> Each of these projects cleared gray areas adjacent to the established central business district, thus eliminating blight that might threaten the city's prime real estate. Moreover, they leveled shabby structures that cluttered the entrance to downtown and that further tarnished the image of the already dingy central cities. Aging waterfronts were frequent targets of redevelopers, and tawdry skid rows also fell under the wrecker's ball. . . . In place of these drab blocks, generally described as economic wastelands, one city after another proposed multiuse projects with retailing, hotels, entertainment, offices, and housing. (Teaford 1990, 148–49)

In other words, just as homely Flint in the mid-1980s required a flagship hotel in order to maintain a semblance of urban respectability, Boston, Detroit, Minneapolis, and Philadelphia needed to create lively twenty-four-hour downtowns in order to retain their status as vibrant metropolitan giants. The relationship that was imagined to link redevelopment and urban vitality was elegantly simple: there was presumed to be a menu of features that any great city would exhibit—including substantial civic institutions, modern downtown hotels, office towers designed to show off cutting-edge architectural practice, and grand outdoor public spaces—and redevelopment projects would shore up those menu items that were threatened or would add new items to the city's array of marvels.

As Beauregard repeatedly notes in his analysis of the rhetoric of urban decline, renewal advocates typically likened their cities to an infected human body. Physically decayed neighborhoods represented cancerous growths, and redevelopment projects constituted the new, healthy tissue that would replace these surgically removed tumors. Project-based urban renewal activities were part of carefully staged campaigns to isolate and destroy threatening slums. Just this approach to redevelopment is revealed in political scientist John Mollenkopf's explanation of how the Boston and San Francisco redevelopment directors fixed on two projects in the mid-1960s. The South End and Western Addition:

> . . . had attracted planners' attention as "blighted" neighborhoods for two decades, and both were zones of entry for in-coming minority groups. But Logue and Herman selected these neighborhoods for large-scale projects because they occupied strategic locations in the geo-political competition for central-city land. Furthermore, these two neighborhoods were located near important dominant institutions which wanted to be protected. (1983, 170)

Ironically, urban design critic Jane Jacobs, whose understanding of neighborhood dynamics was also based on an organic conception of the city, took exception with precisely this element of urban renewal strategy. By producing bordered and frequently single-use projects, urban renewal tended to interrupt the streams of movement and activity that linked various portions of the city. Within project areas this produced the lack of diversity that in Jacobs's view deadened the new urban renewal districts (Jacobs 1961, 241–69).

The urban renewal era ended in 1974 with the passage of the federal Housing and Community Development Act. This legislation introduced Community Development Block Grants, formula-based grants to cities that were not tied to particular redevelopment projects. In subsequent years, some cities continued to carry through substantial urban renewal initiatives that originated before 1974. But in the face of tightening municipal finances, a broader environment of macro-economic uncertainty, and seemingly unchecked central-city decline, the ambitious, project-based developments of urban renewal's heyday became a rarity.

New Modes of Urban Redevelopment

In the wake of the quarter century that was devoted to seeking big-city regeneration via urban renewal's project-centered corrective surgery, several circumstances contributed to the emergence of new forms of urban redevelopment. In the first place, the demise of the urban renewal program, and subsequently the across-the-board retrenchment of federal initiatives aimed at restoring central-city vitality, meant that cities had to identify and perfect their own methods of stimulating private investment. This has resulted in a variety of new approaches to financing and implementing redevelopment efforts. Second, macroeconomic circumstances and the concurrent recognition by many municipal leaders and policy experts that a new era of urban growth was fast approaching also gave impetus to new methods for attracting investment, luring tourists, and reviving neighborhoods. This policy consensus—that the heyday of the industrial city had passed and that in North America, at least, new forms of enterprise would be the engines of future urban growth—can be directly linked with the new modes of redevelopment. Finally, by sometime in the 1970s many observers of American cities had noted that right beside the many inept urban renewal projects dotting inner-city areas were any number of smaller-scale, typically entrepreneurial initiatives that seemed to be bringing back presumably dead neighborhoods. Many of these initiatives have now been hauled under the big analytical tent of gentrification and to some degree treated as harbingers of the postindustrial city, but a generation ago they were rare enough to elicit initial surprise, followed by—we would argue—a considerable degree of imitation in cities across the country.

New and Updated Incentive Techniques

Local and state governments have long sought to attract private investment by granting direct and indirect fiscal subsidies, offering preferential application of regulatory powers (for example, adjusting zoning controls), and otherwise seeking to sustain a "favorable business climate." Political scientist Peter Eisinger, in *The Rise of the Entrepreneurial State* (1988), notes that as early as 1935 the Delaware state government authorized the city of Dover to subsidize manufacturing facilities by issuing tax abatements extending up to ten years. Twenty years later, in 1955, New Hampshire established the first state industrial park authority to develop sites for occupancy by private industrial operations (148), but "parks developed and operated by local governments actually appeared in the 1940s" (178).

During the protracted interest group and legislative maneuvering that preceded the enactment of federal urban redevelopment legislation in 1949, central points of contention were the form and magnitude of the federal subsidy for local redevelopment projects and, ultimately, the size of the property "write down" that could be provided private developers (Gelfand 1975, 115–28). In the subsequent thirty years, as urban redevelopment first evolved into urban renewal then was succeeded by federal initiatives such as CDBG and UDAG, the idea of some form of public subsidy to spur private investment was retained.

State and local governments currently employ a variety of incentive techniques to attract private investment. Undoubtedly the nation's tax-abatement champion is New York City, whose Industrial and Commercial Incentive Board (ICIB, later retitled the Industrial and Commercial Incentive Program) was established in 1977. With New York's economic fortunes still reeling from the 1975 municipal-finance meltdown, the ICIB was mandated to stimulate new nonresidential investment. As measured by the number of subsidized projects (274 between 1977 and mid-1981) and volume of exempted property value ($446 million over the same period), the ICIB was a rousing success. John Mollenkopf reports that during the ICIB's first half-decade its property-tax abatements reduced city revenues by about $50 million per year (1992, 146). After the ICIB was converted to the ICIP in the mid-1980s, the amended program's provisions continued to be very generous: some developers were eligible for full tax abatements running thirteen years, followed by a nine-year phase-in to full tax obligation (Bartlett 1992).

Some cities have also turned to property-tax abatement as a means of spurring residential development and homeownership. In 1990 Cleveland began offering ten-year full property-tax exemptions to purchasers of new single-family dwellings (Stoffel 1991). With the aim of speeding commercial-to-residential conversions in its near-downtown Broad Street district, the city of Richmond, Virginia, is currently offering ten-year abatements on building renovations (Hardcastle 1997). From the municipal standpoint, tax abatement's appeal as an economic development tool is perfectly straightforward. On the one hand, the dollar value of abatements to developers or purchasers of properties can be substantial. On the other hand, tax abatement is an off-budget subsidy: a municipal government forgoes future revenue, but in the short run neither the mayor, the city manager, nor city council members have appropriated funds as a handout to private interests.

Since the 1970s many cities have turned to another off-budget technique, tax increment financing (TIF), as a stimulus for private investment. As a rule, the TIF procedure includes designating particular areas as blighted, estimating the cumulative value of real estate within the designated area and using this figure as a baseline for calculating the "tax increment" to be derived from new investment, and finally, issuing bonds to finance redevelopment expenditures with the anticipated tax increment pledged to pay off the bond debt. Peter Eisinger observes: "Tax increment financing was begun in California in 1952, but it did not spread to other states in any significant degree until the 1970s, when it came to be seen as a way to replace the federal urban renewal program, then in the process of closing down" (1988, 185).

Since the 1970s the TIF technique has become one of the most pervasive means of supporting urban redevelopment. In the mid-1990s, Dallas, Philadelphia, Kansas City, Missouri, and other major U.S. cities were financing large-scale downtown projects with TIF subsidies (Kallenberg 1995; Wallace 1997a; Christian 1996). By mid-1997, Chicago was so enamored with the TIF process that it had designated forty-four separate TIF districts, including most of the downtown Loop area (Washburn and Martin 1997). This latter measure generated considerable local debate; one frequently voiced perspective was that the city's commercial core seemed anything but blighted. However, state TIF regulations tend to permit considerable flexibility in the blight designation, with high proportions of underutilized buildings or even vacant land constituting elements of neighborhood decay (Eisinger 1988, 184). The TIF technique is also controversial because it can divert revenues from jurisdictions whose boundaries overlap, and which, because they also derive revenues from the property-tax levy, share tax proceeds with the "TIFing" municipality. A study of the intergovernmental effects of TIF financing in Chicago estimated that between 1989 and 1995 the local school district's revenues had been reduced by $72 million (Washburn and Martin 1997).

Another means of raising funds for targeted development is through the establishment of special taxing districts. At the present time, the cities of Dallas and Fort Worth are supporting major development projects by way of property improvement districts, within which property owners pay a special property-tax assessment dedicated to local projects. In the Uptown (Dallas) and Sundance Square (Fort Worth) areas, property improvement district funds have been spent on promotional campaigns, street cleaning, local infrastructure, and private security patrols (Kallenberg 1995; 1996).

Reporting on a survey of local government officials conducted in 1989, Susan Clarke and Gary Gaile (1992) found that the two most commonly identified "second wave" economic development tools were two other off-budget items: enterprise zones and permit "streamlining." Although the U.S. Congress did not authorize a national enterprise zone program during the Reagan years, by the early 1990s a majority of states had implemented some form of enterprise zone policy. As a rule, these state-authorized enterprise zones leverage private investment by offering exclusions from state and local taxes, notably the sales and property levies. As in the case of the TIF process, the use of enterprise zones has at times been controversial. In 1992, the *Wall Street Journal* reported that Louisville, Kentucky's enterprise zone had grown from its originally designated 3.8 square miles to 45.7 square miles, at the latter scale including much of the city and even portions of adjoining Jefferson County. As a consequence, enterprise zone tax benefits flowed to businesses—such as the rental car companies operating at Louisville's airport—that were in "areas that can hardly be called poor" (Davidson 1992).

Many cities have also sought to meet a particular concern of real estate interests that often complain that the local regulatory procedures associated with property development are too bureaucratically cumbersome and time-consuming. As a result, cities from Boston to Berkeley, California, have initiated "one-stop" formats for awarding building permits (Diesenhouse 1991; McCloud 1996). Commenting on efforts by former mayor Ed

Koch's administration to stimulate real estate development in New York City during the 1980s, sociologist William Sites underscores how streamlining the project approval process served this broader policy aim:

> Municipal agencies tended to use policy-planning instruments—powers over zoning, development impacts, and the use of public resources—in a flexible, negotiated fashion. Development projects that were legally mandated to pass through a public land-use review process did require a kind of *ad hoc* planning, encouraging adaptation of the planning process to make it more receptive to administration goals. In such cases, plans were increasingly "predeveloped" by developers and city officials, packaged with an agreed-upon set of public amenities, and shepherded through the land-review process by top city administrators. (Sites 1994, 195)

In effect, New York City officials were taking it upon themselves to advocate privately initiated projects and to streamline, by way of political clout, the planning and approval processes.

In addition to the new techniques that have been deployed to induce private investment in the post–urban renewal era, many cities continue to rely on long-standing methods of development support such as manipulation of zoning regulations, ancillary infrastructure improvements, and land acquisition. In recent years both Philadelphia and Boston modified downtown zoning regulations with the aim of spurring new development: Philadelphia by waiving its 548-foot building height restriction (that is, not taller than the head of William Penn's statue atop City Hall!); Boston by allowing building heights up to 460 feet in the North Station area at the eastern end of the downtown (Wallace 1997b; Diesenhouse 1990). It is, of course, commonplace for cities to support new projects such as Norfolk, Virginia's downtown shopping mall, the MacArthur Center, with investments in "roads, utilities, and landscaping" (Hardcastle 1994), or, in the case of Boston's Fort Point area, with "a new road, bridge, rapid-transit spur, ferry, and walkway" (Diesenhouse 1995). Cities also promote development by condemning and acquiring sites that are subsequently transferred to private developers. However, in 1997 the suburban town of Hurst, Texas, raised eyebrows in the real estate and legal communities by using its eminent domain power to condemn a group of private dwellings in order to provide space for an expanding shopping mall. Claiming economic development as the town's "public purpose" in condemning the last ten houses in the Richland Park East neighborhood, Hurst's assistant city manager claimed, "We see the North East Mall as one of the backbones of our business community, and we want to make sure that it remains a viable contributor" (*New York Times* 1997).

Economic Niche Strategies

The authors of a book entitled *Marketing Places* define their text's agenda in the following terms: "Place marketing means designing a place to satisfy the needs of its target markets. It succeeds when citizens and businesses are pleased with their communities, and meet the expectations of visitors and investors" (Kotler, Haider, and Rein 1993, 99). Increasingly, cities' economic development aims follow just this line of reasoning. In order to attract new investment, lure visitors (with money or credit cards in hand), and replenish municipal revenue streams, a city must locate a productive "niche" within the network of urban economies (Pagano and Bowman 1995, 44–67). In *Marketing Places,* this approach to economic development is further linked to the notion of "image positioning": "where the place positions itself in regional, national, and international terms as the place for a certain type of activity or as a viable alternative location/attraction to another place that may have a stronger or more established position" (Kotler, Haider, and Rein 1993, 153). In short, image positioning may require some sleight of hand by the "alternative location/attraction."

The quest by cities for new economic niches is not a random process. Geographer Briavel Holcomb observes that the "category of places which best exemplifies both the construction of new images to replace the old, and the efforts to recreate places to be consonant with the preferred images, are the previously industrial cities now being restructured for the post-industrial, service economy" (Holcomb 1993, 134). Within the context of an industrially anchored economy, the pursuit of desirable economic niches is not unthinkable. Chicago's dominance of the American midwest resulted in large measure from local entrepreneurs' attraction of the rail connections that allowed their city's transportation network to supersede St. Louis's river-based shipping system (Cronon 1991, 63–93 and 112–13). Nonetheless, in the late twentieth century, North American cities, many of them having lost the manufacturers whose rising fortunes had paralleled their own ascent to urban prominence, typically have sought new economic niches within the expanding service economy.

Economic niche strategies tend to follow a relatively small number of predictable paths: the development of convention and sporting facilities that will attract trade shows, professional meetings, major sporting events, or even professional sports franchises; the enhancement of cultural institutions and historical sites that burnish a city's reputation and define it as a place worthy of tourists' interest; the development of entertainment destinations whose markets may be, for the most part, local or regional, but whose attractions are likely to generate substantial spending by long- and short-term visitors alike (Beauregard 1998). Among the contemporary array of such entertainment destinations, gambling casinos seem to have won a special place in the hearts of municipal officials.

In the business press and among the public at large much of the attention that is devoted to convention-and-tourism-derived economic development focuses on the fortunes of megaprojects such as New York City's Jacob Javits Center or Chicago's McCormick Place, or on the relative merits of the half-dozen or so cities that dominate the convention trade. In fact, cities across the United States seek a share of this market. Providence, Rhode Island, set between the larger, attraction-rich convention cities of New York and Boston, opened a new convention facility in 1993 with the explicit aim of luring cost-conscious regional conference and trade groups. In the words of one of the convention center's staff: "The main reason they come here is cost and accessibility. As soon as we can get a group here, we can please them" (Braccidiferro 1994). In 1992, the St. Paul *Pioneer Press* reported that its home city was losing its niche in the competition for conventions and trade shows. Saddled with an aging convention center, St. Paul was unable to compete with nearby Minneapolis for large-scale events, while smaller and state-based groups were opting to hold their meetings in cities such as St. Cloud, Duluth, and Rochester, Minnesota. Indeed, in the decade preceding this newspaper account, the number of local convention and tourist bureaus in Minnesota had increased from ten to thirty-two (Iverson 1992).

Marketing Places seems to suggest that a locale's production of historical ambiance is as manageable as the construction of a highway or parking garage. Some cities have had success in intentionally upgrading their historic aura. Among large American cities, Baltimore, initially by way of its Inner Harbor redevelopment and subsequently through the gentrification of adjoining neighborhoods, has in the last generation greatly increased its reputation as a historic city and tourist destination (Frieden and Sagalyn 1989, 259–61; Levine 1987). In the case of much smaller Lowell, Massachusetts, whose mills were the flagships of the U.S. textile industry for about thirty years during the mid-nineteenth century, the designation of its downtown area as a national urban park in 1978 coincided with a crucial corporate relocation, the renovation and conversion of a number of old mill structures, and the arrival of a robust stream of tourists (Gittell 1992, 65–93). Nor does the sprucing up of historical districts require especially old or historically significant sites. At present, Los Angeles is pursuing a redevelopment plan along Hollywood Boulevard, whose oldest remaining structures date from the early twentieth century and were not closely allied with the development of the film industry. The Hollywood Entertainment Museum will occupy the converted food court area of a shopping mall that was built around 1980. With mass transit access to downtown Los Angeles, and given the boulevard's location in the Hollywood area, redevelopment officials expect the street's two new museums and its restored movie houses to pull tourists (Newman 1996).

Convention center managers, restaurateurs, shop owners, hotel managers, and local economic development officials alike seek to promote their particular cities as destinations with well-defined images. It is due to such well-defined images that Las Vegas and Atlantic City have for decades attracted millions of out-of-town gambling enthusiasts. An emerging wrinkle in the destination game is the development of facilities such as urban theme parks and entertainment centers whose attractions anchor local redevelopment initiatives. New York City's redevelopment of the Times Square area aims to create a theme park whose restaurants, shops, game rooms, and theaters evoke Times Square's long-standing identity as an exciting big-city entertainment district (Reichl 1999). The facilities and experiences of the new Times Square are not re-creations of the old Times Square. The contemporary district is much more the product of comprehensive planning that has aimed to communicate a sense of personal security to visitors while sustaining the visceral experience of viewing or walking through the district. This latter objective is advanced by the use of glaring signage and the introduction in various venues of all manner of state-of-the-art entertainment technologies (Muschamp 1993; Shepherd 1996).

Ironically even in Las Vegas, whose destination identity would seem to be assured, a new wave of casinos has sought to employ similar techniques in order to redefine their attractions as suitable destinations for families on holiday. Much of what differentiates these new casinos from their predecessors of a generation past is the addition of facilities and entertainments targeting youth audiences. In 1990, the newly opened Mirage casino facility included "a tropical rainforest, waterfalls that turn into volcanoes, a dolphin habitat, rare white tigers, and more." By late 1993, The Mirage's owner had opened another casino, Treasure Island: "Complete with pirate ships, the casino is the scene of a waterfront battle each evening where the buccaneers defend their booty from the British" (Becker 1994). Coincidentally, the City of Las Vegas and real estate interests holding property downtown, several miles from the center of new casino development along the Strip, have sought to upgrade downtown Freemont Street as a pedestrian passage and focus of "adult entertainment." Even as the casino industry seeks to broaden Las Vegas's economic niche, within the city separate redevelopment tracks are defining distinguishable family entertainment and adult entertainment areas (Kopytoff 1996).

Place Enhancement Strategies

The Philadelphia Gateway project, on the north end of Philadelphia's downtown area, illustrates the third element characteristic of new urban redevelopment strategies. The core of the Gateway project is a twelve-story parking garage erected in 1992 by a private developer who leased the publicly owned site. Plans for this project's second phase included a multi-screen cinema complex atop the parking facility, and adjoining the original structure, a second building holding "nightclubs, theme restaurants, and shops." On the one hand, the developer sought to define an "entertainment destination." The Gateway project's immediate neighborhood had a limited residential population, and due to the project's siting along a major expressway, the theatre operators anticipated tapping the metropolitan film market. On the other hand, by creating a mixed-use project, the developer sought to draw local customers—such as downtown office workers lingering after hours—and stimulate additional investment in the vicinity. The Gateway project's sponsors ultimately aimed to create a local environment whose mix of attractions and accessibility to the pedestrians would enable it to knit itself into the surrounding cityscape (Kirk 1995).

Many of the most prominent inner-city redevelopment projects of the 1950s and 1960s—such as Baltimore's Charles Center, Boston's Government Center, or Chicago's Sandburg Village—were single-use environments whose modernist architectural presentation further set them apart from their adjoining neighborhoods. By the 1970s, Jane Jacobs's gospel of mixed uses had finally won converts among real estate developers, architects, and city planners, but by that time anxieties over big-city decline and escalating criminal activity produced developments that, while nominally for mixed use, were also willfully "defensible." Detroit's Renaissance Center, mixed-use on the inside but separated from the adjoining downtown area by a ten-foot berm, exemplified this compromise design strategy. In 1977, a commentator in the *Saturday Review* characterized the Renaissance Center, as well as the similarly designed IDS and Peachtree centers (in Minneapolis and Atlanta, respectively), as "urban dinosaurs"—devastating small businesses on nearby streets and feeding from massive public-development and routine service expenditures (Conway 1977).

Duncan Fulton, principal architect of the Columbus Square project in Dallas's Uptown area, which includes conventional apartments, loft-style residential spaces, and street-level retailing, expresses a sense of the city that is worlds apart from the attitudes driving urban renewal–era design: "In creating Columbus Square, we looked at model urban communities in New York, Paris, and London and fashioned a building with European esthetics and the practicality inherent in a New York or Boston neighborhood" (Kallenberg 1995). Obviously, Fulton's project is pitched to an upscale market with a taste for nostalgic urban glamour, but just as crucially, his commitment to street-accessible siting, modest building scales, and mixed uses reflects a familiar pattern in new urban projects. Sometimes working on smaller sites, often incorporating older "leftover" structures within otherwise new developments, and typically animated by an urban vision appreciative of the "traditional" streetscape, many contemporary developers seek to situate new construction so it contributes to the street life and practical pedestrian use of the adjoining city.

The developers and designers of contemporary sports facilities have not been immune to these trends. Following a generation of stadium development on suburban sites, where mammoth sporting facilities are located just off expressway ramps and centered on huge surface-parking areas, recently built baseball stadiums, including Coors Field, Oriole Park at Camden Yards (Baltimore), and Jacobs Field (Cleveland) have been consciously designed with the enhancement of the surrounding city in mind. In the press, much attention has been devoted to their relatively small scale and traditional design features. From the standpoint of urban economic development, just as striking are their "contextualized" siting and mixed-use character—these stadiums function as sporting event–centered multiple-retailer complexes purveying food, sports paraphernalia, and nonsporting entertainment. Each of these stadiums maximizes pedestrian and mass transit accessibility, and the foot traffic they generate is intended to spur retailing and entertainment activity on adjoining streets. In short, apart from their central function as sports centers, these new facilities seek to recreate densely used, multiple-purpose commercial areas (Viuker 1992; Kamin 1994).

The Political Economy of Contemporary Urban Redevelopment

The new aims and techniques of urban redevelopment result from emerging trends in the global economy in conjunction with shifting national-government policy priorities. Economic globalism has produced particular consequences in certain cities, and it has affected the thinking of municipal officials, economic development professionals, and private developers. However, there are also a variety of local and largely political factors contributing to the shape of contemporary urban redevelopment. In U.S. cities, the crucial political correlates of the new-style regime of urban redevelopment include the rise of the nonpartisan, pragmatist mayor; the long-term ebbing of planning and land-use conflict; and the emergence of nonprofit organizations as advocates of housing and neighborhood economic development.

Mister Fixit Mayors

A *New York Times* account of the 1997 Los Angeles mayoral race pitting incumbent Republican mayor Richard Riordan against Democratic challenger Tom Hayden noted Riordan's adoption of "the prevailing bipartisan mantra of minimalist government mixed with activist volunteerism" (Purdum 1997). This characterization undoubtedly understates the degree to which Mayor Riordan attempted to deploy his administration's considerable fiscal resources in alliance with private development activity, but just as surely, it touches on a philosophical grounding shared by many contemporary U.S. mayors. Long gone are mayors such as John Lindsay of New York City or Richard Lee of New Haven, Connecticut, who made use of "city hall as a bully pulpit in their efforts to bridge racial and class divisions" (Eisinger 1998, 320). In the 1990s, mayors such as Riordan, Rudolph Giuliani (New York City), Richard M. Daley (Chicago), and Edward Rendell (Philadelphia) emphasized frugal fiscal management, crime reduction, maintenance of a business environment congenial to new private investment, and restored civic confidence. A principal consequence of this scaled-down, collaborationist approach to municipal leadership has been for mayors' economic development priorities to follow the lead of private sector initiatives. And during the expansionist 1990s there were many such private initiatives to support, though they tended to follow a handful of frequently visited paths: hotels and upscale commercial development in downtown areas; high-end residential construction and rehabilitation in near-downtown locations, often on obsolete industrial sites; and the unveiling of a new generation of mixed-use sporting and high-tech entertainment venues.

The watchword of contemporary U.S. mayors is public-private partnership. Mayors Daley, Giuliani, Rendell, and Riordan presumed that corporate investment is the key to local economic prosperity, and correspondingly, that to interrupt the flow of private capital with undue municipal regulation is to court disinvestment and economic stagnation. Thus, Richard M. Daley proudly asserts: "Our goal is to bring down the walls of regulation." A local observer of Mayor Daley, as well as of his father, the legendary Richard J. Daley, has offered this comparison of the two: "He thinks more like a businessman than a politician. His dad ran the city on patronage; he's running it like a business—outsourcing, privatizing. He hates studies and reports; he wants quick action" (Atlas 1996, 39).

Though admirers of Richard M. Daley find in his approach to the mayoralty a leadership style in keeping with turn-of-the-millennium political economic realities, there is another interpretation that comes to mind. In his review of journalist Buzz Bissinger's admiring profile of Philadelphia's Ed Rendell, *A Prayer for the City* (1997), urban historian Robert Fishman observes:

> The Mayor's version of urban liberalism leaves him very little power to achieve liberal goals. Where the bosses of the past relied on patronage jobs, lucrative contracts and solid neighborhood support to control city government, Rendell seems to function best as a freelance negotiator trying to broker deals with the real powers in the city and in corporate America. (Fishman 1998)

Rendell succeeded as mayor by maintaining a relatively firm hold on municipal finances, the bureaucracy, and city employees unions, then delivered for his Philadelphia constituents by leveraging private sector–initiated development projects.

There is an additional element that structures the political economic environment producing the contemporary Mister Fixit mayors. In the last couple of decades, campaigning for municipal office has become highly capital intensive, and among the local constituencies most inclined to make sizable campaign contributions are developers and other real estate interests. This trend is especially evident in Chicago, where as recently as the 1970s citywide election campaigns continued to be relatively low-cost affairs driven by intensive door-to-door canvassing operations. In his 1995 reelection campaign, in which he faced very weak opposition, Richard M. Daley raised over $5.4 million, compared to the $545,000 contributed to all other candidates. Corporate and other business contributions accounted for over 40 percent of these funds, a figure that does not include individual contributions by property owners and business executives (Gierzynski, Kleppner, and Lewis 1996, 26–28). Interestingly, although the volume of business dollars far exceeded that of overall labor union contributions to the Daley campaign, the plumbers union, long concerned with the provisions of Chicago's building code, raised $55,000 for the mayor's reelection effort (Gibson 1995). Nor is Mayor Daley's campaign fund-raising advantage unique. A month before the 1997 Los Angeles mayoral election, Richard Riordan had raised $2.4 million to finance his campaign. His opponent, California state senator Tom Hayden, had managed to generate only $200,000 in contributions (Purdum 1997). In short, mayors such as Daley and Riordan, whose policy priorities converge with the scenarios of major development and business interests, can expect to amass formidable campaign war chests.

The Declining Ferocity of Urban Land-Use Conflict

In the 1960s, cities' efforts to rebuild their downtowns, extend their expressway systems, and rebuild residential neighborhoods were repeated precipitators of local political conflict.

> By 1961 one did not have to read Jane Jacobs to discover criticisms of the renewal process. In one city after another, individuals less articulate than Jacobs but just as outraged were expressing complaints and raising questions about the justice and economic feasibility of urban renewal. . . . Especially bitter were those who expected to be displaced from renewal sites. (Teaford 1990, 153–54)

The 1954 reshaping of the original urban redevelopment law—which, among other things, redubbed the program "urban renewal"—spurred cities around the United States to initiate far more ambitious clearance and rebuilding schemes. And as if to add fuel to the newly sparked fire, in 1956 the U.S. Congress passed the Interstate Highway Act. Cities' subsequent efforts to slice their geographic cores with these roadways further threatened the residents of near-downtown, low-prestige, and substantially minority inner-city neighborhoods. Thus, by virtue of the overwhelming physical changes focused on inner-city neighborhoods in the 1960s, there was the great likelihood that intense political conflict would ensue.

Political controversy over redevelopment was not just a matter of the number of blocks to be cleared or expressway miles to be routed. As John Emmeus Davis notes in his summary of the sources of redevelopment conflict in Cincinnati's West End during the late 1960s: "Added to these . . . conditions underlying the West End revolt was another condition not engendered by urban renewal: the black movement for civil rights" (Davis 1991, 148). Urban renewal, which was often derisively rephrased as "negro removal," collided with and added force to the growing political consciousness of African American inner-city residents. Two participants in the West End urban renewal debate later described the neighborhood's response to the City of Cincinnati's redevelopment agenda: "They wanted the kind of total community development necessary to promote a fundamental change in the social class of blacks in Cincinnati's West End. And they believed that this view stood diametrically opposed to that of city officials who, the residents felt, equated urban renewal with massive black removal" (Jenkins and Lewis 1982, 105). Indeed, by the late 1960s, as younger civil rights activists began to call for black power, the rhetoric of civil rights had converged with the assertively localist philosophy embedded in federal War on Poverty initiatives such as the Community Action Program, whose enabling legislation had called for the "maximum feasible participation" of low-income residents in shaping ameliorative neighborhood programs (Fainstein and Fainstein 1974, 1–57; Piven 1974).

Urban renewal's primacy as a source of urban political conflict was not just a result of programmatic scale and impact. The 1954 U.S. Housing Act mandated "local citizen participation in developing and executing the urban renewal program," and as urban renewal's notoriety grew, and—just as crucially—as community organizers learned to work the planning process, efforts to block or reshape renewal schemes by means of the program's citizen participation protocols became commonplace. In his 1969 introduction to a study of three Boston urban renewal projects, Langley Carlton Keyes Jr. describes the political salience of urban renewal's citizen participation provisions:

> While federal rules do not go beyond the requirement to hold the hearing, a negative response from the majority of neighborhood residents would clearly be an inauspicious start for a program dependent on local concern and involvement for its ultimate success. At bare minimum, a neighborhood rehabilitation program presupposes the involvement and approval of the majority of those elements in the local community who are the greatest potential source of support, and conversely, of opposition—were they to go into opposition. (Keyes 1969, 7)

To assure federal redevelopment officials of a proposal's local support, and ultimately to begin the process of redevelopment, local consultation was necessary. By focusing on the hearing process that accompanied redevelopment planning, opposition forces could marshal support, and if they could deliver their constituents to the public hearings, they could possibly kill unwanted proposals. Thus, urban renewal both stimulated neighborhood antagonism and offered a straightforward and well-understood mechanism for voicing that antagonism.

Contemporary redevelopment plans play out in an entirely different local political environment. Neighborhood-based opposition political movements, animated by broad considerations of social justice and aggrieved by the legacy of specific past redevelopment initiatives, are a rarity. The various techniques for stimulating private development do not command the kind of widespread public attention attracted by urban renewal. And possibly of greatest import, the decision-making processes that result in the authorization of new development initiatives do not occur in public arenas subject to influence by opposition forces. In other words, the 1960s Boston community organizer's ultimate mobilizing trick—bringing out neighborhood residents to humble redevelopment tsar Edward Logue at a public hearing—is simply not available today.

A second feature contributing to the quiescence of contemporary redevelopment politics is the late-twentieth-century U.S. cityscape itself. Unlike American cities at mid-century, whose urban renewal and expressway schemes required surgical cuts in densely built-up central districts, contemporary cities characteristically hold thousands of acres of underused industrial and transportation-infrastructure land, as well as open land as yet undeveloped in the wake of previous clearance efforts. Among northeastern U.S. cities, redevelopment initiatives are currently occurring in the old factory area of Brooklyn's Greenpoint across the East River from Manhattan, in Boston's Fort Point on the eastern edge of that city's traditional commercial core, and in Providence, Rhode Island's former jewelry district (Redburn 1994; Diesenhouse 1995; Abbot 1997). In such neighborhoods, which historically have not held substantial residential populations, the arrival of investors and upscale residents does not stoke significant local resentment.

Ultimately, the ideological climate that prevails in contemporary U.S. cities also works to reduce the likelihood that new development schemes will produce substantial political conflict. Chicago mayor Daley's pledge to "bring down the walls of regulation" is the coin of the municipal economic development realm. So many U.S. cities have suffered sustained population and business decline that the prospect of turning the corner into a new era of urban growth tends to receive unquestioned assent. Susan Fainstein (1991, 23) has noted how this attitude has transformed the planning process in major cities: "If the argument that what is good for business is good for everyone is not wholly accepted, neither is it opposed by a widely held alternative formulation." In a practical sense, this ethos produces municipal administrations that can freely court a variety of investors and development schemes—far more than they could a generation ago. Conversely, opponents of new development begin in a very disadvantaged rhetorical position; they have to substantiate their opposition to the desperately needed flows of dollars, new buildings, and jobs that are presumed to result from private investment.

The Rise of Community Development Corporations

In the past generation, surely the most striking neighborhood-level institutional development in U.S. cities has been the proliferation of community development corporations (CDCs). Estimates of the number of CDCs run from one thousand to five thousand (Vidal 1992; Dreier 1997, 12). Typically, CDCs are grassroots organizations that mobilize local and nonlocal resources with the aim of promoting neighborhood improvement. Probably the modal CDC activities are the production and management of affordable housing and neighborhood economic development work. Many CDCs, some with roots extending back to the 1960s, were founded as opposition groups that sought to block or reshape city-sponsored redevelopment efforts. Apart from their contemporary policy-implementation or service-delivery functions, a great number of CDCs continue to advocate local economic development, housing, and social service measures that respond to the particular needs of racial minority or low-income neighborhoods (Goetz 1993).

From the standpoint of urban neighborhood policy, the maturation of the CDC movement has been most welcome. As a rule, these constituent-tied organizations seem to build and manage low-cost housing much more effectively than public housing agencies. Moreover, in many inner-city neighborhoods where the legitimacy of mainstream institutions—corporations, municipal service-delivery bureaucracies, and so on—has been on the wane for decades, CDCs have played a crucial role in sustaining local community allegiance (Medoff and Sklar 1994). However, the spread of the CDC model appears to have had a curious effect on municipal redevelopment agendas. As the federal government no longer directly supports low-income housing production and as many local public housing agencies have become administrative backwaters, mayors and other municipal leaders have been relieved of the responsibility to craft redevelopment agendas that give serious attention to the production of housing whose cost will be within the means of less affluent residents.

There have been exceptions to this generalization. During the administration of Mayor Ray Flynn in the 1980s, the City of Boston proceeded with an ambitious program of affordable-housing development, with the bulk of this activity carried out via CDCs (Dreier 1997, 12–15). In 1993, Chicago CDCs mounted a successful affordable-housing campaign that pressured Mayor Daley into increasing the city government's support for nonprofit housing construction (Reardon 1993). Nevertheless, because CDCs have come to shoulder most of the subsidized housing production burden in U.S. cities, the municipal economic development agenda has been narrowed. While CDCs do the heavy lifting involved in leveraging financial resources, locating appropriate sites for development, and negotiating with neighborhood constituencies, municipal governments are left to court the developers of large-scale commercial and entertainment facilities and upscale residential complexes.

The Ascendant City of Leisure

In many respects Walter McQuade's survey of early-1960s Boston is a "chronicle of a death foretold." Since the early 1960s, Boston—like Brooklyn and Lower Manhattan, Chicago, Cleveland, Detroit, and scores of other U.S. cities—has lost substantial portions of its old industrial economy. Concurrently, the regional centrality of downtown retailers in Boston—and again, in many other U.S. cities—has declined in the face of massive suburban commercial development. And finally, like most of its older industrial metropolis peers of the Northeast and Midwest, Boston has, in the past few decades, experienced substantial population loss (Teaford 1990).

Nevertheless, the forty years that have passed since McQuade portrayed a Boston in economic stasis have not been a period of unmitigated urban decline. For example, many U.S. central cities have remained important corporate nodes, housing numerous business headquarters and a wide variety of ancillary business-service firms. Each year cities such as Atlanta, Chicago, New Orleans, New York, San Francisco, and Washington, D.C., continue to draw millions of convention-goers and tourists. Other cities, including Boston, Los Angeles, Minneapolis, and Seattle, have retained or developed important cultural institutions, which have solidified their regional and national prominence. Moreover, in each of these cities gentrification of older neighborhoods and, more recently, new upscale residential development have repopularized some of their inner-city districts as commodious and, indeed, prestigious places of residence.

The emergent postindustrial metropolis in the United States is also a redesigned city, and paradoxically the new spaces appearing in late-twentieth-century cities often incorporate or evoke older urban forms. Witness Bernard Frieden and Lynne Sagalyn's description of the renowned Faneuil Hall/Quincy Market complex in Boston, which was restored in the mid-1970s by developer James Rouse and architect Ben Thompson:

> The reconstruction . . . both preserved and changed Quincy Market: it was partly a cleaned up gem of 1826 architecture, partly a contemporary shopping arcade. Work crews had stripped away 150 years of alteration—interior walls, add-on sheds, roof extensions—to reveal the original structure in its graceful simplicity. But they had also tampered with that historic building. They cut a hole in the first-floor ceiling to create a rotunda with a view up into the great dome above the second floor. They took out the old multi-paned windows and mounted large sheets of glass on pivots. Where produce merchants had once put up canvas awnings to cover outside stalls, they built glass canopies with overhead sections that could slide down like garage doors in bad weather. . . . Another old-fashioned touch came from wooden push-carts: on opening day some forty of them were dotted around the market, operated by artists, weavers, jewelry makers, and others selling unusual hand-made products. (Frieden and Sagalyn 1989, 1–2)

Aside from the much-noted architectural eclecticism of this project, which has had a tremendous influence on subsequent inner-city commercial developments, the other striking features of the Faneuil Hall/Quincy Market complex are its pedestrian friendliness and mixed-use array of attractions and businesses. In the new city of leisure, shoppers are very likely to be sheltered from the elements and provided with near-site parking, but as they go about the business of shopping, they navigate smartly ornamented spaces designed to be easily accessible on foot and offering a variety of amusements (Zukin 1993).

This approach to designing office complexes, shopping centers, and even sporting facilities—described as the "theming of America" by design critic Ada Louise Huxtable (1992)—has become a staple of contemporary urban redevelopment initiatives. The transformation of the city into a consumer's playground entices much-needed discretionary spending inside the borders of the central city, and through creative restoration and new construction allows otherwise declining cities to retain evocative pieces of their physical heritage. In the past decade Coors Field has been but one of a number of new sporting facilities reflective of these trends in consumption-oriented urban design. In Toronto, the baseball Blue Jays' SkyDome includes hotel accommodations, a McDonald's outlet, and the local Hard Rock Cafe. Moreover, as a mixed-use sports and entertainment complex, the SkyDome is an important anchor for the city's ambitious waterfront redevelopment area. In Baltimore, Oriole Park at Camden Yards represents a variation on the same theme: a baseball stadium, a renovation project (the baseball club's offices occupy a restored warehouse adjoining the historicist ballpark), and a prominent destination within a larger harborside entertainment district.

In the contemporary U.S. city, sports can no longer be characterized as mere games. Sports franchises build their fan pools by assuming the mantle of civic identity and achievement. As emotional compasses for audiences near and far, sports clubs have become important economic magnets: they bring crowds into the city and induce these crowds to make substantial cash expenditures. Sports stadiums such as Coors Field, the SkyDome, and Camden Yards center larger entertainment districts, and at a time when more conventional government facilities beg for investment, they represent well-endowed and, at least on occasion, much-admired civic monuments. Ultimately, the symbolic and material importance of sports clubs and sporting facilities embodies the ascendancy of the city of leisure as a model of postindustrial urban economic development.

3

The New Comiskey Park

Economics, Politics, and

Professional Sports Franchise Retention

By the summer of 1990, from any seat in the left-field grandstand of the venerable Comiskey Park an observer of a Chicago White Sox contest could spot the upper reaches of Comiskey's successor ballpark looming over the first-base grandstand roof. For five years the fate of this odd couple of structures—the one a sprawling heap of white-painted brick capped with an erector set of stadium lights, the second a soaring composition of beige concrete and reflecting-glass facade detailing—had been intimately connected. During these years the principal owners of the White Sox baseball franchise, Jerry Reinsdorf and Eddie Einhorn, had laid the groundwork for abandoning the old ballpark, had negotiated with officials of at least three municipalities over the terms for building a new White Sox home, and had finally won a State of Illinois–financed "New Comiskey Park" costing in excess of $150 million.

Representatives of the state-mandated Illinois Sports Facilities Authority (ISFA) had in turn negotiated a relocation settlement with residents of South Armour Square, the small residential enclave adjoining the original Comiskey Park that became the site of the new ballpark. The efforts of the South Armour Square residents to deal with ISFA offer a fascinating window for assessing the opportunities and constraints confronted by working-class neighborhood people seeking to negotiate with powerful governmental and corporate institutions. Just as the breathtaking new Comiskey Park towered above its turn-of-the-century antecedent, the neighborhood impact of the new sports arena was expected to reach past South Armour Square into adjoining areas such as Bridgeport and North Armour Square. Another revealing element of the new Comiskey Park's legacy is its curious disconnection from these areas.

In the following pages we trace the transition from old to new Comiskey Park, focusing on the maneuvers of the White Sox owners to find a new home, the efforts of City of Chicago officials to retain the ball club, and finally, the stadium itself as a site for baseball playing and profit making. In chapter 4 we turn to the new Comiskey Park and its community context. There we view community in three ways in order to evaluate the new sports arena in reference to its immediate neighbors in South Armour Square, as an institutional anchor within a larger segment of Chicago's South Side, and as a potential magnet for metropolitan identification and loyalty.

The Baseball Palace of the World

In the early months of 1910, White Sox owner Charles Comiskey oversaw the construction of his eponymous home field. Comiskey Park's architect was Zachary Taylor Davis, who consulted White Sox pitcher Ed Walsh in designing the new facility. Possibly due to Walsh's involvement, the spacious dimensions of Comiskey (362 feet along the right- and left-field foul lines, 420 feet from home plate to center field) quickly earned it a reputation as a pitcher's ballpark. For its time, the original Comiskey Park was indeed a grand facility. It cost Charles Comiskey approximately $750,000 to build, offered seating to nearly 30,000 fans, and was enclosed by grandstands reaching well beyond first and third bases. In a city often given to hyperbole, Comiskey Park was known as the "baseball palace of the world" (Gershman 1993, 92–94).

The original Comiskey Park's three-quarter-century history was checkered. During the 1910s the White Sox were among baseball's more successful franchises, but following the 1920 season several members of the American League champion 1919 White Sox were banned from major league ball for throwing the World Series to the Cincinnati Reds. Most notable of the "Black Sox" of 1919 was "Shoeless" Joe Jackson, one of the great hitters of the early twentieth century. From the 1920s through the 1940s the White Sox were extremely anemic, though even during this period Comiskey Park had its moments. For example, the first major league All-Star game was played there on July 6, 1933. For many years during the 1930s and 1940s baseball's Negro League All-Star game was an annual Comiskey Park event. Joe Louis's defeat of James Braddock and ascent to boxing's heavyweight title occurred on June 22, 1937, at Comiskey. Chicago's "other" professional football club, the Cardinals, won their only NFL championship by defeating the Philadelphia Eagles 28–21 at Comiskey Park on December 28, 1947 (Hayner 1990).

Located at the intersection of 35th Street and Shields Avenue on Chicago's South Side, Comiskey Park was in several respects an embodiment of the city of broad shoulders. The ballpark was about a mile east of the Union Stockyards complex, and as one former White Sox player recalled, "when you could smell the stockyards, that meant the wind was blowing out, blowing with the hitter" (Gershman 1993, 92). For many

The visual tunnel effect produced by the original Comiskey Park's upper grandstand

years Mayor Richard J. Daley reserved a box seat at Comiskey Park and regularly attended White Sox contests. Indeed, on the evening of September 22, 1959, against the backdrop of Cold War anxieties, Mayor Daley's administration caused considerable local consternation when his fire chief authorized the sounding of civil defense sirens in celebration of the White Sox clinching their first American League championship in 40 years. The mayor explained: "The City Council passed a resolution decreeing that there should be hilarity in the streets and shouting and celebration" (Hayner 1990).

During the post–World War II period, the fortunes of the White Sox and Comiskey Park were closely associated with Bill Veeck, a flamboyant baseball entrepreneur who was chief owner of the ball club first in the late 1950s and then for several years in the mid-to-late 1970s. Following the White Sox championship season of 1959, Veeck installed the ballpark's "exploding scoreboard," from which fireworks were detonated in response to the rare White Sox home run and whose sound effects included "35 tapes, 32 seconds in length, that combined the best in shrieks, crashes, roars and howls. Fans delighted to the weird cacophony of train wrecks, live battles, diving planes and a circus calliope" (Reidenbaugh 1987, 70). During Veeck's second stint as White Sox chief executive, a

The original Comiskey Park's last days, with the new ballpark looming beyond the first base–side grandstand

similarly unorthodox promotional event proved much less delightful and probably contributed to the baseball franchise's change of direction in the following decade. On July 12, 1979, the White Sox invited a local radio disk jockey to host a "disco demolition" event between contests of a White Sox–Detroit Tigers double header. Fans who brought disco records had enjoyed admission for only ninety-eight cents. As the records were ignited, much of the crowd rushed out from the grandstands and onto the playing field. The damage to the Comiskey Park turf was substantial. Moreover, the "shouting and celebration" were sufficiently excessive to result in the cancellation—and White Sox forfeiture—of the evening's second baseball game (Hayner 1990). A few years later, White Sox co-owner Jerry Reinsdorf described Comiskey Park as having become the "world's largest outdoor saloon" during the regime of his predecessor (Fitzpatrick 1986).

The New White Sox Regime

In January 1981, Bill Veeck turned over the reins of the White Sox to a new ownership group headed by Jerry Reinsdorf and Eddie Einhorn.

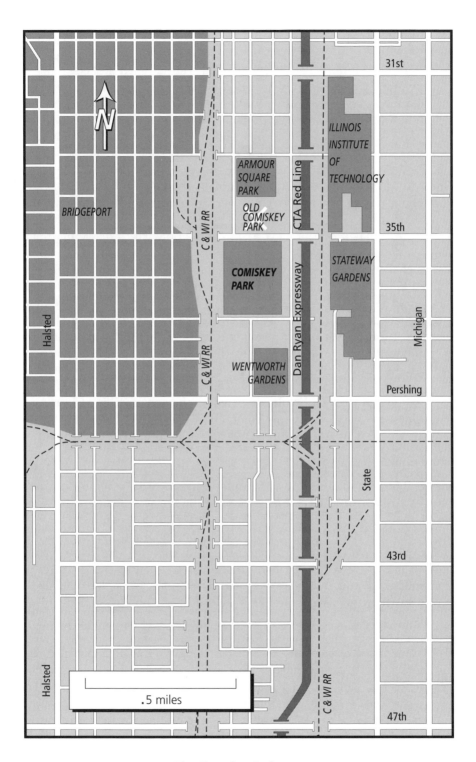

The Comiskey Park Area

Reinsdorf and Einhorn had become friends during their student days at Northwestern University Law School. Reinsdorf had subsequently made his millions in real estate, and within a few years he would also become the principal owner of the Chicago Bulls professional basketball team. Einhorn was a CBS executive who had previously prospered as an independent producer of televised sporting events. Upon taking over the White Sox, Reinsdorf and Einhorn committed themselves to turning the franchise into a first-class operation. Although the elderly Veeck had often been characterized as an innovative sports marketer, it was clearly the intent of the new White Sox owners to turn away from his carnivalesque techniques in favor of a more contemporary approach to delivering their sport product (Markus 1981; McNamee 1988).

The challenges confronting Reinsdorf and Einhorn were formidable. Although Bill Veeck had produced a mild on-field and box office resurgence in the mid-1970s, the White Sox played in Major League Baseball's oldest facility, whose maintenance had been substantially underfinanced for many years, and their ball club was not among the most competitive in the American League. Moreover, with the Tribune Company's acquisition of the Cubs in mid-1981, the city's preferred baseball club was controlled by a powerful corporation possessing immense marketing capacity. Over the next several years the White Sox owners pursued an array of strategies that, although not always complementary, were generally aimed at modernizing the franchise's operations, redefining its core market, and increasing cash flow.

In 1982, the Chicago City Council, with the support of Mayor Jane Byrne, approved the issuance of $5 million in industrial revenue bonds to finance the construction of a bank of skyboxes attached to Comiskey Park's upper grandstand deck. Yet even as the White Sox management was upgrading Comiskey Park and widening its potential revenue stream, the club's owners were claiming that in the long run their ball club would have to move into a new facility. The franchise's view of the situation is encapsulated in this statement prepared by a structural engineer advising White Sox management, which Jerry Reinsdorf released to the local press on July 11, 1986:

> The purpose of this letter is to emphasize some of the points we raised at yesterday's meeting. As we indicated, we were very surprised at the rapid deterioration that has occurred at Comiskey Park since the extensive renovation project three years ago. Unfortunately, we foresee the likelihood of significant expenditures on an annual basis to keep the park in safe and usable condition through the 1989 season. Beyond that time there are no realistic long-term solutions since the deterioration is irreversible. Simply put, Comiskey Park is nearing the end of its useful life. (Krallitsch 1986)

The "baseball palace of the world" was not only a hazard to sports fans, it was a drag on the finances of the White Sox franchise. The White Sox sought a new, publicly financed stadium.

White Sox–sponsored marketing research also instructed the ball club that its most exploitable fan base was in Chicago's western suburbs. Indirectly, this may have contributed to the franchise's shift in television strategy: to reduce conventional broadcasting (which had been by WGN-TV, now a corporate cousin of the Cubs) and begin to move to cable television. Eddie Einhorn commented, "You want to see Fisk? You want to see Luzinski? Then you gotta pay to see the game. The future is pay television in some form, because we need additional income to survive" (McNamee 1988). Again, the emphasis on cash flow is obvious, but Einhorn's hard line is also reflective of an assumption that a more affluent audience would be willing to pay for the opportunity to see the heroics of White Sox stars such as Carlton Fisk and Greg Luzinski.

Clearly in conjunction with the ball club's wish to move to a new stadium, by the mid-1980s Reinsdorf and Einhorn had begun to explore alternative hometowns for the White Sox. The wish to find greener pastures was the flip side of what might be called the team's "South Side problem." The South Side problem had two components. The first was summarized by a local journalist: "A perception that the neighborhoods around Comiskey Park are dangerous began during the riots of the late 1960s—attendance was 589,496 in 1969 and 495,355 in 1970, both seasons in which the team was also a big loser on the field" (Hersh 1986). In a pattern of neighborhood racial transition that dated to the 1950s, most of the South Side residential areas near Armour Square and Bridgeport were now home to majority African American populations. Moreover, as Chicago had deindustrialized since the 1960s these same areas had become increasingly poor. In the view of the White Sox owners, due to neighborhood conditions, bringing free-spending fans into Comiskey Park was an increasingly daunting challenge.

Then there was the second component of the South Side problem: that although Comiskey Park had once been integral to the Negro League circuit, the contemporary White Sox did not draw a substantial audience of African American baseball fans. A journalist assessing this situation noted in 1991 that among the overwhelmingly suburban membership of the White Sox fan club, there were no members who resided in the largely African American inner-ring suburbs of Maywood and Markham (Cattau 1991). Ironically, one possible reason for the White Sox's particular failure to win African American patronage may have been the long-standing reputation of the Bridgeport neighborhood as a white enclave fiercely hostile to incursions by racial minorities. In any event, quite unlike Cubs management, who enjoyed the "friendly confines" of Wrigley Field, set within the larger "neighborhood of baseball," Lake View, White Sox management felt itself to be exiled in an unfriendly setting with few good prospects for the future. When pressed at one point about the likelihood of a White Sox move, Jerry Reinsdorf observed: "If it happens, it would be part of white flight, but that isn't the reason for the move. The fans moved away from the South Side. Why can't we?" (Hersh 1986).

The Addison White Sox?

By the summer of 1985, representatives of the White Sox were meeting with City of Chicago officials to discuss the construction of a publicly financed stadium that would house both their ball club and, in all likelihood, the Chicago Bears professional football team. City officials were attempting to defend a triangular bargaining terrain involving the White Sox, the Bears, and the Cubs. Even as Jerry Reinsdorf and Eddie Einhorn were convinced that Comiskey Park was an obsolete, inauspiciously located facility, the owners of the Bears were both dissatisfied with Soldier Field as a sporting arena and unhappy with their lease agreement with the Chicago Park District, the proprietor of Soldier Field. Cubs ownership was also convinced that its ballpark was an impediment to that franchise's on-the-field and bottom-line success.

However, at this time White Sox ownership—more than the Bears or Cubs management—took long steps in pursuit of a suburban option. In late 1984 the White Sox purchased a 140-acre site in the northwestern suburban town of Addison, and the following year a White Sox subsidiary, CWS development, applied to the Illinois Finance Development Authority, a state agency, for $100 million worth of tax-free bonding capacity to finance a new sports arena (Goozner 1986). In conjunction with its bond application, the White Sox released plans for a retractable dome stadium seating 55,000 fans and offering 15,000 parking spots. The press account describing the arena plans also notes that the stadium's seating could be modified to produce a "basketball configuration" (Presecky and Fuentes 1985). At least one implication of this design feature was that Jerry Reinsdorf, by this time the principal owner of the Chicago Bulls NBA franchise as well as the White Sox, might consider bringing his basketball team— and its emerging superstar, Michael Jordan—to the Chicago suburbs.

For much of 1986 the White Sox pursued an agreement with local and state officials to finance a new stadium in Addison. The ball club commissioned an economic impact study that projected over 1,300 new jobs and a $41 million increase in annual income for DuPage County residents (Presecky and Fuentes 1985). White Sox representatives made the rounds of Addison's and DuPage County's institutional leadership. At one presentation Jerry Reinsdorf assured his audience that "we're not going to bring bad people to the ballpark," and "traffic will be set up so that people can't get into the neighborhoods" (Fitzpatrick 1986). At first, local political figures such as Addison mayor Anthony Russotto offered the White Sox a hearty welcome, but soon after the franchise's announcement in July 1986 that Addison was its first choice for a new stadium, local opposition materialized. At a public hearing on July 15, the president of a homeowners association commented: "Our main concern is the lifestyle of the people. They moved to a neighborhood because it's tranquil. They moved out of the city and now they don't want the city coming out here" (Papajohn 1986).

In addition to the predictable opposition of homeowners concerned about property values and their neighborhood's ambiance, environmental activists began to object to the project's impact on adjoining wetland areas. Opponents of the Addison project had a handy means of demonstrating their strength. The village government approved adding a referendum item to the upcoming November election ballot as a means to tap local sentiment regarding the stadium proposal. The White Sox hand in the run-up to the referendum was diminished, to some degree, by the persistently articulated expectation that a portion of the new stadium's cost would be financed by an increase in the DuPage County sales tax levy. Although the Chicago White Sox had spent an estimated $100,000 to make their case, on November 4, 1986, the anti–White Sox forces carried the Addison referendum by a narrow margin (43 votes out of 7,531 ballots). Though the ballot measure was only advisory and White Sox and Addison municipal officials continued to negotiate, the White Sox owners' Addison gambit was beginning to unravel (Euchner 1993, 145–46). Within weeks the team's prospective suburban move came completely undone as Illinois governor James Thompson and Pate Philip, state senator from Wood Dale in DuPage County and Senate Republican leader, disavowed the White Sox–Addison deal. By December 1986, the White Sox were once again negotiating with the City of Chicago.

The Southern Strategy

In July 1986, while addressing a crowd of suburban business and civic leaders regarding his Addison plans, Jerry Reinsdorf candidly observed, "It is true that at the same time we are going to be trying to make a deal with another city. But that city understands that they're the back-up. We want to talk to a couple of other cities and try to zero in on one of them just in case this deal doesn't work out" (Fitzpatrick 1986). Indeed, within days of Reinsdorf's speech the *Chicago Sun-Times* reported that the White Sox had been in contact with Denver officials and that Washington, D.C., Indianapolis, and Buffalo might also be interested in snagging the ball club (Gibbons 1986). On November 4, 1986, the date of the Addison advisory referendum, the Indiana lieutenant governor placed an advertisement in the *Chicago Tribune* headed with the come-on "Indiana Is Making a Wild Pitch" and followed by a brief letter addressed to "Mr. Reinsdorf." The letter's text suggested that the White Sox should consider a stadium location in northwestern Indiana, where a site and financing could be had without recourse to a referendum. Somewhat maladroitly, given the depths of many Chicagoans' second-city anxieties, the letter also opined that "Indiana's Dunelands is to Chicago what the Meadowlands is to New York" (*Chicago Tribune*, 1986). The White Sox did devote some energy to exploring stadium sites in northwest Indiana.

The owners of the White Sox recognized that from various economic, political, and symbolic standpoints their major league baseball franchise was a precious commodity, and from the winter of 1986 to the summer of 1988 they took full advantage of this circumstance. With the breakdown of the Addison proposal, Jerry Reinsdorf and his associates quickly rediscovered the Chicago bargaining table and negotiated a three-way deal with city and state officials. On December 5, 1986, the Illinois General Assembly approved a stadium funding package to finance a $120 million facility. The White Sox, as sole tenants of the new ballpark, would pay an annual rent of $4 million for twenty years, and after twenty years—and the retirement of the state-issued bonds—the club would pay $2 million annually in rent. This new White Sox ballpark would be built adjoining the original Comiskey Park. The legislature's approval of the ballpark deal hinged in part on aggressive lobbying by Governor Thompson, who collared Republican votes in a number of ways, including linking the White Sox package to the Democratic leadership's support for a bill benefiting Illinois horse-racing interests (Briggs and Wheeler 1986).

However, for most of 1987 the initiation of the White Sox stadium project was held up as Governor Thompson and Chicago mayor Harold Washington quarreled over control of ISFA, the new agency that would issue stadium bonds and oversee the construction process (Hornung 1987). By October 1987, Washington and Thompson had patched up their differences, but in the meantime the White Sox, ever conscious of their status as desired commodity, had introduced a new player into the drama: St. Petersburg, Florida. In 1987, St. Petersburg and Pinellas County, Florida, had started construction of the 43,000-seat Suncoast Dome, a $138 million stadium that lacked a high-profile tenant such as a major-league baseball or professional football franchise. Consequently, St. Petersburg municipal and business leaders were anxious to haul in either an expansion team or a relocating franchise (Euchner 1993, 146–151). From their standpoint, the White Sox easily qualified as a worthy trophy. From the perspective of the White Sox, entering into negotiations with representatives of St. Petersburg at minimum applied pressure on Chicago and

Illinois officials to move ahead with the new ballpark on 35th Street.

In January 1988, ISFA announced that due to the previous year's delays in getting the White Sox stadium project off the ground, spring 1991 rather than spring 1990 would bring opening day for the new ballpark. In the meantime, White Sox management and St. Petersburg officials had entered into a serious courtship. Over the course of the next six months, the White Sox commissioned a study to determine whether Al Lang Field—a spring-training ballpark located in St. Petersburg—could stand in as the team's home until the Suncoast Dome was completed. St. Petersburg officials offered the White Sox a highly advantageous rental arrangement covering their first ten years as Suncoast Dome tenants, in effect offering rent-free use of the stadium if the baseball franchise failed to turn a profit. A Florida-based investment group also chipped in with the offer of a low-interest $10 million loan to the ball club (Kass 1988a). Finally, on June 7, 1988, even as Illinois officials rushed to approve a new stadium deal more favorable to the White Sox, the Florida state legislature authorized $30 million in construction assistance to speed the completion of the new St. Petersburg stadium (*Chicago Tribune,* 1991).

In Chicago, the reaction of the media to these proceedings was explosive. For example, on May 11, at a point when White Sox–ISFA negotiations were at a low point, a *Chicago Tribune* editorial questioned ISFA officials' "sincerity or their judgment" and pleaded with the White Sox to hold off on talks with St. Petersburg until the adjournment of the Illinois state legislature's spring session:

> Intentionally or not, this . . . again nudges the Sox toward St. Petersburg. . . . Maybe the Sox owners have no intention of staying in Chicago, and are only using these talks to win more goodies from St. Petersburg. . . . But if the stadium authority persists in refusing to negotiate, it virtually guarantees that the Sox will move, and puts much of the blame on itself. (1988b)

Following the same line of interpretation, sports commentators adopted an even more hysterical tone. The next day, Bob Verdi wrote in the *Tribune:*

> If meetings were mortar and if promises were pipes, the White Sox presently would have a facility large enough to accommodate the entire population of Florida instead of every reason to move there. . . . Should Reinsdorf and Einhorn depart for clearly a better situation in St. Petersburg, they will be gone, out of sight, out of mind. But not forgotten will be those striped suits who helped arrange the going-away party. They are the ones who will have to stand up for a change and explain what happened. They are the ones who will have to answer questions from voters who put them in office. They are the ones who will beg for an expansion franchise and be laughed at by major

league baseball, because major league baseball understands that the White Sox are not doing the squeezing, but are the ones getting squeezed. . . . And a major league baseball franchise must be fairly special, because there are only 26 in existence. Does he [Governor Thompson] want the St. Petersburg White Sox on his resume? (Verdi 1988)

It was the White Sox who were seeking to renegotiate the terms of the December 1986 stadium agreement, and it was the White Sox ownership that was casting about for a back-up. Verdi's perception of who was squeezing whom is, at the least, arguable.

Nonetheless, as May slipped into June and White Sox–ISFA–Illinois state legislature maneuvering proceeded ever more relentlessly, Verdi's logic was heard. One Republican state legislator commented to a *Tribune* reporter, "It's a difficult thing for Democrats or anybody else to sell to voters—that you voted for Reinsdorf and Einhorn but not for schools. But this White Sox issue could generate some heat later. No leader or legislator wants to be collared with the mantle of losing the Sox. That's not good politics either" (Kass 1988d). Although the White Sox had signed an agreement to relocate to St. Petersburg if the State of Illinois failed to offer new stadium terms, on June 30, the final evening of the state legislative session, Governor Thompson once more cajoled narrow majorities in both the state House and Senate to approve a reworked White Sox stadium deal. The deciding vote in the Illinois House of Representatives was cast at 12:03 AM, July 1—for purists, three minutes past the legislative session's legally mandated time of adjournment (Sherman 1991b).

As in 1986, the July 1988 legislative package underwrote the construction of a new White Sox stadium in the immediate vicinity of the old Comiskey Park. However, the second time around the stadium deal offered the White Sox considerably more favorable terms. The overall stadium authorization increased from $120 million to $150 million, with the State of Illinois ($5 million annually), the City of Chicago ($5 million annually), and the proceeds of the local hotel-motel tax providing the main revenue streams to repay the stadium bonds. The White Sox, in turn, signed a twenty-year lease to occupy the new Comiskey Park. Over the course of this lease, if the ball club's season attendance fell below 1.2 million it accrued no rent obligation. When season attendance exceeded 1.2 million, the White Sox pledged to pay ISFA 20 percent of gross ticket revenues and 33 percent of parking and concession revenues. Possibly most remarkable was ISFA's commitment over the second ten years of the lease to buy up to three hundred thousand White Sox tickets annually if attendance fell below 1.5 million. In regard to land acquisition matters, the state legislature granted ISFA "quick take" eminent domain powers and access to $10 million to fund property-owner buy-outs and relocation expenses (Wright 1989; Pelissero, Henschen, and Sidlow 1992, 68–69).

Whether or not the White Sox were serious in their exploration of St. Petersburg as their new hometown has been the subject of considerable debate in Chicago. Certainly, during the first six months of 1988 the franchise devoted a considerable amount of energy, as well as some hard cash, to assessing what kind of reception, politically and economically, they would receive in south Florida. And, as sports political economist Charles Euchner (1993, 148) has noted, by moving into the rapidly growing Florida market before any other major league baseball team, the White Sox would have been ensured a substantial regional base of support. On the other hand, the White Sox would have been moving from the country's third-ranking media market to the twenty-fourth. We can illustrate the fiscal implications of this point in two ways. First, when the White Sox negotiated a new local television broadcasting deal with WFLD-TV/Channel 32 in 1986, the team doubled its television revenues, from $4 million to $8.3 million, an increase directly attributable to the size of Chicago's media market. During the same period, baseball's Kansas City Royals—playing in the twenty-ninth largest media market—earned $2 million annually, while the Cleveland Indians, whose metropolitan area ranked twelfth, earned $3 million from its television contract (Bremner 1986).

A more direct indication of what the Chicago market means to the White Sox was provided to us by Julie Taylor, Director of Guest Services for the White Sox:

> If we sold all the seats for the whole year we could not pay the players' salaries, but with skyboxes and a good marketing of signs, television contracts, and so on, we can do that and more . . . maybe some profit. You see that Boston Market sign out there in the outfield. That is a new sign, and it cost that company $500,000 for the year, plus they have to sponsor a big fireworks show, that is, about $80,000. On the other hand, do you see that small Fontanini sign in the upper deck? It costs $30,000 for the year, and they also have to sponsor an event during the season. (Taylor, personal communication, 1995)

In short, there seems to be no question that by very early in the 1980s White Sox management had determined that the kind of baseball operation they wanted to run required a new kind of stadium. Moreover, although the White Sox did not feel a strong sense of obligation to either their old ballpark or its surrounding neighborhood, as their options narrowed even South Armour Square could be reconceived as an acceptable site for a new stadium. Euchner's summary of the matter seems wholly correct: "According to many participants, ranging from the commissioner's office to the White Sox management itself, St. Petersburg was just a tool for the White Sox to use against Illinois legislators—a suitor to be teased and then cast aside when the Illinois deal was concluded" (1993, 150).

The City's White Sox Game Plan

As the White Sox put into play their drive for a new ballpark, the political environment in Chicago was as murky as at any time since the 1960s. In 1979, incumbent mayor and longtime Democratic Party insider Michael Bilandic was ousted by an insurgent candidate, Jane Byrne. Byrne campaigned for mayor as a reformer, promising to rid the city of the "evil cabal" of Democratic Party kingpins who had ruled in the years following the death of Mayor Richard J. Daley. Quick on the heels of her resounding general-election victory over a weak Republican opponent, Byrne came to terms with the established City Council leadership, including Aldermen Edward Vrdolyak and Edward Burke, and her administration locked into a generally conventional program of economic development measures (Kleppner 1985, 118–33). Byrne supported the City's financing of skybox upgrading in the original Comiskey Park and cooperated with the private committee seeking to bring a World's Fair to Chicago in 1992. Although the Byrne administration's approach to economic development was unimaginative (though possibly the mayor's flirtation with the staging of a Formula One automobile race in downtown Chicago would qualify as perversely visionary), the mayor's race relations strategy was highly unconventional and, indeed, fraught with risk. On the one hand, Mayor Byrne, whose Democratic primary upset of Michael Bilandic had been largely dependent on strong support in the city's South and West Side African American neighborhoods, engaged in striking symbolic gestures, such as her brief move into the notorious Cabrini Green public housing complex in 1981. On the other hand, Byrne's penchant for replacing African American with white political appointees, most notably on the city's school board, earned her widespread mistrust among what had been her base voting constituency (Grimshaw 1992, 156–64; Rivlin 1992, 62–79).

In the mayoral election of 1983, Congressman Harold Washington first defeated Byrne and Richard M. Daley—son of the city's famous "Boss"—in the Democratic primary, then narrowly outpolled a Republican state legislator in the general election. Over the next several years Washington, the city's first African American mayor, battled a hostile City Council majority and a municipal bureaucracy that included many holdovers from the old Democratic Party regime. Yet race was but one element of the "Council Wars" that broke out in the mid-1980s. Washington had been swept into office by a movement that included not only thousands of rank-and-file African American voters, but also an array of grassroots activists who viewed his campaign as a vehicle for articulating a new vision of municipal policy making. During the Washington administration's first year, tremendous effort was directed at producing *Chicago Works Together* (City of Chicago 1984), an economic development scenario that emphasized job creation as the centerpiece of City development policy, as well as "balanced growth," attention to neighborhood-grounded economic issues, and citizen participation in municipal decision making. Beyond producing this ambitious economic development blueprint, Harold Washington also appointed an unprecedented number of grassroots activists and nonprofit organization veterans to important administration posts. Thus, the Washington regime threatened various entrenched Chicago interests not simply because of the mayor's ethnic identity and constituent base, but also because many other features of municipal business-as-usual were likely to be renegotiated (Clavel and Wiewel 1991; Bennett 1993).

Given these circumstances, as the White Sox began to make noises regarding the inadequacy of Comiskey Park, the Washington policy team, and Harold Washington in particular, found themselves in an uncomfortable position. As economic development officials Robert Mier and Kari Moe recalled, "Mayor Washington undertook such projects reluctantly. They were not consistent with his development philosophy of small, widely dispersed projects with lots of opportunity for community involvement." Nevertheless, the city's volatile political environment meant that Washington had to deal, in some fashion, with the wishes of the White Sox owners. The mayor "believed if he lost a professional sports team, even to the suburbs, neither he nor any other black candidate for mayor could win the next election" (Mier and Moe 1991, 86).

Thus, by mid-1985 the Washington administration had begun to explore potential sites, financing mechanisms, and developers in an effort to placate the city's restive professional sports franchises. At this time, the most likely site for a new stadium was on the city's Near South Side, on obsolete railroad-owned property. The Near South Side site was centrally located and offered the opportunity to transform an eyesore right on the edge of the city's downtown area. Initially, the Washington administration thought in terms of building a domed stadium that could accommodate two professional sports teams, in all probability the White Sox and Bears, though there was some discussion of the White Sox and Cubs sharing a ballpark (McCarron 1985b; Mier and Moe 1991). From the administration's standpoint, the appeal of a multitenant project was twofold. First, the new sports palace offered the prospect of meeting two franchises' needs, and second, at a time of considerable fiscal constraint for the city government, a shared stadium represented a more efficient investment. Washington administration personnel also devoted some effort to defining a link between franchise/stadium negotiations and broader, more characteristic policy priorities such as industrial retention. At one point, one of Mayor Washington's advisors observed, "Losing a major-league baseball team is no different than losing a Wisconsin Steel" (McCarron 1985a).

However, fortune did not smile on the Near South Side stadium project.

Neither the White Sox nor the Bears were interested in playing in a domed stadium, and given the emerging consensus among professional sports people that baseball/football complexes tend to produce unsatisfactory seating arrangements, neither club seemed keen on the prospect of cohabitation. Moreover, neighborhood interests in the South Loop area adjoining the prospective stadium site were overtly hostile. At the south end of the Loop a new residential community, Dearborn Park, had been developed in the mid-1970s, and in its vicinity a slow process of loft conversion and new in-fill residential construction was beginning. Residents, property owners, and residential developers were united in opposing a stadium project that promised noise, occasional traffic jams, and acres of unsightly parking lots (Golden 1986; Euchner 1993, 142–144).

By the spring of 1986 the Bears had pulled out of the Near South Side stadium talks, but Washington administration officials continued to promote a proposal for a White Sox–only, open-air facility until the end of the spring 1986 Illinois General Assembly session. Its projected cost was lower than that of earlier versions of the project, and it could be built with little direct public appropriation of funds. When the state legislature failed to act on this proposal, the White Sox announced their intention to move to Addison. Five months later, after the Addison voters failed to embrace the White Sox, the Washington administration renewed negotiations with Jerry Reinsdorf and his associates and arrived at the initial 35th Street stadium arrangement. Apart from neighborhood opposition to the South Loop site, the Washington administration's "return" to the Armour Square area had various, probably overlapping sources. In mayoral advisor Robert Mier's recollection, the new site preference was "totally driven by costs" (Mier and Moe 1991, 87). Unlike the Near South Side location, which would require substantial public infrastructure improvement (in Mier's estimate, from $30 to $50 million), the construction of a new ballpark on or adjoining the site of the existing stadium would demand minimal highway, transit, or utility upgrading. A second mayoral aide, Al Johnson, reported that Harold Washington may also have been animated by a sentimental sense that the White Sox ought to remain a South Side institution. And another possibility was discussed in the press: that building for the White Sox near 35th Street allowed the City to hold the South Loop site in reserve, just in case the Bears resumed their quest for a new playing field (McCarron and Egler 1986).

Ironically, Harold Washington's pursuit of his underlying economic development priorities by way of the White Sox stadium deal contributed, in part, to the breakdown of the first 35th Street White Sox stadium agreement. Mayor Washington held up the appointment of ISFA personnel until Governor Thompson agreed to accept more expansive affirmative action standards in the awarding of stadium construction contracts. By the time this dispute was settled, in October 1987, the amorous White Sox had once more joined the municipal dating game and were arm and arm with St. Petersburg (McCarron and Egler 1987). Washington's death in late November 1987 further unsettled relations among the City, ISFA, and the White Sox, and as the new Comiskey Park agreement was renegotiated over the next seven months, the city government's role diminished. Though Washington's successor as mayor, Eugene Sawyer, attempted to sustain his predecessor's program, he also sensed that neighborhood resistance in South Armour Square was emerging. From the moment he began his two-year stint as mayor, Sawyer was a far less commanding figure than Washington, and rather than risk a confrontation with a mobilized African American neighborhood, he kept a low profile as ISFA, holding Governor Thompson's political resources in reserve, and resumed deal making with the White Sox (Kass 1988b; 1988f). As the city government's involvement diminished, the fiscal expectations of the White Sox increased, and the new Comiskey Park came to be James Thompson's pet project (McCarron 1990b). From the standpoint of the White Sox, who had accepted the stadium site they did not prefer, and given the acquiescence of the city government and an ISFA anxious to build Governor Thompson's monument, the second new Comiskey Park deal offered the opportunity to build the kind of home field they desired, even if it was not to be located in the setting of their choosing.

The New Comiskey Park

The construction of the new Comiskey Park took two years, and predictably, the various intermediate steps were not without incident. The period of greatest uncertainty preceded groundbreaking. During the summer and early fall of 1988, ISFA officials and residents of the South Armour Square neighborhood negotiated a relocation settlement that would enable the state agency to acquire the site for the new ballpark. We will focus on the political maneuvering that accompanied ISFA-neighborhood negotiations in chapter 4. Like many other large-scale public works projects, the new Comiskey Park was also beset by cost overruns that required reevaluation of just what ISFA could afford to build (McCarron 1990a). For a short time at the end of 1988, the head of ISFA, Peter Bynoe, squabbled with Mayor Sawyer's economic development advisor, Robert Mier, over the allocation of tax-exempt bonding capacity controlled by the City of Chicago (Hornung 1988). ISFA wanted to ensure that the entire bond issue underwriting Comiskey Park construction would be tax exempt, thereby reducing its debt repayment outlays. This holdup was resolved when Mayor Sawyer agreed to meet ISFA's bonding needs in full (Karwath and Seigenthaler 1988). Groundbreaking for the new ballpark occurred in early

A shopper's paradise: the outfield concourse of the new Comiskey Park

May 1989, and blessed by very impressive contractor diligence, the completed new Comiskey Park was available for the White Sox home opener on April 18, 1991.

The new Comiskey Park was the first open-air major-league baseball stadium to be built in more than a decade, and in various ways its design reflected new thinking about the presentation of professional baseball as well as the new realities of sports economics. The stadium's physical bulk was considerably greater than its precursor across 35th Street. In the words of *New York Times* architecture critic Paul Goldberger, the new facility looked "more like a high football stadium than a low baseball park" (1990). Nevertheless, the new ballpark's architects, Hellmuth, Obata, and Kassabaum, Inc. Sports Facilities (HOK), created a sculpted exterior facade that bore some resemblance to the old ballpark's arched window openings, and the new facility's seating capacity of 44,702 was actually several thousand less than that of the oft-expanded original Comiskey Park.

Inside the new ballpark are the features that most directly reflect the new realities of sports economics: ninety skyboxes arrayed in two tiers above the lower grandstand, a glass-walled "Stadium Club" beyond the right-field foul pole that provides fine dining and a bird's-eye view of the baseball proceedings, and a mall-like pavilion area beyond the outfield

bleachers that offers numerous eating, souvenir hunting, and amuse-
ment—that is to say, spending—options. Press reaction to the new
Comiskey Park was initially quite favorable, as encapsulated by paired
April 17, 1991, *Chicago Tribune* headlines: "Architect Strove to Incorporate
Traditional Values" and "New Facility as Modern as Other Was Outdated."
Yet even in its inaugural days, the new Comiskey Park's chief virtues were
typically presented in the negative:

> Gone is the myriad of poles, which, depending on the seat, blocked out the
> pitcher's mound, home plate, or first base. Gone are the tight aisles and con-
> fining concourses, which had fans packed together like so many ballpark hot
> dogs. Gone are the terrible dugouts, which might have been the worst view
> in the house, and gone is the majors' smallest clubhouse, which put Sox at a
> homefield disadvantage. The truth is, most Sox players hated old Comiskey.
> (Sherman 1991a)

Even in the new stadium's early days one element of its design won few,
if any, admirers. In order to accommodate the banks of high-revenue-gen-
erating skyboxes, HOK had to position the lower-priced upper grandstand

Morrie O'Malley's: one of the handful of neighborhood business establishments in the
vicinity of the new Comiskey Park

seating at a dizzying elevation. Architect Philip Bess (1989), whose alternative White Sox stadium proposal will be discussed in chapter 4, observed that the most distant upper-deck seats in the old ballpark were nearer the playing field than the most proximate upper-deck seat in the new Comiskey Park. As a construction worker at the ballpark observed in 1990, "that upper deck is steep. They'd better stop serving beer up there after the sixth inning" (McCarron 1990b).

Over the longer term, and following the completion of highly praised stadium projects such as Oriole Park at Camden Yards in Baltimore, the consensus regarding Comiskey Park's physical character has turned negative. Michael Gershman, author of a thoroughgoing survey of American baseball stadiums, characterizes the White Sox's new home field in this way:

> This is a ballpark without a heart, a mallpark, a superficially attractive "environment" where fans who decry "the yuppies at Wrigley Field" are blind to lawyers in uniform gingerly elbowing their way to the taco stand. Even though it's an open-air park with Play-All grass turf, baseball is secondary to chatting and people-watching. (1993, 227)

Our contacts in the Bridgeport neighborhood typically have been less than enthusiastic about the second Comiskey Park. Commented one long-time White Sox fan: "When you go into the upper deck, which I did just once, you need a parachute to get down" (Lou Knox, interview, August 11, 1999). Dennis Beninato, co-owner of the Hickory Pit restaurant on South Halsted Street, expressed admiration for the overall layout and "amenities" of the new ballpark, but added: "It just has no character" (interview, August 3, 1999).

Many baseball fans have come to view the new Comiskey Park as an impressive but unendearing arena. However, it is when one exits the baseball stadium and considers its siting and design within its neighborhood context that one confronts the real shortcomings of the new home of the White Sox. In the first instance—and quite apart from the matter of neighborhood demographics that seems to have pained the White Sox owners in the 1980s—the immediate vicinity of Comiskey Park presents some formidable planning dilemmas. One of the ballpark's presumed advantages, the ten-lane Dan Ryan expressway running north and south parallel to the ballpark's left-field pavilion area, also cuts off Comiskey Park from the city to the east. To the west along 35th Street, just beyond the parking lots, a 350-foot-wide railroad viaduct just as decisively divides the ballpark from the Bridgeport neighborhood on its west. In short, building a sports facility that could be physically linked to adjoining commercial and residential areas was, from the outset, a substantial challenge.

The selected design solution—to ring Comiskey Park with a "sea of asphalt," one hundred acres of surface parking accommodating over seven thousand cars—has exaggerated the ballpark's isolation (Pastier 1989). The immediate surroundings of the stadium, apart from some plantings and the huge access ramps to the interior, are barren. Not even benches are provided for weary pedestrians or awe-struck baseball aficionados seeking to relax and ponder the edifice towering overhead. Clearly the owners of the White Sox had in mind an automobile-dependent transportation plan and provided accordingly (with some mass transit back-up—the Chicago Transit Authority's Red Line runs along the expressway and has a station at 35th Street). HOK, for its part, simply acquiesced to this unidimensional framing of Comiskey Park. The principal architect, Rick deFlon, characterized his role in this way: "I'm a dinky little stadium architect. I'm not trying to design cities" (Pastier 1989, 58).

ISFA assisted the White Sox in severing the link to one institution in the adjoining neighborhood: McCuddy's Tavern, a bar that had served White Sox fans since early in the century, stood south of 35th Street on the new stadium site. It was not allowed to relocate near the new Comiskey Park. Then in 1992 the White Sox secured the passage of a municipal ordinance prohibiting vendors (of programs, food, t-shirts, and so on) from operating on public property within one thousand feet of the ballpark (Joravsky 1995). The territory surrounding Comiskey Park would be devoted to a single purpose: moving fans into and out of the ballpark as expeditiously as possible. It was as if the franchise were saying, "Please attend our contests and support the Sox. But there will be no dillydallying or frivolity along the way!"

Beyond the ballpark's immediate vicinity, there is no evidence that the new Comiskey Park has renewed the vigor of the nearby neighborhood economies. In table 5 (in the appendix) we present employment figures drawn from the two zip codes adjoining Comiskey Park. In addition to retailing jobs (which include jobs in "eating and drinking places"), we have displayed the number of jobs in the Illinois Department of Employment Security's "miscellaneous and all other service industries" category, which includes "hotels and other lodging places" and "motion pictures, amusement, and recreation."

Over the six years covered by these figures, retail and miscellaneous service jobs in the zip code areas nearest the new Comiskey Park declined by 663, a testament not so much to the flaws of the new ballpark's design as to the inconsequential job-creation impact virtually any stadium project would have. Nevertheless, it is reasonable to assert that, given the approach to designing and situating the new ballpark that was adopted by the White Sox and ISFA, Comiskey Park has clearly not set off streams of auxiliary economic development.

It is also evident that the new ballpark has not contributed to upgrading its immediate environment. The principal connection between Comiskey Park and surrounding neighborhoods is 35th Street, which to the east passes across the Dan Ryan expressway and under a narrow railroad viaduct before entering a mixed area including a university campus (the Illinois Institute of Technology), a large public housing complex (Stateway Gardens), and Chicago's new Police Department headquarters. This long stretch of 35th Street offers few prospects for commercial development that might benefit from the nearby baseball stadium. However, west of Comiskey, after passing under a wider viaduct, 35th Street enters the Bridgeport neighborhood, a working-class area that over the years developed many ties to the old ballpark. Yet along the first five blocks of 35th Street west of Comiskey Park there are but three businesses—two snack shops and a sports apparel dealer—whose clientele overlaps with the White Sox fan base. Farther west in Bridgeport, merchants on Halsted Street, the neighborhood's main commercial strip, were unanimous in relating to us the view that Sox-derived business has suffered since the 1994 major-league baseball players' strike. The traffic-management practices of the White Sox and the City of Chicago have further cut into the economic spillover of Comiskey Park events. Bartender Lou Knox at Schaller's Pump, a long-standing neighborhood tavern on Halsted Street, pointed out that cars cannot directly enter Bridgeport following ball games: "After the game you've got to go east. To get back around here, you have to go down to 31st Street or 39th Street. I don't understand it" (interview, August 11, 1999). To the east is the Dan Ryan expressway, the transportation corridor presumed to carry all White Sox fans into and away from South Armour Square.

The Comiskey Park traffic-management scheme has also not generated good will between the ball club and its residential neighbors to the south. Marcella Carter, an elderly resident of the Wentworth Gardens public housing complex, told us:

> One night I came home from church and could not turn onto Princeton Avenue. They had turned the street one-way as they were guiding traffic out of the ballpark. We have had trouble getting in and out of our homes after games ever since. Many times I'll drive forever around my house because of games. The police will not let us in. They want you to park your car far away and walk. On one occasion I was led back onto the Dan Ryan! (Interview, July 6, 1999)

Ironically, permit-parking restrictions on the residential side streets of Bridgeport to the west have pushed more cars into the parking lots directly adjoining Comiskey Park, which is an economic boon for the ball club. However, this practice has probably harmed businesses west of the ballpark, while the residential area most proximate to Comiskey Park has not been spared the rigors of game-day automobile congestion.

Although there is a local consensus that the new Comiskey Park has not brought prosperity to neighborhood merchants, most of the Bridgeport business people whom we have contacted feel that on-the-field success by the White Sox could be the impetus for a substantial turnabout in their own fortunes. Table 6 (in the appendix) presents White Sox home attendance and won/lost figures for the ten seasons from 1989 through 1998. These figures are consistent with the merchants' view. Following an attendance trough during the mid- to late 1980s, fans began to return to the old Comiskey Park during its last year of operation—a season characterized by much franchise and media tub-thumping over the passing of the venerable baseball palace of the world, but also a season that was the first of a half-decade's resurgence of the ball club's performance. Attendance at the new ballpark peaked in 1991 (its first season), and the White Sox continued to draw well, averaging more than thirty thousand spectators per contest, until the players' strike terminated the 1994 season in early August. Had the White Sox played a full schedule of home games in 1994 they could have expected to draw 2.4 million fans. By 1995, when attendance at the nearly full schedule of games at Comiskey Park fell short of the more truncated 1994 season's figure, the White Sox on-the-field record had also begun to flag.

Table 6 also suggests that the new Comiskey Park's "halo effect," its attraction of fans due to the novelty of the new home field, was quite short-lived. Even in 1993, just two years following the opening of the new stadium, and with a very strong White Sox team on the field, attendance fell 10 percent below the 1991 figure. Nevertheless, by acquiring a new home field in tandem with a very favorable leasing arrangement from ISFA, the White Sox transformed their fiscal circumstances (see table 7 in the appendix). With a new ballpark, the White Sox of the early 1990s experienced a substantial increase in gate revenues, an income jump also attributable to fielding a stronger ball club, but most strikingly, the franchise's stadium revenues (suite rentals, concessions, parking, advertising, and souvenirs) tripled between 1990 and 1991.

This latter trend represents a sore point for some local merchants, several of whom voiced to us the view that the arena that was handed to the owners of the White Sox by the City of Chicago and the State of Illinois allows the ball club to corral food and beverage, apparel, and souvenir expenditures that otherwise might have fallen into their hands. More broadly, neighborhood followers of the White Sox accuse owner Jerry Reinsdorf of some extremely dubious decision making in the mid-1990s. For example, Reinsdorf is accused of heading up the intransigent faction of franchise owners in the face of the player walk-out in 1994, which occurred when the White Sox were holding first place in their division. On numerous occasions we have encountered Sox fans who maintain, without qualification, that had the 1994 season been completed, the White Sox would have emerged with the World Series championship. For such partisans of the ball club, Reinsdorf quite simply robbed them of what was theirs. Then, late in the 1997 season, even as the White Sox were fighting to catch the eventual division champion Cleveland Indians, the franchise traded several key players for future prospects. This purported backing out of the pennant race has come to be known locally as the "white-flag" deal.

Of course, the White Sox have not been fiscally immune to the effects of declining team competitiveness and shrinking attendance, and they posted operating deficits in 1994, 1995, and 1996. Although the White Sox once more fielded a division-champion team in 2000, attendance fell below the two million mark (average game attendance was 24,347, placing the Sox ninth among the American League's fourteen franchises), and a decade following its construction, there is little reason to expect that the new Comiskey Park might still generate a neighborhood economic boom. Oftentimes commentators on the problems of the ball club, stadium, and neighborhood compress their charges into an indictment of the new sporting facility: too many bad seats, and more shopping mall than ballpark—or, as Dennis Beninato observed, a park with "no character." However, as we have attempted to illustrate in this examination of the new ballpark and its economic spillovers, the recent difficulties experienced by the White Sox and merchants in the vicinity of the new Comiskey Park have multiple sources that reflect human as much as architectural content. In the following chapter, as we discuss the community impacts of Comiskey Park, we seek to elaborate in more detail the human problems that have beset the White Sox, their ballpark, and their neighbors.

4

Rebuilding Comiskey Park

The Elusive Link between Stadium Construction

and Community Development

During the frenzied negotiations involving White Sox executives, City of Chicago officials, Illinois state legislators, and Governor Thompson in the spring of 1988, journalists and some participants in the bargaining frequently alluded to the larger purposes to be served by the new sports facility. One scenario of presumed community benefit emphasized the deteriorating condition of the neighborhoods adjoining Comiskey Park, which would be corrected by a gleaming new facility, the seasonal importation of sports fans, and a new generation of businesses thriving in the shadow of the reborn sporting palace. For other figures who helped to give shape to the new Comiskey Park deal, notably Governor Thompson, the retention of the White Sox was a symbolic gesture communicating a more fundamental notion: that the City of Chicago was not a declining industrial center, but rather a dynamic metropolis whose leaders understood the importance of professional sports within an emergent postindustrial economy and possessed the foresight and resources to retain a municipal icon as resonant as the White Sox baseball franchise.

In the decade since the new Comiskey Park opened, the White Sox franchise has had only mixed success, and the ballpark's neighborhood economic impact has been meager. And there is another, even less auspicious strand of the new Comiskey Park's community development legacy. This involves the decision-making process that produced the stadium siting choice adopted by the Illinois Sports Facilities Authority, including the negotiations between ISFA and South Armour Square residents. Although some South Armour Square residents clearly benefited from the relocation agreement that was reached with ISFA, either by winning a substantial cash payment or accepting a new residence constructed in an adjoining neighborhood, the remaining residents, tenants of a public housing complex and a senior citizens residence south of the new stadium, as well as their truncated residential area, have not thrived as neighbors of the White Sox.

One of the ironies of the new Comiskey Park decision-making process is that although the City of Chicago and the State of Illinois were tactically boxed in by the White Sox owners' overtures to other cities, there were other articulate voices in Chicago that proposed stadium solutions that might have offered real community development benefits to South Armour Square, Bridgeport, and the greater South Side of Chicago. A group called Save Our Sox mounted an effort to retain the White Sox franchise that turned on renovation of the original Comiskey Park and having it declared a national monument. Architect Philip Best produced a plan for a new stadium ("Armour Field") that promised to preserve the ambiance of older ballparks while also serving as a development node for the surrounding neighborhood. We conclude our discussion of the redevelopment of Comiskey Park by examining the demise of McCuddy's, a neighborhood tavern that stood across 35th Street from the old stadium for the greater part of its history, and whose demolition serves as an apt symbol for the City and the White Sox owners' inept understanding of how the White Sox franchise might have been sustained as a powerful civic icon for residents of Chicago.

The South Armour Square Neighborhood Coalition/Illinois Sports Facilities Authority Negotiations

In early December 1986, when White Sox and City of Chicago officials reached their first agreement on the construction of a new Comiskey Park, the accompanying memorandum of understanding specified: "The stadium will be constructed in the immediate area surrounding West 35th Street and South Shields Avenue." This language required that the new ballpark be built either to the north of the old stadium, that is, on the site of Armour Square Park, and in all likelihood extending into the mixed industrial and residential area to the north of that park; or alternatively, to the south and across 35th Street from the original Comiskey Park in the small, largely residential neighborhood of South Armour Square. The various parties to the decision to locate the new ballpark south of the older facility do not agree on the specifics of how the siting choice was made. The negotiations between South Armour Square residents and ISFA reveal both the difficulties confronting neighborhood residents of modest means seeking to protect their interests and the tendency for development advocates to overlook the human costs associated with moving physical projects from the two-dimensional drawing board to three-dimensional reality.

South Armour Square covers about fifteen city blocks, from 35th Street on the north to Pershing Road (formerly 39th Street) on the south. On its eastern margin is the Dan Ryan Expressway; to the west a railroad viaduct crossing 35th Street separates South Armour Square from Bridgeport. Preceding the construction of the new Comiskey Park, South Armour Square had approximately fifteen hundred residents. Five hundred lived in eighty-nine privately owned dwellings, including 179 residential units. The other thousand residents lived in the TE Brown Apartments, a senior citizens complex with 116 apartments, and Wentworth Gardens, a low-rise public housing complex with 432 units (Voorhees Neighborhood Center 1995). The neighborhood's two principal institutions continue to be the Progressive Baptist Church and Abbott Elementary School. Before the construction of the new Comiskey Park, South Armour Square also included a number of commercial establishments, including McCuddy's Tavern and Tyler's Soul Food Grill, businesses that had long catered to Comiskey Park visitors.

Although South Armour Square covers a very small area and has never been especially prosperous, it is a locale that has generated a considerable degree of resident loyalty. As described by the attorneys who sued the White Sox, the City of Chicago, and ISFA in the wake of the ISFA–South Armour Square Neighborhood Coalition (SASNC) agreement reached in 1988, South Armour Square "was a close-knit neighborhood. Most residents knew one another; called each other by their first names; were generally on friendly terms; and relied upon one another for help and protection, particularly those who were aged, handicapped, or otherwise infirm" (*Laramore* v. *ISFA* 1989a, 11). Nor in the late 1980s was South Armour Square a physically decayed neighborhood. In the words of a local journalist, "It's a quiet, clean, and well-tended neighborhood, with one school, one church, and one grocery store. Some of the lawns have flourishing vegetable and flower gardens" (Joravsky 1987, 15–16). In late 1986, a local resident related to another reporter a more utilitarian, though not unflattering view of the area, emphasizing the "good city services provided by the 11th ward organization" (Smith 1986). Nevertheless, this small African American neighborhood was politically vulnerable, a tiny, racial minority–occupied section of a ward whose residents are otherwise white and by tradition tied to the city's powerful Democratic Party organization. As one political activist seeking to explain how the White Sox and the City came to their siting agreement observed, "Those people have never been organized, they have no groups. They are not important in either city or ward politics" (Euchner 1993, 134).

During 1987 and 1988 the residents of South Armour Square did manage to organize themselves and shaped a plausible strategy to protect their community from the emerging plan to set a stadium complex in their very front yards. As early as January 1987, a small contingent of SASNC members picketed the bill-signing ceremony formalizing the initial agreement between the City and the White Sox to build a new Comiskey Park. At about this time SASNC contacted Sheila Radford-Hill, who was then working on a local juvenile delinquency project. She became the group's community organizer. As Radford-Hill put it, "Our strategy is to make noise loud enough and insistent enough to be heard across the city" (Joravsky 1987, 15). In addition to assembling demonstrators at stadium-related public events, SASNC sought support from other groups critical of the new Comiskey Park plan, notably among them the Save Our Sox (SOS) organization.

In the case of SOS, the legacy of South Side Chicago's racial divisions inhibited SASNC's coalition-building. As Mary O'Connell, one of the founders of SOS, recalled, the largely white membership of her group and the overwhelmingly black constituency of SASNC had a difficult time coming to terms. At the single joint meeting of the two groups, the representatives of SASNC sat on one side of a local restaurant, while the SOS members grouped themselves at tables along the opposite wall of the dining room (interview, July 6, 1995). Nor, in O'Connell's recollection, was the dialogue across the divided tables especially effective. By early 1988, as the White Sox began to signal their willingness to leave Chicago altogether, SOS gave up its animating commitment to the rehabilitation of the old baseball park. From this point on the group no longer objected, as a practical matter, to locating a new ballpark south of 35th Street. Given the franchise owners' willingness to move to sites as far afield as St. Petersburg, SOS's governing objective shifted to retaining the White Sox somewhere on the South Side, and preferably near the old ballpark.

In addition to using agitation as a means of drawing attention to their plight, SASNC representatives pursued the more traditional interest-articulation strategy of contacting local officials. Some effort was devoted to communicating with local legislators such as 11th Ward Alderman Patrick Huels, but SASNC never found an advocate among its cluster of City Council and state legislative representatives. A more willing recipient of their direct petitions was Mayor Harold Washington, the city's first African American mayor and a vocal champion of the city's working-class and neighborhood populations. Representatives of SASNC met with Washington on at least two occasions, once shortly after their demonstration at the January 1987 bill-signing event, and again in mid-1987 (Joravsky 1987; Laramore v. ISFA 1989b, 132–33). There is no reason to doubt the recollection of various observers, notably mayoral advisor Robert Mier, that Mayor Washington was determined to keep the White Sox in Chicago, even if this meant relocating some local residents and commercial enterprises (Mier and Moe 1991, 86–87). Moreover, before he died in November 1987, it is unlikely that he could have known just what degree of demolition would be dictated by the south-of-35th Street siting of the new Comiskey Park. Residents of South Armour Square thought at the time, and evidently continue to think, that Washington would have acted to minimize the new stadium's impact on their neighborhood (South Armour Square Focus Group 1996). However, once Washington passed from the scene, South Armour Square residents no longer had even a prospective ally on the fifth floor of City Hall.

The final prong of the SASNC strategy involved negotiating with ISFA while simultaneously holding out the prospect of legal action unless a satisfactory resolution to resident concerns over stadium siting and, if circumstances required, relocation support was achieved. To this end, SASNC retained an attorney, Mary Milano, who was affiliated with one of Chicago's leading law firms, Baker and McKenzie. Milano worked closely with SASNC leaders, such as organization president George Marshall. Her role in achieving a settlement between ISFA and the residents was especially important during the summer of 1988, following the state legislature's approval of the second new Comiskey Park package.

In 1988, Illinois Sports Facilities Authority was the grand title of a public corporation mandated to build and oversee operations of a single structure, the new Comiskey Park, and made up of a board of directors and staff numbering approximately a dozen persons. ISFA spent its first months in a limbo defined by Mayor Washington's and Governor Thompson's disagreement over personnel appointments and contracting priorities. Thus, when the organization took shape in early 1988, it was already facing the prospect of the White Sox backing off from the December 1986 stadium agreement and heading south. In the recollection of ISFA chairman Thomas A. Reynolds, offered in a deposition collected in conjunction with the *Laramore* v. *Illinois Sports Facilities Authority* lawsuit,

> I formed a judgment that the possibility that the White Sox would move to St. Petersburg was real. And therefore, we had no more than four or five months at the outside to conclude a deal with the White Sox. And that we had to play the cards that were given to us by the legislature in terms of boundaries and by the direction I got from the Mayor and the Governor.

Further specifying the "direction" that had come from Harold Washington, Reynolds added: "I came to the conclusion if we didn't rehab it . . . we'll build it across the street on the south side of 35th Street" (*Laramore* v. *ISFA* 1992b, 45 and 50).

Thus, in Reynolds's mind, given Washington's preference for a new stadium in South Armour Square, once ISFA dealt with the proposition that ballpark funding go to rehabilitating the existing Comiskey Park (an idea once more punctured by a negative engineering report), the siting of the new ballpark was predetermined. This view has been challenged by other parties to the development process. In his deposition for the *Laramore* v. *ISFA* lawsuit, Robert Mier asserted that from the city government's standpoint, no final decision regarding the siting of the new Comiskey Park was made before Harold Washington's death in November 1987 (*Laramore* v. *ISFA* 1989b). A third view of the impetus for the siting of the ballpark was offered, again in a *Laramore* v. *ISFA* deposition, by a Department of Planning staff member, Maria Choca, who visited White Sox executive Howard Pizer in June 1987. Choca recalled that Pizer showed her a site map of the new ballpark on which "the circular part of the ramps were on the north side of the street and there was ultimately some type of bridge that conveyed pedestrians across 35th Street into the stadium" (*Laramore* v. *ISFA* 1992a, 56). This description conforms to the pedestrian-access ramps that bring fans into the new ballpark from the parking areas on the stadium's north flank. If Choca's recollection is accurate, the White Sox would seem to have been moving ahead with plans for a South Armour Square site even before ISFA swung into action.

In any event, ISFA's rush to determine a site for the new ballpark and reach an agreement with affected residents and commercial interests is not subject to dispute. ISFA held no public hearings to discuss alternative stadium sites. Correspondingly, the design of the new ballpark was assigned to HOK, the architectural firm that had been working with the White Sox for the previous several years. Ultimately, ISFA was able to win a stadium siting/relocation agreement with SASNC representatives on August 3, 1988, less than five weeks after the Illinois General Assembly's authorization of the second new Comiskey Park agreement.

During July 1988, SASNC began to fragment. In seeking to win local acquiescence to a land-acquisition plan, ISFA developed a relocation package that was especially attractive to homeowners, whose properties were clustered at the 35th Street end of South Armour Square. The homeowners could choose one of two options: (1) sale of their property scaled to appraised value plus a $25,000 "cash incentive," with additional moving and attorney fees also paid by ISFA, or (2) the construction of a new, comparable dwelling by ISFA in another neighborhood (again, with ISFA underwriting relocation expenses). Tenants whose buildings would be demolished were eligible for a settlement of up to $5,000 if they signed on to the SASNC-ISFA agreement. No compensation was offered to the remaining South Armour Square residents living in the TE Brown Apartments or Wentworth Gardens (Kass and Luft 1988).

Not many weeks before, SASNC president George Marshall had adopted a hard line in addressing ISFA: "This stadium deal is a land grab, that's all it is. And we aren't leaving easy. We're committed to this struggle to the end." For her part, attorney Mary Milano had likened South Armour Square's situation to that of a "township . . . in South Africa" (Joravsky 1988, 3). But in the weeks leading up to the neighborhood settlement, Milano, Marshall, and other homeowner-members of SASNC found it advantageous to bargain with ISFA. In contrast, the public housing residents, senior citizens, and other renters, who had no representatives on the committee that was meeting with ISFA, maintained a less compromising stance. Some members of the press, and quite clearly Mayor Eugene Sawyer, assumed that renter resistance to the South Armour Square siting of the new Comiskey Park was fanned by outside agitators. Following a meeting with local residents on July 6, Mayor Sawyer explained to a *Chicago Tribune* reporter: "Most of the people have legitimate concerns, but you could see some . . . in here manipulating and trying to make me look bad. . . . I see my opponents had their people in there ready to criticize me for keeping the White Sox. But this is Harold Washington's site. This is his legacy" (Kass 1988e). In Sawyer's mind, loyalists to the late mayor, many of whom were promoting the prospective mayoral candidacy of 4th Ward Alderman Timothy Evans, were using the Comiskey Park siting debate to discredit his own leadership.

Regardless of its causes, the division among South Armour Square residents was real. SASNC, whose members were mainly renters, never took a formal vote to approve or disapprove the agreement reached by its negotiating committee. In the minds of SASNC's renter-members, their efforts to win a just settlement had been scuttled by a combination of ISFA cleverness in offering a handsome relocation package to the homeowners and the self-interested action of SASNC's negotiating committee. The original SASNC effectively ceased to exist as an organization on the evening of August 3, 1988, when the agreement with ISFA was announced to a packed house at Abbott Elementary School. In early 1989, a new group of attorneys retained by the remaining South Armour Square residents filed suit against ISFA, the City of Chicago, and the White Sox, claiming that the public officials and sports franchise owners had conspired to dismember the neighborhood south of 35th Street in the interest of finding a desirable location for a publicly financed sports facility.

The construction of a new baseball park south of 35th Street and the demolition of the northern section of South Armour Square was not the only choice available to the White Sox owners and ISFA. Even before the first new Comiskey Park deal was reached in 1986, efforts were afoot to counter the prospective demolition of the original ballpark and reduce the degree of residential displacement. The first of these alternative stadium development schemes was advanced by the Save Our Sox group, whose goal was to retain the old Comiskey Park and, by documenting its historical significance, have the renovated sports facility anchor an urban national park. The second ultimately rejected option was the brainchild of local architect Philip Bess, who proposed to build a new ballpark with a design that would evoke the sporting environments of turn-of-the-century stadiums. According to Bess, his ballpark design would be responsive to the needs of the franchise while at the same time serving as a catalyst for real neighborhood economic development.

Save Our Sox

When the White Sox franchise announced its interest in moving from the original Comiskey Park to a new facility, a group of die-hard Sox fans organized to block the loss of their beloved baseball team. Save Our Sox (SOS) challenged the White Sox ownership's contention that Comiskey Park was structurally unsafe and too costly to maintain. This group of forty to fifty fans, mainly drawn from the neighborhoods adjoining Comiskey Park, formed in 1986. SOS was convinced of the structural integrity of the ballpark but recognized early on that Jerry Reinsdorf and Eddie Einhorn were not interested in hearing their pleas. Mary O'Connell of SOS told us:

> We were so surprised to hear the ownership making these proposals. I have been a White Sox fan all my life, and we could not let that happen. Our interest was to preserve the old Comiskey. Some of the questions we asked included: why should it be torn down and if there is money to build a new ballpark why not restore the old one? (Interview, July 6, 1995)

From the White Sox owners' standpoint, the structural layout of the old Comiskey Park represented an unalterable barrier to the franchise's ability to substantially increase its on-site revenues. An integral feature of early-twentieth-century baseball park architecture was the system of posts rising from the lower grandstand area to provide support for the upper deck of seats, with the posts then extending to an upper deck roof. In the case of Comiskey Park, the post system was set beneath an upper deck with a relatively modest slope, which reduced the distance from rear upper deck seats to the baseball field below. However, there was a downside to this structural arrangement: approximately two thousand seats in the old Comiskey Park had an obstructed view of the playing field. Furthermore, the confined space between the lower grandstand and upper deck substantially reduced the number of premium rental skyboxes that could be grafted onto the old ballpark's structure.

Realizing the economic implications of these structural realities, the SOS leadership turned to a novel strategy. According to O'Connell:

> Posts generated obstructed views at the old Comiskey, thus, with the assumption of removing them to increase revenue, every report on the old Comiskey Park's viability would turn negative. Under this assumption it would be very costly to renovate the ballpark. It was this large cost which provided the justification for the construction of a new stadium. (Interview, July 6, 1995)

Given the single-mindedness of the White Sox owners' insistence on a new stadium, SOS's counterproposal was ingenious: to designate Comiskey

Park a national monument, and by so doing, to attract fiscal resources sufficient to finance a thorough renovation of the old ballpark. Trading on Comiskey Park's place in local and national history, the national-monument proposal hinged on presenting old Comiskey as a Chicago social institution, something much more than a mere baseball stadium. SOS's leadership thus sought to link the fate of a physical structure to the broader flow of Chicago's local history and cultural particularity.

The Old Comiskey Park as a South Side Social Institution

At the core of SOS's national-monument proposal was the notion that Comiskey Park had long been an entertainment mainstay for South Side Chicago's working-class population. This was in no small measure due to the ballpark's location within walking distance of factories employing thousands of blue-collar workers:

> Close to the park were the Union Stockyards and the International Harvester plant, somewhat further the steel mills of South Chicago. These and other factories nurtured blue collar neighborhoods like Bridgeport, Canaryville, and Hegewisch. There, people worked hard and lived simply. By necessity, entertainment had to be close at hand or at least a bargain. Even if the White Sox lost 90 or more games a season, Comiskey Park always was accessible and affordable. It also offered real working-class heroes to cheer. (Bukowski, O'-Connell, and Aranza 1987, 4)

Several generations of South Siders had attended events at Comiskey Park. It was a place where the fans could identify with their heroes, in part, according to the authors of the national-monument proposal, because their hard-work ethic in the factory was reflected in the performance of the White Sox players: "They hustled on the field the same way their working-class fans hustled on the job" (Bukowski, O'Connell, and Aranza 1987, 5). Thus, the old Comiskey Park was not simply located in the heart of Chicago's South Side. The action on the playing field paralleled the lived experience of the fans who flocked to watch their beloved team perform.

The working-class character of Comiskey Park took other, more instrumental forms as well. Local steel manufacturers recruited employees by advertising at White Sox games. The 1953 White Sox scorebook contained the following ad from US Steel: "Join a Major League Team: Work at United States Steel Corporation, South Works" (Bukowski, O'Connell, and Aranza 1987, 15). Owner Charles Comiskey's commitment to Chicago's blue-collar workers was evidenced by the generous provision of inexpensive bleacher seats—numbering more than ten thousand (Gershman 1993, 227).

In a city of often fractious racial and ethnic relations, Comiskey Park even managed to function as something of a racial common ground. Among the events hosted by the park were the heavyweight championship boxing match between Joe Louis and James Braddock in 1937, witnessed by a mixed-race crowd of more than forty-one thousand. Minnie Minoso, a black Cuban Sox player in the 1950s and 1960s, was a Comiskey Park favorite. Bill Veeck, two-time owner of the White Sox and progenitor of its famous exploding scoreboard, was deeply committed to increasing the number of black major-league baseball players. Many years after they left Veeck's White Sox, a number of his former players continue to express enormous respect for their one-time boss. In the words of retired White Sox player Al Smith, "He was like a dog. He didn't know about color" (Cattau 1991, 6). Comiskey Park was also the occasional home of the Negro League's Chicago American Giants, who regularly drew ten to twenty thousand fans to their games. In 1933, the Negro League initiated its East-West all-star game at Comiskey Park. It became an annual South Side Chicago event drawing the attention of black baseball fans and, later, white professional baseball scouts from across the country. For many African Americans, attending a White Sox game was a significant event in their lives. Some sent accounts of a game home to relatives in the deep South. According to historian James Grossman, such correspondence "was some heavy-duty bragging" (Cattau 1991, 6).

Renovating Comiskey Park as a National Monument

From the standpoint of architecture, the SOS proposal aimed to return Comiskey Park to its glory days of the mid-1930s, in keeping with the ballpark's appearance following its major expansions in 1926 and 1933. This period overlapped the careers of three popular White Sox players, Luke Appling, Urban Faber, and Ted Lyons, who subsequently won admission to Major League Baseball's Hall of Fame. Among the design elements that would be returned to their 1930s character were the ballpark's brick-and-masonry facade, which would be stripped of the white paint first applied in 1960; dozens of unblocked window openings, which would once more be graced with awnings; and sidewalk ticket booths, which would sport their original "mushroom roofs." At the same time, "the clubhouse, team offices, and press facilities should be modernized as necessary" (Bukowski, O'Connell, and Aranza 1987, 11). The ballpark's surrounding area would be upgraded as well. Cobblestone paving adjoining the ballpark, as well as restoration of the Armour Square Park Fieldhouse beyond the left-field grandstand and McCuddy's Tavern across 35th Street, would further contextualize the baseball facility. In addition, loans and technical assistance to local residents would be used to encourage neighborhood improvements in keeping with the ballpark renovation. Finally, the SOS leadership anticipated that the renovation of Comiskey Park would also address structural problems within the stadium and reduce the number of obstructed-view seats.

SOS drew its inspiration for making Comiskey Park a national landmark from the successful creation a few years earlier of the urban national park commemorating the textile-mill district in Lowell, Massachusetts (Bukowski 1987; Gittell 1992, 65–93). Given the ballpark's lengthy connection to the life of South Side Chicago, as well as its striking architecture, SOS leaders concluded that it represented a national monument easily as significant as the Lowell millworks. SOS recommended that ISFA purchase the ballpark from the White Sox owners and, in turn, donate it to the National Park Service. Once the ballpark was designated a national monument, the Park Service would have access to federal funding and a mandate to oversee the renovation project. An adjoining museum would feature exhibits complementing the ongoing use of the ballpark for professional baseball and other entertainment events. Year-round programming at the museum, much of it devoted to the history of the White Sox, would serve as an independent draw for visitors to the Comiskey Park area.

Proponents of the urban national park concept also sought to link the restoration of Comiskey Park to neighborhoods and cultural sites in the larger area surrounding the ballpark. For example, visitors to Comiskey Park might also wish to tour the nearby Illinois Institute of Technology, whose campus includes twenty-two structures designed by the renowned modernist architect Ludwig Mies van der Rohe. Other nearby attractions that could be highlighted for the inquisitive urban tourist were the Armour Square Park Fieldhouse, designed by another famous Chicago architect, Daniel Burnham; legendary blues clubs to the south of the Comiskey Park area; numerous historic churches; and several port-of-entry neighborhoods for one or another group of Chicago's heterogeneous ethnic population (Bukowski, O'Connell, and Aranza 1987 14–15).

In short, SOS conceptualized its plan to renovate Comiskey Park as the centerpiece of a sophisticated "heritage tourism"–oriented economic development program for the "forgotten south side." The report presenting the SOS proposal concludes:

> A similar plan has been undertaken with great success in Lowell, Massachusetts. There, a 137-acre national park has helped revive an economically depressed area. Focusing on the non-trendy theme of New England's textile industry, the park has brought 600,000 people a year to a town never considered a tourist attraction. . . . Renovation of Comiskey Park can do for Chicago what Faneuil Hall has for Boston and Harborplace for Baltimore. Unlike those projects, however, this would be no copy of the generic Rouse

Company plan. Instead, it would take full advantage of Chicago's architecture, its history—and its great baseball tradition. (Bukowski, O'Connell, and Aranza 1987, 15)

For all of its creativity, the SOS proposal did not receive the public or official attention it merited. SOS's leaders frequently advocated their group's perspective in the local press, and the organization staged demonstrations both at Comiskey Park and in the Loop. However, SOS veterans sense that their efforts to preserve Comiskey Park were overshadowed in the media by the nearly concurrent mobilization of Lake View activists hostile to the Chicago Cubs' proposal to add lights to Wrigley Field. SOS also sought an alliance with the South Armour Square Neighborhood Coalition, which proved unfruitful, and with Philip Bess, the architect who proposed a scaled-down, neighborhood-sensitive new baseball park. But the SOS vision and Bess's plan for a new baseball park were not convergent ideas. Ultimately, SOS never won a substantial following among rank-and-file White Sox fans. Mary O'Connell told us, "When Reinsdorf threatened to move the team, much of our support decreased. That was due to fear of losing the team" (interview, July 6, 1995). To the degree that White Sox fans and other local baseball enthusiasts became aware of the SOS proposal, the prospect of retaining the franchise in Chicago and outfitting it with an up-to-the-minute new facility was probably much easier to digest than the SOS plan to offer major-league baseball in a carefully recast cultural site.

Armour Field: The "Urban Ballpark" Proposal

Early in 1987, following the signing of the initial new Comiskey Park agreement, Philip Bess, a Chicago-based architect, began to circulate plans for an "urban ballpark" that would replace the original Comiskey Park (Botts 1988). Bess's agenda was twofold: (1) to revive old ballpark-design principles by way of a new stadium project, and (2) to use a new stadium project as an anchor for auxiliary neighborhood development. For the next two years Bess sought to convince public officials and White Sox ownership of the plausibility of his alternative design strategy, but he was ultimately unsuccessful. By reviewing Bess's proposal in some detail we can observe a considerably more nuanced approach to stadium design and community development than was manifested by the course of action chosen by the White Sox and ISFA.

Bess's urban-ballpark design was driven by his desire to reproduce the positive elements found in turn-of-the-century baseball facilities. Taking advantage of these positive elements, Bess contended, requires that a sports arena be designed with the adjoining community—both as a physi-

How the on-field action might have been framed by architect Philip Bess's "urban ball-park" (picture courtesy of Philip Bess)

cal and social organism—in mind. A commitment to urbanism character-izes the overall stadium-design agenda and serves as the link between ar-chitecture and neighborhood improvements. Thus, the architect is man-dated to produce a physical design in which neighborhood features and a stadium's physical particularity go hand in hand (Bess 1989, 18–22).

According to Bess, the generation of sports-facility design represented by the projects completed in the 1960s and 1970s willfully disregarded these considerations. Structure rather than purpose became the defining rationale of stadium design, and the relationship between a stadium and its surround-ings was not given any serious consideration. The results were unimagina-tive, cookie-cutter facility layouts, the isolation of complexes amid acres of surface parking, and the universal locational preference for automobile-friendly sites along expressway corridors. This "suburban ballpark" model was even adapted to inner-city locations in which a variety of alternative design strategies were available. Moreover, the design uniformity of structures such as Atlanta–Fulton County Stadium (1966), Riverfront Stadium (completed in Cincinnati in 1970 and subsequently renamed Cinergy Field), and Veterans Stadium (Philadelphia, 1971) forced a standardized viewing experience on fans. In the above stadiums, playing-field dimensions are almost identical, resulting in a boring uniformity quite at odds with the ballpark variability characteristic of pre–World War II major-league baseball (Klein 1987). Unlike early-twentieth-century ballparks such as Yankee Stadium, Wrigley Field, and Comiskey Park, stadiums constructed according to suburban-ballpark design are overscaled and lack the architectural variation, the intimacy between the fans and the athletes and playing field, the localized social identity, and the spatial idiosyncrasy that makes for a unique sporting experience.

Critical to Bess's thinking about the new White Sox ballpark was the connection between the sports facility and nearby structures, which drove his view of how the urban ballpark could become a stimulus for associated economic development opportunities. According to Bess,

> One of the challenging aspects of stadium design is to integrate the facility into the city. Generating local development as a result of a project of this kind can be accomplished. Suburban-style stadium developments need not respond to integration since they utilize superblocks. Here you have to take into consideration the existing boundaries. The physical layout of the community in the form of streets, blocks, parks . . . should be preserved. (Interview, July 17, 1995)

Taking local geography into account, Bess identified Armour Square Park, just north of the original Comiskey Park, as the site for his proposed Armour Field.

The Bess Proposal

Bess's master plan for a stadium on the site of the ten-acre Armour Square Park included six thousand parking spaces and adjoining-neighborhood development. Specifically, 23.9 acres were allocated to parking (11.4 acres for surface parking and 12.5 acres for four two-and-one-half-story garages). Bess further specified an adjacent development area for replacement housing (on 5.8 acres of existing vacant lots) and for nearly nine acres of mixed-use, loft-style construction that would provide 200,000 square feet of commercial/retail space, 250,000 square feet of office/studio space, and 480 units of market-rate housing at 2,000 square feet per unit. An additional forty-eight market-rate housing units were projected on 3.4

acres of land west of the railroad viaduct. Finally, the 7.4-acre site of the old Comiskey Park would become a public park anchored by a 55,000-square-foot field house (Bess 1989, 45).

The proposed mixed-use private development adjoining the new base-ball facility would comprise six-story buildings housing retailers, taverns, and restaurants on the ground floor, offices and studios on the second floor, and residences on the top four floors. Bess projected that an investment totaling $95 to $100 million would be required to "fill out" the area directly adjoining the baseball park. It was also in these blocks immediately surrounding Armour Field that Bess wished to see the development of a new "civic" structure such as a church or public library (Rapoport 1987).

Bess proposed to build a 44,250-seat open-air, natural-turf, baseball-only facility, and despite Bess's traditionalist design orientation, Armour Field would be equipped with the typical accoutrements of a contemporary sporting palace: sixty-six luxury skyboxes, a 2,500 square feet indoor/outdoor stadium club, and a ground-level restaurant. The architect estimated that the cost of Armour Field would be $63 million, substantially less than the initial $120 million committed to ISFA. However, auxiliary stadium-development expenses, such as the construction of the four parking structures, would substantially increase the total project price tag. Paramount to Bess's urban-ballpark strategy was maximizing the game-viewing experience, which he aimed to achieve by reworking features expressed in the design of stadiums built during the early-twentieth-century "golden era" of baseball park construction as represented by Fenway Park (Boston), Ebbets Field (Brooklyn), and Wrigley Field. For example, the distance from the top seat in the upper deck (directly behind home plate) to home plate at Wrigley Field is 210 feet, while at the old Comiskey Park that same distance was 150 feet. Bess's design specified this ballpark dimension at 225 feet. In contrast, HOK set the same dimension at 250 feet in its design for the new Comiskey Park, a figure in line with other modern facilities, such as Riverfront Stadium (262 feet) or Royals Stadium (now Kauffman Stadium) in Kansas City (265 feet). In a direct evocation of Wrigley Field's neighborhood environment, Bess also anticipated that his relatively low-slung ballpark profile would allow residents of the new structures adjoining the ballpark to view the game from their buildings' balconies (Bess 1989).

The Armour Field proposal also avoided extensive displacement of residents. Positioning the facility in Armour Square Park to the north of the old Comiskey Park ensured that homes in the northern part of South Armour Square would be spared. In reference to the ISFA stadium initiative, Bess, in his pamphlet illustrating the Armour Field proposal, commented:

> The ISFA proposal requires the demolition of 78 privately-owned dwellings, and displaces approximately 220 families. Our Master Plan would require the

> demolition of about 25 buildings containing approximately 50 dwelling units to accommodate one of the parking garages; but no families would be displaced from the neighborhood because we propose that an equal number of replacement housing units be built right in the neighborhood, on the new east/west block south of 35th Street, and on currently vacant lots on Shields, Princeton, and Wells Streets. (1989, 29)

As Bess sought to drum up public support for the Armour Field project, this commitment was welcomed by the residents of South Armour Square in line to be displaced by the ISFA-sponsored project. In the words of one resident to whom a northerly site for the new stadium seemed the more sensible solution: "I'm a sports fan. I'm an athlete. But why displace people? . . . That's more room than we have over here" (Devall 1988).

The Demise of the Armour Field Plan

Like the SOS proposal, Philip Bess's Armour Field plan failed to achieve three-dimensional reality. Bess had devoted some effort to communicating with other groups seeking to reorient the new Comiskey Park juggernaut, but for the most part he directed his project-promotion energies at ISFA, HOK, and the owners of the White Sox. Though buoyed by some highly flattering media coverage, the Bess plan—seemingly more economical than the project mandated by the Illinois state legislature, but also requiring a more complicated planning process—never won over the hearts and minds of the powerful groups seeking a quick resolution to the Comiskey Park issue.

Bess wrote to ISFA as early as July 1987—that is, several months before it was a functioning authority—informing it of his urban-ballpark plan. His intention was to begin cultivating the interest of the authority in the hope of eventually winning the opportunity to offer a formal presentation of his stadium proposal. Months later, in April 1988, Bess sent a letter to HOK seeking the architectural firm's aid in helping "to create a climate of opinion among baseball executives and city officials that will make the urban ballpark less a fantasy than a preference" (1988a). Shortly thereafter, he wrote a letter to Jerry Reinsdorf and Eddie Einhorn outlining the advantages of his plan for the residents of South Armour Square, while emphasizing how the franchise's support of the Armour Field proposal could redound to its own benefit:

> Most importantly for South Armour Square residents and the public officials concerned for their future, it requires only a small amount of neighborhood rearrangement, and no neighborhood dislocation. Most importantly for you, an opportunity now exists for the White Sox to have not only a new ballpark, but to generate some good will as well.

In the same letter, Bess offered an additional perspective on how the owners' adoption of the Armour Field plan could burnish the reputation of the team: "The White Sox can become famous as the team that gave the urban ballpark back to baseball, perhaps even setting the trend for the future of baseball park design in America" (1988b). Similar letters and public presentations followed in the summer of 1988, in which Bess urged both the White Sox owners and ISFA to enter into a discussion of how best to build a neighborhood-friendly baseball park.

Bess spent approximately two years attempting to convince various constituencies that his plan was worthy of serious attention. For part of this time he was nominally allied with SOS and SASNC, but the construction of Armour Field was not SOS's real priority. As for SASNC, the South Armour Square residents did not add much political force to Bess's proposal. Bess, though an able publicist of his stadium plan, did not substantively contribute to SASNC's mobilizing efforts. Bess was never able to win a formal hearing from either the White Sox or ISFA. By early 1988 ISFA seems to have been firmly committed to an expeditious solution to the new Comiskey Park puzzle. The White Sox just wished that Philip Bess would go away. Though he acknowledged that Bess had already begun a campaign to generate interest in the Armour Field project—even before ISFA, presumably the body that would authorize a specific stadium site and architectural plan, had held its first meeting—White Sox executive Howard Pizer disingenuously observed to a local journalist: "It would seem to me someone genuinely interested in putting forth a proposal for anything other than publicity purposes would talk to the prime tenant" (Rapoport 1987). By mid-1987 the White Sox may have already locked in on the design produced by their long-time stadium consultant, HOK, though they did not acknowledge this publicly.

There are several additional factors accounting for the disinclination of the White Sox owners and other parties to give Philip Bess a serious hearing. In the first place, HOK did not like the proposal. Speaking to a journalist in July 1987, Rick deFlon, the HOK partner responsible for the new Comiskey Park design, objected to Bess's plan to locate commercial and residential space directly across the street from the ballpark: "I'm not convinced that it makes sense" (McCarron 1987b). The White Sox may have found the revenue-generation potential of the suburban model so despised by Bess far more alluring than the prospect of occupying a sports palace knit into the fabric of a functioning city neighborhood. The suburban model permitted more skyboxes, and its encompassing parking lot precluded neighborhood establishments from siphoning off food, apparel, and sports-trinket purchases (Euchner 1993, 158). City of Chicago officials did not seem inclined to address the multiple planning challenges presented by the Armour Field proposal. In the aftermath of the White Sox owners' flirtation with St. Petersburg, neither Harold Washington nor Eugene Sawyer may have wished to take time to debate the merits of the Bess proposal. Indeed, during the spring and summer of 1988, Mayor Sawyer, beset by "disloyal" African American political activists and facing a special election to fill out the term won by Harold Washington, was determined to make a record for himself as an efficacious chief executive. Given this cast of mind, the mayor was inclined to seize the opportunity for decisive action rather than embracing a scenario promising extended negotiations among the architect, the franchise, and the neighborhood.

One element of the Bess proposal was sure to dampen its appeal among some local residents and, in all likelihood, their political representatives. By common acknowledgment, Armour Square Park had long functioned as a racial barrier between largely African American South Armour Square and the residential blocks mainly occupied by whites to the north of the park (Peterman 2000, 93). Bess was aware of this stumbling block: "The proposal would have faced resistance from one of the neighborhoods to the north. We would probably be tied up in court since that was public property and belonged to the Chicago Park District" (interview, July 17, 1995). Indeed, in mid-1987, *Chicago Tribune* reporter John McCarron summarized a conversation with 11th Ward Alderman Patrick Huels (City Council representative for Bridgeport and areas to the east, including South Armour Square) in this fashion: "Armour Square should not be moved, since the white ethnic neighborhood to the north likes it just where it is" (McCarron 1987b, 2). In further corroboration of this point, Harold Washington advisor Timothy Wright, in his *Laramore* v. *ISFA* deposition, recalled that as early as December 1986, when the state-enabling legislation for the original new-ballpark plan was taking shape, state senator Timothy Degnan, who also represented the Bridgeport and Comiskey Park areas, took pains to ensure that Armour Square Park was excluded from the area subject to condemnation for the new baseball stadium (*Laramore* v. *ISFA* 1992c).

Finally, the close and possibly inappropriately cozy relationship between the private and the public sectors that was mandated by the state legislature's authorizing legislation gave the White Sox owners and their collaborators, HOK, the inside track on dictating the resolution of the Comiskey Park design and siting issues. Philip Bess explained:

> The assumption by the City was that whatever the White Sox wanted was good for Chicago residents. If one takes that approach then whatever the White Sox proposed was good for the public. The ownership of the White Sox, especially Reinsdorf, was fascinated with the Royals Stadium in Kansas City. Every team owner wanted one just like that. Why? Because it was the prototype at the time—1973—of not only the suburban-style stadium, but

also the baseball-only facility. That's big and HOK had designed it. Well, the team recommended HOK, and the City responded that HOK is good for Chicago. It is an interesting logic. (Interview, July 17, 1995)

Such was the fate of a new-stadium proposal that offered an array of attractive benefits to baseball fans, the White Sox owners, and the adjoining neighborhood. Even as it sustained the mystique of the classic baseball park, Armour Field offered the prospect of very profitable operations to the Chicago White Sox. The Bess proposal also held down residential displacement, and to the extent that some relocation was necessary, sought to accommodate local people within their neighborhood of long standing. The Armour Field proposal also could have served as a model for urban-ballpark design. In Bess's words, "Our design of Armour Field itself was governed by a concern that it be a genuinely urban building, constrained by its block, with an architectural presence, scale, and monumentality befitting its status as a public building" (1989, 33). Oddly enough, the Armour Field proposal seems so promising, especially in light of stadium design trends during the past decade, that one must wonder if it might not have engendered neighborhood changes far more profound than either its main supporter, Philip Bess, or it various detractors ever imagined. We will return to this matter in our concluding chapter.

The South Armour Square Aftermath

With the August 1988 signing of the relocation agreement between the South Armour Square homeowners and ISFA, SASNC's constituency was reduced to the residents of the TE Brown and Wentworth Gardens apartments. Feeling a deep sense of betrayal by its previous allies in the confrontation with ISFA, the remnant of SASNC redirected their efforts on two fronts: (1) an exploration of local economic development opportunities apart from the new Comiskey Park project, and (2) the pursuit of legal action challenging the agreement reached with ISFA. Over the next several years, each of these strategies reached a dead end, and SASNC expired as a functioning neighborhood movement.

Attempting to Revitalize South Armour Square

The new Comiskey Park project resulted in the closing of twelve businesses in South Armour Square. In 1994, SASNC won a community planning grant from the City of Chicago to conduct a market feasibility study exploring the possibility of developing a neighborhood shopping center. SASNC contracted with the Nathalie P. Voorhees Neighborhood Center at the University of Illinois at Chicago (UIC), which had led a community planning exercise in South Armour Square in 1987, to do the background research on the shopping center project. The UIC researchers conducted a market survey of the neighborhood and discovered that over 40 percent of local grocery purchases were made at convenience stores, a finding that suggested that a well-situated local food market could generate business from a substantial share of local households. Similarly, the market survey revealed that more than half of the area's residents dined in restaurants at least once per month. There were only three full-service eating establishments in the vicinity; a new restaurant could provide residents with additional dining options and also serve the approximately 1,600 employees of nearby businesses. Finally, the Voorhees Center report weighed the pros and cons of including either a video rental store or an entertainment arcade in the prospective shopping complex.

The SASNC and UIC researchers also examined a number of shopping-center design alternatives and concluded that the best choices for principal tenants of the center were the grocery store and restaurant. The grocery store was projected to generate $1.2 million in annual sales, while the restaurant could anticipate sales volume in excess of $400,000 each year. Given residents' concerns about gang activity and the possibility of attracting large numbers of nonlocal youths, SASNC hesitated to seek either a video rental store or an entertainment arcade as a shopping-center tenant. SASNC and the Voorhees Center identified what they considered the best site for the proposed complex: the intersection of Pershing Road and Wentworth Avenue, at the southeast corner of South Armour Square. The proposed shopping center would be of modest size, providing space for approximately a half-dozen commercial establishments (Voorhees Neighborhood Center 1995).

Probably the most novel proposal that emerged from SASNC's effort to plan the local shopping center was its advocacy of a complex that would be owned and managed by the community. As a consumer-owned cooperative, the shopping development would have broader-than-usual aims: (1) to meet community needs for local goods and services, (2) to employ local residents, (3) to maintain local ownership and control, (4) to ensure the offering of high-quality goods and services, and (5) to capture local spending and retain it within the neighborhood. SASNC would select the tenants to occupy spaces in the shopping complex and would use the commercial activity to support its broader neighborhood development agenda. The shopping-center report asserted that "community ownership of the development is key to the South Armour Neighborhood Coalition's efforts to rebuild its community." The estimated cost of shopping development was $1.7 million.

The South Armour Square shopping-center proposal was never realized. What was left of an initially fragmentary neighborhood lacked the political resources and expertise necessary to push even this small-scale development project to fulfillment. Former SASNC organizer Sheila Radford-Hill told us that her group's leaders just lacked that "junk-yard-dog mentality" (interview, August 26, 1999). Having lost homeowner spokespersons such as George Marshall, SASNC's leadership pool was substantially reduced. Lacking the internal resources to develop and publicize its shopping-center proposal, SASNC turned to external agents whose priorities did not include South Armour Square. The site of the proposed complex was in the city's third ward, represented by Alderman Dorothy Tillman. SASNC sought the support of Alderman Tillman, but she never publicly committed to assist the shopping-center project. Similarly, SASNC looked to the Roman Catholic Archdiocese of Chicago for assistance with site assembly, but once more, no significant support was forthcoming. Looking back on this exercise some years later, elderly local resident Marcella Carter recalled: "Dorothy Tillman did not want us there. She did not want to work with us. The Archdiocese of Chicago did not want to help us. We called and called. No one cared. No one wanted to help" (interview, July 6, 1999).

The South Armour Square Lawsuit

In the wake of the agreement between ISFA and the Armour Square homeowners, SASNC retained a new attorney, James Chapman, who had considerable experience in civil rights litigation. On February 9, 1989, Chapman filed suit in federal district court on behalf of SASNC and forty-nine residents of South Armour Square, Bridgeport, and Fuller Park, another area near the new Comiskey Park (*Laramore* v. *ISFA* 1989a). The *Laramore* suit charged that ISFA, the White Sox, and the City of Chicago had engaged in a series of racially discriminatory actions in conjunction with their effort to build the new Comiskey Park. In particular, it charged that ISFA's enabling legislation, the stadium-development agreement reached by ISFA and the White Sox, and the City's enactment of a zoning change permitting the south-of-35th Street siting of the new ballpark were designed "to force black residents of South Armour Square to sell their property to the Authority," resulting in the "intentional destruction of South Armour Square as a viable community" (*Laramore* v. *ISFA* 1989a, 20 and 22). The suit identified four legal counts against the defendants: violation of the right to equal protection under the law (guaranteed in the 14th Amendment); two counts that identified a racial motivation for ISFA, White Sox, and City actions—violation of Titles VI and VIII of the Civil Rights Act of 1964; and an "arbitrary and capricious" application of municipal zoning procedures (*Laramore* v. *ISFA* 1989a, 27–29). With respect to remedies, the plaintiffs requested that the court halt the construction of the new Comiskey Park, require the defendants to replace the destroyed homes in

South Armour Square, award compensatory damages to all plaintiffs, and award punitive damages to all plaintiffs (*Laramore* v. *ISFA* 1989a, 29).

Later in 1989, federal district court judge Ilana D. Rovner dismissed counts two and three of the *Laramore* petition but allowed the plaintiffs to proceed with the effort to prove that State of Illinois, White Sox, and City of Chicago actions violated the South Armour Square residents' 14th Amendment protections. Over the next several years, attorneys representing each side jousted over the defendants' effort to win a summary dismissal of the remaining two counts of the *Laramore* petition. In the meantime, James Chapman deposed a variety of individuals involved in the new Comiskey Park decision-making process and collected numerous pertinent documents. The results were presented to the federal district court in late 1994 with the aim of blocking the defendants' motion for a summary judgment. Chapman's detailed fact collecting, nevertheless, came to naught, and in 1996 federal district court judge Wayne R. Anderson dismissed the remaining counts of the *Laramore* petition (Chapman, interview, September 9 and 16, 1999). Judge Anderson's summary comments concluding his ruling are illuminating:

> There is absolutely no evidence that the southern site for the new Comiskey Park was selected for racial reasons—that is, that the stadium was built on its present site because defendants wanted to displace or injure African Americans. Indeed, the evidence is undisputed that the White Sox wanted a new, contemporary stadium for purely economic reasons. (*Laramore* v. *ISFA* 1996, 33)

Thus, South Armour Square's renters, senior citizens, and public housing residents may have received a raw deal, but this was because they happened to be in the way of the new Comiskey Park juggernaut, not because they were African American.

Missed Opportunity: The Destruction of McCuddy's

Under the best of circumstances, the construction of a megaproject like the new Comiskey Park, set in the midst of a complex neighborhood environment, is a difficult task. As we have seen, in the face of a profit-directed professional sports franchise and various local and state government officials anxious to please the ownership of this franchise, the residents of South Armour Square—a tiny, racial minority–occupied neighborhood with limited political, economic, or organizational resources—were unable to protect their local interests in a comprehensive way. While a fraction of the neighborhood population was able to win satisfactory compensation from ISFA, the majority of South Armour Square residents did not receive any significant benefits as an offshoot of the deal-making process that retained the White Sox in Chicago. Moreover, as we demonstrated in chapter 3, the impact of the new Comiskey Park on the larger adjoining area has been insignificant. We conclude our discussion of the Comiskey Park redevelopment effort by noting another interesting blind spot in the White Sox/ISFA vision of the new baseball facility: the missed opportunity to solidify the new Comiskey Park as a metropolitan icon by linking the present to the past via McCuddy's Tavern.

Both the SOS and Bess proposals aimed to tie stadium development to the adjoining neighborhoods' long-standing identity. In each case, advocates sought to present major-league baseball in a physical setting that matched their particular sense of tradition. Each of these alternative proposals viewed a professional sporting facility as an institution whose character could be enhanced by and, in turn, could enhance its local neighborhood environment. Such thinking clearly did not loom large in the minds of White Sox and ISFA executives. Indeed, its foreignness to their approach to stadium development is especially highlighted by their cavalier treatment of the owners of McCuddy's, a modest local bar directly across 35th Street from the original Comiskey Park. What is striking about the shuttering of McCuddy's is that if the White Sox and ISFA had retained but this single piece of the old Comiskey Park neighborhood environment, they could have reduced the subsequent neighborhood backlash to their overall stadium design and day-to-day mode of operation and at the same time helped secure the new ballpark's status as a worthy sports pilgrimage site.

McCuddy's was more than a neighborhood bar. Over the decades it had become one with the ballpark, a crucial link between the White Sox and the surrounding neighborhood. By the 1980s, the tavern did business only during the baseball season, approximately eighty days per year. Many baseball fans drew a close association between McCuddy's and Comiskey Park, with the tavern extending the magic and fantasy of the sports world into the pragmatic world of South Side Chicago. As one frequent patron of McCuddy's, *Chicago Tribune* columnist John Kass, told us: "It wasn't much of a bar, but it was an icon for suburbanites who wanted to be reminded of who they were" (interview, August 5, 1999).

The tavern was built by John McCuddy, whose friend Charles Comiskey had given him a tip as to the location of his new stadium. Since 1910, thousands of baseball fans had visited the bar; many claimed that one could not be a true White Sox partisan without having spent time in McCuddy's. There the lore of old-time baseball was ubiquitous. Some of the most pervasive stories hark back to the New York Yankee dynasty of the 1920s and Babe Ruth. According to one well-circulated account, after the third inning of every game the Babe would cross from the ballpark to McCuddy's for a quick beer and then dash back to continue his assault on the White Sox. Frances McCuddy, granddaughter of the founding owner, maintained that Ruth once wrecked the carpet in the bar with his baseball spikes as he rushed among the tables trying to finish four sandwiches and as many beers while positioning himself for the quick sprint back across 35th Street (Kass 1988c).

Many Chicago politicians visited McCuddy's on the White Sox Opening Day. Indeed, Governor James Thompson, immediately before signing the agreement to hold the White Sox in Chicago, stopped by McCuddy's to "high-five" the assembled patrons and pledge to retain the bar as an irreplaceable component of the Comiskey Park environment. However, McCuddy's was located just about where third base would be in the new facility, and the development agreement mandated that ISFA control all properties on and directly adjoining the site of the new baseball park. According to the "quick take" provisions of the agreement, ISFA could file suit to obtain adjoining commercial parcels, then settle with their owners following acquisition of their property. The history and local cultural heritage associated with the tavern disappeared in the one hour it took to demolish McCuddy's in March 1989 (Davis 1989).

Over the next couple of years, ISFA and Pat Senese, owner of McCuddy's, negotiated regarding a site for a new tavern. Senese accepted a $235,000 pay-off from ISFA, but the authority did not commit itself to a new site for the bar. Senese was left with a bitter taste from these proceedings: "And it's not the money either, I don't want the money. It's the place. It's the name that should remain across the street. Do you just break history off like a stick? Wash it away? I want my grandchildren to see that sign up there. That's what I want" (Kass 1988c). Senese and his wife Pudi wanted to reopen McCuddy's during the winter of 1991, a few months in advance of opening day at the new ballpark, and on a site across 35th Street or elsewhere in the near vicinity. This scenario was not convergent with ISFA's priorities. According to Executive Director Peter Bynoe, "We bent over backwards for McCuddy's. We spent a lot of time walking that neighborhood looking for a site for them. They were paid for their property like everyone else, but they want more. They want to be on-site, and in my opinion that's not legally possible" (Joravsky 1991, 3). Bynoe was referring to the stadium development agreement granting exclusive right to the White Sox to sell food, alcohol, and other beverages. From the Seneses' viewpoint, the alternative sites that were made available for their business were too far from the new ballpark. As a result, 1988 was McCuddy's last season.

More than a decade later, the Senese family still hopes that McCuddy's will return as a cultural icon connecting the history of the White Sox to contemporary Chicago. The bar stand, various banners and bats, and more than two hundred framed photographs, some dating back to the early 1900s, have been placed in storage, and the family has copyrighted the tavern's name. For Pat Senese, McCuddy's belongs to the family and belongs across the street from the new Comiskey Park: "We can't just sell it. We want to own McCuddy's. I'd love to have my grandson work here" (Skertic 2000). A recent *Chicago Sun-Times* editorial also endorsed the return of McCuddy's, arguing: "Packed with baseball memorabilia, McCuddy's was the kind of place that stadium designers today try to recreate at the new ballparks around the country. . . . If ever there was a time to bring back McCuddy's and its wonderful decor, now would be it" (*Chicago Sun-Times* 2000). So far, neither the White Sox nor ISFA has chosen to respond to such pleas.

The fate of McCuddy's encapsulates the broader failure to link stadium development and effective community development in the new Comiskey Park project. On the one hand, the old Comiskey Park served as an important neighborhood anchor in a declining section of South Side Chicago. Given the ambiguous economic and environmental impacts that sports facilities are likely to have under even the most favorable conditions, either the renovation of the old ballpark or the construction of a new one as an engine for neighborhood improvement would encounter substantial hurdles. At the very least, these would include physical planning issues such as siting, access, and—given the historical character of the old ballpark—the challenge to develop a new or renovated structure that could sustain the intangible but real "presence" of Comiskey Park. There were also social considerations to be addressed in the stadium development process: how to minimize residential displacement and, perhaps more dauntingly, how to develop a sporting facility that could offer community space or even jobs to neighborhood residents. On the other hand, the drive to improve Comiskey Park was animated by the priorities of the White Sox ownership: to field a successful baseball team and to efficiently move large numbers of sports fans into and out of their sports complex, and in so doing, to turn a handsome profit. The latter group of considerations, in large part, determined where the new Comiskey Park was located, how it was designed, and how it was worked into its neighborhood context. Given the White Sox owners' aim to run a profitable corporation, it is not surprising that they were unwilling to consider alternative stadium designs or to induce ISFA to negotiate a South Armour Square agreement acceptable to most of that neighborhood's residents. It is remarkable, however, and indicative of White Sox and ISFA narrow-mindedness, that saving McCuddy's, a relatively inexpensive but highly symbolic gesture, was not included in the final development plan. The vast majority of contemporary Comiskey Park visitors have no idea that a demonstrably decent neighborhood was undermined in the interest of building a new sports palace; a powerful impression much discussed by a host of White Sox fans is that the vicinity of the new ballpark is a carefully laid out, oppressively sterile physical setting.

5

Bringing Light
to Wrigley Field

Thousands of Chicagoans, if pressed to describe their quintessential experience as residents of the city, would recall an afternoon spent at Wrigley Field. For those who take the history and lore of baseball very seriously, Wrigley Field is, quite simply, a pilgrimage site. It was at Wrigley Field during the 1932 World Series that Babe Ruth reputedly "called" his subsequent home run to center field. Within the firsthand memory of many Chicagoans are the summer and early autumn of 1969, when the Cubs, already considered a long-suffering ball club, drove toward the National League pennant, but ultimately failed to win it. A sunny afternoon in the grandstand at Wrigley Field, with the city's lakefront skyline visible to the east and sailboats speckling the blue surface of Lake Michigan beyond, is an indisputably exhilarating experience. Given the Chicago Cubs' lack of on-field success, much of the enthusiasm for the ball club surely is attributable to their home field, one of the last of the old-time ballparks worked into the fabric of a city neighborhood, and the very last major-league baseball park to install playing-field lights.

It was Wrigley Field's very uniqueness, however, that was a concern for the Tribune Company following its acquisition of the Chicago Cubs in the early 1980s. As a revenue generator, Wrigley Field impeded the Cubs franchise. Not only did Tribune Company executives presume that night baseball could spur attendance at Cubs games, the company's main broadcasting affiliate, WGN-TV, was anxious to increase the number of Cubs contests that could be slotted for evening presentation. But the upgrading of Wrigley Field would not prove to be a simple matter. Residents of the adjoining section of Lake View, sometimes called Wrigleyville, were well-organized and included many vociferous opponents of nighttime baseball, and both state and municipal statutes, which had been passed at the behest of local residents, inhibited the scheduling of evening baseball contests. In order to upgrade its ballpark and remarket its baseball franchise, the Tribune Company would have to wage an aggressive public relations campaign, as well as win the support of a goodly number of politi-

At the corner of Clark and Addison Streets, just before game time at Wrigley Field

cians both in Chicago and in the state capital, Springfield.

In the present chapter we survey the economic environment giving impetus to the Tribune Company's wish to reconfigure its historic stadium, and we explore how the Tribune Company marshaled economic impact-data in support of its proposal. A particularly fascinating feature of the decision-making environment surrounding the upgrading of Wrigley Field is the Tribune Company's multiple identities as owner of a professional sports franchise; broadcaster, via WGN television and radio, of both entertainment and public affairs programming; and local opinion shaper by way of the *Chicago Tribune*. Nighttime major-league baseball had become commonplace elsewhere decades earlier; by the mid-1980s many Chicagoans probably assumed that a lightless Wrigley Field would remain a permanent feature of city's environment. However, the power of the Tribune Company was such that neither politicians nor organized Wrigleyville residents could withstand its push to transform the ballpark.

In chapter 6 we examine—from a number of other vantage points—the place of Wrigley Field in Lake View. First, we will look at how local residents sought to maintain the neighborhood environment that many assumed could only include a lightless Wrigley Field. We then explore, given

The view from the right field upper deck at Wrigley Field: outfield seating including the stadium's bleacher section and the roof decks on the east side of Sheffield Avenue

the evolving character of the Lake View neighborhood, the varied economic impacts that have resulted from the stadium-lights compromise. We conclude by describing how the transformation of Wrigley Field has contributed to the theming of Lake View as a sports-entertainment district, a process of neighborhood redefinition that may begin to chip away at some of the local eccentricities that have given the neighborhood its distinctive character.

Night Play in Major-League Baseball

Nighttime baseball was brought to the major leagues by the Great Depression, which coincided with a substantial drop-off in baseball attendance. The Cincinnati Reds franchise, which had been particularly beset by the decline in gate revenues, introduced baseball under the lights at their home ground, Crosley Field, on May 24, 1935. To host evening baseball contests, the Reds had convinced other club owners to waive a National League prohibition of nighttime baseball. The Reds had recognized that in the previous season, 70 percent of their income had resulted from a mere 15 contests: Opening Day, holiday games, and Sunday games. The

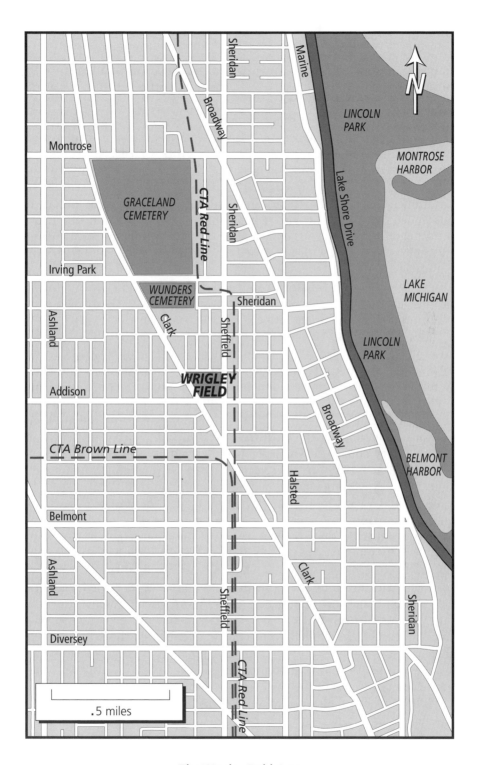

The Wrigley Field Area

franchise contended that evening baseball would increase attendance by making the game time accessible to a greater proportion of the city's working population (Pietrusza 1993).

After the Reds began to schedule evening contests, many baseball officials supposed that the appeal of these events was mainly in smaller-sized cities, not in metropolitan giants such as New York, Chicago, and Philadelphia. Conventional wisdom also presumed that the entertainment day was segmented, with the evening hours the principal time for more serious entertainment such as theatre and musical performances. Some observers contended that night play also reduced the number of children who could attend baseball games, thus contributing to a loss of support for the game by future generations. Others worried that night baseball would transform ballplayers from athletes to actors. Clark Griffith, owner of the American League's Washington Senators, commented: "There is no chance of night baseball ever becoming popular in the biggest cities. . . . High-class baseball cannot be played under artificial light" (Gershman 1993, 152).

Cubs owner Philip Wrigley shared Griffith's view, arguing that evening baseball was "just a fad . . . a passing fancy" (Gershman 1993, 155). After 1948, when the Detroit Tigers added lights to Briggs Stadium, the Cubs were the only major-league club whose home field did not accommodate nighttime baseball. Despite Philip Wrigley's initial reservations about evening baseball, in 1941 the Cubs had made plans to illuminate their ballpark, but following the Japanese attack on Pearl Harbor in December 1941, Wrigley donated the unassembled light equipment to the U.S. government (Heuer 1985). In later years, Wrigley cited neighborhood conditions when explaining why he had not brought lights to Wrigley Field. In 1968 he told a local journalist: "When we owned the [minor league] Angels in Los Angeles, we built a park in the same type of neighborhood that Wrigley Field is in. Then we put in lights. And the neighborhood went down lickety-split" (Watson 1968). Indeed, Wrigley's cultivation of neighborhood good will was such that when another National League franchise owner pressured him to add lights in the early 1960s, he turned to the local neighborhood organization, the Lake View Citizens Council, to circulate petitions in opposition. Wrigley later—and rather circuitously—thanked the citizens council for its efforts "to enlighten the general public there is a very good reason for not putting up lights at Wrigley Field rather than it is just a peculiar whim on my part which has erroneously been suggested so many times in the past" (Heuer 1985, 27).

Philip Wrigley's reluctance to upgrade his ballpark was the exception to the rule. Among the other major-league franchises, the rapid spread of nighttime baseball can be attributed to the power of economics. In Crosley Field's first season of night baseball, average attendance for the seven evening contests was 17,713. Attendance at the Reds' other 69 home games, all played during daylight hours, averaged 4,699. Nor was the Reds' experience unique. When the Brooklyn Dodgers began to host night baseball at Ebbets Field in 1938 their season's afternoon games averaged about 4,000 in attendance; their games played under lights drew 30,000 fans per contest (Gershman 1993, 156–57).

Corporate Ownership and the Drive to Add Lights to Wrigley Field

In December 1980, William Wrigley, son and heir of the recently deceased Philip and Helen Wrigley, learned that he owed a huge amount of estate and inheritance taxes, approximately $40 million, to the federal, California, Illinois, and Wisconsin governments. On June 16, 1981, the financially pinched Wrigley agreed to sell the Cubs to the Tribune Company for $20.5 million, thus ending his family's sixty-year association with the ball club (Heuer 1985, 27). The Tribune Company's holdings include the *Chicago Tribune*, WGN-TV, and WGN-Radio. At the time, WGN-TV was a pioneering cable flagship broadcaster, and was thus on the lookout for hours upon hours of entertainment content. In addition to these Chicago-based properties, the Tribune Company also owned a number of other television and radio stations across the country.

In the early 1980s, a handful of major-league clubs were reaching huge new television markets by signing exclusive contracts with nationally broadcasting cable stations. Ted Turner's "superstation," WTBS, presented Atlanta Braves contests throughout the United States (Danielson 1997, 79–80). The only limitation on these arrangements was exercised by the Major League Baseball network television contract, which permitted the selection of national game-of-the-week broadcasts. But as a rule, these franchise/cable outlet contracts gave teams such as the Braves regular national television audiences without recourse to the network game-of-the-week slot.

Like WTBS, WGN-TV was broadcasting nationally, and according to John Madigan, executive vice president of the Tribune Company, the acquisition of the Chicago Cubs offered "the opportunity to control live programming which is the most important thing to a television and radio station—live programming, good programming" (Gershman 1993, 218). The goal of the Tribune Company was to make the Cubs a nationally known entertainment product. One of the principal means to accomplish this objective was to upgrade Wrigley Field, thus increasing the number of Cubs games that could be broadcast in prime time. The Tribune Company made sure to acquire the numbers to back up this proposition. In 1985, it commissioned a local firm called Market Facts, Inc., to survey sports television viewing habits in the Chicago metropolitan area. Of those responding to the Market Facts survey, 38 percent indicated that if the Chicago Cubs played night games at Wrigley Field, they would be more likely to view Cubs baseball on television. About half of the respondents indicated that nighttime baseball at Wrigley Field would not affect their viewing habits. Fewer than 12 percent thought that the introduction of evening baseball would reduce their viewing of Cubs games on television (Chicago Cubs 1985a).

Wrigley Field: Chicago's Favorite?

The public sentiment revealed in this and other surveys conducted in the mid-1980s buttressed the Tribune Company's end-of-the-decade campaign to bring lights to Wrigley Field. A majority of respondents to the Market Facts metropolitan survey identified the Cubs as their favorite baseball team. The proportion of Cubs partisans was even greater (77.4%) among self-identified baseball fans. The results of this survey revealed an interesting mixture of opinions about Wrigley Field. Among baseball fans, nearly one-third (31.7%) opposed the installation of lights or thought that if lights were installed their use should be permitted only for postseason play. Fifteen percent of this group opposed nighttime play under any circumstances. However, nearly two-thirds of the respondents (64.6%) were willing to accept unrestricted evening play or a limited regular season and postseason schedule of night games (Chicago Cubs 1985a).

The sources of respondents' affection for Wrigley Field are not surprising, but when asked about the future of the ballpark, respondents revealed a striking diversity of opinion. Just under 60 percent characterized Wrigley Field as "excellent" or "very good," while 11.9 percent selected the lowest pair of ratings ("fair" and "poor"). The most prized features of the ballpark, each selected by approximately one-quarter of the respondents, were its "traditional ballpark characteristics," "seating/layout," and "friendly/comfortable" character. Asked whether they preferred the illumination of Wrigley Field or the construction of a new Cubs stadium, over one-third (35%) of the respondents indicated that they would choose a new ballpark (Chicago Cubs 1985a). In short, although Wrigley Field was a demonstrably well-loved sporting facility, for a substantial fraction of the metropolitan population its presence was not crucial in defining their support for the Cubs franchise.

The Cubs commissioned a second survey 1985, this one sampling residents of the area adjoining Wrigley Field. It also produced results that were used by the Tribune Company to advance its case for upgrading the ballpark, but this survey additionally revealed a degree of local ambivalence regarding Wrigley Field. Residents living within one mile of the ballpark were asked to respond to the statement that "the Cubs are an asset to the neighborhood." An overwhelming majority of them supported this proposition, though people living within a half-mile of the stadium were less likely (77.6%) than those living between a half-mile and a mile away (91%) to view the ball club as a local asset (Chicago Cubs 1985b).

Pulling the Switch on the Lights Issue

In March 1982, within a year of the Tribune Company's purchase of the Cubs, the team's outspoken general manager, Dallas Green, announced that he supported the installation of lights at Wrigley Field. According to Green, unless Wrigley Field was modernized the Cubs would "have to think about playing in another ballpark" (*Chicago Tribune* 1988c). If not heard around the world, Green's comments were at least heard around Lake View. Within weeks, local residents formed an organization called Citizens United for Baseball in Sunshine (CUBS), whose mandate was to block the illumination of Wrigley Field. CUBS was supported, in turn, by the area's long-standing neighborhood organization, the Lake View Citizens Council. Leaders of the two groups mobilized local residents and quickly persuaded both state and local legislators to introduce bills aimed at blocking nighttime baseball at Wrigley Field (Heuer 1985).

The state legislation, which was introduced by two legislators well-known to Lake View residents, John Cullerton and Ellis Levin, specified that:

> Baseball, football, or soccer sporting events played during nighttime hours, by professional athletes, in a city with more than 1,000,000 inhabitants, in a stadium at which such nighttime events were not played prior to July 1, 1982, shall be subject to nighttime noise emission regulations promulgated by the Illinois Pollution Control Board. ("Constitutional Law" 1987, 372)

Governor James Thompson, a resident of Chicago's North Side, commented as he signed the bill into law: "Wrigley Field is located in an old, established neighborhood. . . . [Night baseball] would impose an undue hardship on nearly 60,000 residents who live within a four-block area of the stadium" (*Chicago Tribune* 1988c). A year later, the Chicago City Council approved legislation that had been introduced by aldermen Bernard Hansen and Jerome Orbach, whose wards, the 44th and 46th, were most affected by Wrigley Field events. The Hansen/Orbach legislation prohibited nighttime sports events in facilities with a seating capacity exceeding 15,000 and located within five hundred feet of one hundred or more housing units (Elie 1986). The provisions of the city ordinance, like those of the state legislation, regulated the operations of a single sporting facility: Wrigley Field.

In the fall of 1984 the Cubs advanced to postseason play for the first time since 1945. Although the National League's playoff schedule awarded three home games to the Cubs, Commissioner of Baseball Bowie Kuhn, in order to permit evening television broadcasts of three of the five playoff contests, switched one of the Wrigley Field games to the home field of the Cubs' opponent, the San Diego Padres. After winning the first two games of the series at Wrigley Field, the Cubs lost the three remaining games in San Diego. Among diehard Cubs fans, this turn of events produced much weeping and probably some gnashing of teeth. In the eyes of many Chicagoans, mischief originating in the baseball commissioner's office had not yet run its course. On December 18, 1984, newly appointed Commissioner of Baseball Peter Ueberroth announced that if the Cubs once again advanced to the National League playoffs, they might be required to play their "home" games in a stadium permitting nighttime baseball. The next day the Cubs filed suit in Cook County Circuit Court challenging the state and municipal bans on evening baseball at Wrigley Field (*Chicago Tribune* 1988c).

The Cubs in-court luck was no better than their on-the-field performance in the playoffs. In the spring of 1985, Judge Richard Curry ruled against the baseball club. In his opinion he went so far as to comment: "Tinkering with the quality-of-life aspirations of countless households so that television royalties might more easily flow into the coffers of twenty-five distant sports moguls is . . . repugnant to common decency" (Gershman 1993, 220). In October 1985, the Illinois Supreme Court upheld Judge Curry's decision. Nevertheless, the Tribune Company had begun its counterattack. Company lobbyists were already in contact with state legislators and City Council members in an effort to win repeal of the 1982 and 1983 statutes.

City of Chicago officials, clearly concerned at the prospect of the Cubs leaving Wrigley Field, began to examine the impact of upgrading the ballpark. The city's Economic Development Commission retained a marketing firm, Elrick and Lavidge, Inc., to examine public reaction to various Wrigley Field options. Elrick and Lavidge divided its sample of residents according to the distance of their homes from the ballpark. It found, to no one's surprise, that those living nearest Wrigley Field were the most opposed to the installation of lights (see table 8 in the appendix). Among those who opposed the lights, the ballpark's near neighbors were only half as likely as more distant residents to say they would accept the installation of lights if it was necessary to prevent the Cubs from leaving Lake View. The three reasons most frequently cited by those who supported the installation of lights were to increase attendance, to keep the Cubs at Wrigley Field or at least within the city, and to benefit the team, for example, by making it more competitive. The reasons most frequently cited by opponents of the lights were the negative neighborhood impacts of increased traffic and trash, fan rowdiness, and noise, factors that would especially affect people living within a half-mile of the stadium. Quite tellingly, fewer opponents of lights cited directly baseball-related factors such as the tradition of daytime play (Economic Development Commission 1987).

The Relocation Threat

In the wake of the Cubs' rebuff by the Illinois Supreme Court, Chicago was awash in speculation regarding the future of both the ballpark and baseball franchise. One scenario that City of Chicago officials certainly contemplated placed the Cubs and the Chicago Bears in a domed multipurpose stadium somewhere within the city limits. Another persistent rumor suggested that the Cubs would move to a suburban site, with the northwest suburban town of Schaumburg frequently identified as the team's future home (Cappo 1985). Cubs representatives did meet with Schaumburg officials for "exploratory" talks in the summer of 1985 (Gibson 1985). Though upgrading its property at Clark and Addison Streets clearly remained the ball club's preference, keeping the door to the suburbs slightly ajar seemed to serve the Cubs' rhetorical purposes. In the words of Donald Grenesko, the Cubs' vice president for operations: "Lights are still our first choice and without them we cannot stay at Wrigley" (McCarron and Burton 1986).

Such talk left many Chicagoans uneasy. An editorial in the local weekly *Crain's Chicago Business* (1985) contended that the vacating, and ultimately the demolition, of Wrigley Field would represent the loss of a Chicago trademark:

> A domed stadium may be a good deal for the Bears and the White Sox. And we can't recall anyone praising the delights of watching games at Soldier Field, Comiskey Park, or the Chicago Stadium. But Wrigley Field is one of Chicago's greatest treasures—right up there with the Chicago Theatre and the rest of the preservationists' causes. As Cubs General Manager Dallas Green recently gushed to *Chicago Tribune* columnist Jerome Holtzman: "I'm not the same guy I was in '81 and '82. . . . Wrigley Field is a landmark. It's Chicago."

In the same editorial, *Crain's* called for a compromise between the Tribune Company and opponents of lights at Wrigley Field:

> Tribune Company made it clear that the Cubs will play night baseball sooner or later—at Wrigley Field or elsewhere. The company's compromise offer—no more than 20 night games a year and expanded seating in the upper decks— sounds reasonable to us. If the company can be held to those terms, we'll back it. The Wrigley neighbors should do likewise.

Concurrently, the baseball franchise commissioned an economic impact analysis by the consulting firm Melaniphy and Associates. The Melaniphy report, which appeared in 1986, estimated that the Cubs contributed $90.7 million annually to the city's economy. This included $37 million in direct economic benefits and $31.4 million in indirect benefits. The consultants arrived at the latter figure by summing $12.2 million in concession purchases; $8.1 million in restaurant and tavern expenditures; $3.6 million in parking revenues; $3.5 million in Cubs' purchases from local vendors; $2.5 million in hotel and public transit expenditures; $600,000 for taxis, bus charters, and gasoline; $600,000 in local retail and street vendor purchases; and $300,000 for towing and parking fines. The analysts employed a multiplier of 3.2 to estimate a further $22.3 million Cubs contribution to the Chicago economy, deriving from the baseball-generated income of neighborhood and other city residents. With respect to local governments, the report set the annual revenue contributions as follows: City of Chicago, $2.8 million; Cook County, $26,000; State of Illinois, $2.9 million (Melaniphy and Associates 1986).

As if to trump the Cubs-sponsored research, in 1986 the City of Chicago's Department of Economic Development (DED) released its own study of the economic impact of the city's baseball franchises. Although the DED report (1986) noted that the Melaniphy estimate of the Cubs' economic impact was based on an unjustifiably high multiplier, it reworked the Melaniphy numbers to produce a "peak year" impact of $115 million. The DED also contended that previous research had underestimated governmental revenues:

> The Department added two other sources of tax revenues to the list identified by the [Cubs] consultant. About 2.5 percent of state income taxes are returned to the City of Chicago; thus, a baseball team will generate at least $23,000 for city coffers. More significantly, the consultants [for the White Sox and the Cubs] did not consider the fact that multiplier activity generated by a baseball team will lead to added tax revenues. Using rough ratios of City, County, and State revenues to economic activity, we made a very crude estimate of how much revenue this added activity produces. (Department of Economic Development 1986, 7)

The result of these multiplier calculations: additional State of Illinois, Cook County, and City of Chicago revenues in the ranges of $1.8 and $2.5 million, $77,000 and $107,000, and $230,000 to $319,000, respectively (Department of Economic Development 1986).

The magnitude of these figures was not lost on public officials. During the City Council's Wrigley Field deliberations in early 1988, Robert Mier, Commissioner of Economic Development and the City's "point man" on stadium issues under Mayor Harold Washington and his successor, Eugene Sawyer, observed: "I have always taken business seriously when they say they have problems and are going to move. I've seen too many say that, and when there is no solution, they move" (Strong 1988). In the years following the Tribune Company's acquisition of the Chicago Cubs, the corporation's oversight of the ball club and efforts at surveying local attitudes had probably not produced a public relations breakthrough. Nonetheless, city officials had come to view the Cubs and Wrigley Field as very important local assets. Interestingly, all parties to the Wrigley Field lights conflict seem to have accepted the economic-impact estimates produced by private and City analysts. Neither the accuracy of these numbers, nor the substantive question of the Cubs' real contribution to the Chicago economy, was ever debated. By 1988 the City and the Tribune Company, if no one else, were ready to strike a compromise with respect to the modernization of the Cubs' home field.

The City Council Approves Lights at Wrigley Field: Mayoral Transition and Political Compromise

Responding to continued pressure from the baseball commissioner's office and against the backdrop of Washington administration–initiated negotiations seeking to forge a compromise between Lake View residents and the Cubs franchise, in June 1987 the Illinois state legislature passed a bill, with but a single dissenting vote in its two houses, exempting Cubs' playoff contests from the state's noise pollution statute (*Chicago Tribune* 1987a; 1987b). In effect, the state legislators were passing on to the Chicago City Council the option to reverse its 1983 ban on evening play at Wrigley Field. Meanwhile, aides to Mayor Harold Washington were seeking to broker an agreement that would attend to the concerns of CUBS and the Lake View Citizens Council over traffic and parking problems, litter, and noise, while permitting the Cubs to install lights at Wrigley Field (Washington and Hollander 1986). As was suggested in the *Crain's* editorial of June 1985, the ball club's commitment to a limited seasonal schedule of night games came to be the core of the resulting arrangement.

Mayor Washington's populist inclinations prompted him to acknowledge the neighborhood opposition to lights at Wrigley Field, and yet, as he also demonstrated during the protracted negotiations preceding the deal to build a new Comiskey Park, Washington was loath to lose any of the city's major-league sports franchises. This surely reflected his assessment of the economic impact of professional sports and the collateral political fallout that would result from franchise relocation, but just as important, Washington was a lifetime Chicagoan who at a personal level could not accept the departure of a civic emblem such as the Cubs.

By late 1986 Washington initiated discussions involving Cubs executives, Lake View residents, and city officials. The effect of these talks was to bring two of the three sides within hailing distance of an agreement. In early 1987, Don Grenesko of the Cubs announced that the ball club would be willing to accept an eighteen-game-per-year (plus any playoff games) limit on night baseball (Braden 1988). For its part, the City insisted that the Cubs suspend alcohol sales in the late innings of their games, reduce the number of late-afternoon game times, and cooperate with neighbors and the City on litter and traffic-control measures. Although city officials felt that they were advancing the interests of local residents, CUBS representatives never bought into this line of negotiation. In mid-September 1987, the Solutions Sub-Committee of the Lake View Task Force, the forum for the City, the Cubs, and neighborhood residents to discuss the Wrigley Field situation, prepared a twenty-four-item set of "Findings and Proposals," none of which directly considered the addition of lights to Wrigley. Indeed, the authors of this document concluded that "until some of these programs have been put in place, and all of our questions and concerns satisfactorily dealt with, there is simply no basis on which to discuss the issue of night baseball" (Lake View Task Force 1987, 5).

On November 4, 1987, Mayor Washington noted that in order for a Wrigley Field compromise to be reached, "somebody will have to bleed a little." Charlotte Newfeld of CUBS replied: "If the mayor does decide against this community, there will be blood" (Spielman 1987b). By the time of Washington's sudden death on November 25, City Council had assigned a compromise agreement for committee review and was expected to approve the Wrigley Field deal within a few weeks.

Eugene Sawyer, elected mayor at a rancorous City Council meeting in the early morning hours of December 2, pledged to carry on Harold Washington's policy agenda. In practical terms, this included his support of the Wrigley Field agreement. However, Sawyer did not possess the hold on the City Council that Washington had achieved following his reelection in early 1987, and over the next three months the city's uncertain political future clouded the council's Wrigley Field deliberations. In late January 1988, Alderman Bobby Rush, a Sawyer antagonist and chair of the Energy, Environmental Protection, and Public Utilities Committee, began a series of public hearings that seemed to reopen all aspects of the Wrigley Field debate. On the one hand, an array of Lake View residents and merchants spoke in opposition to lights. On the other hand, John Madigan of the Tribune Company offered this emphatic comment: "Without the ability to play limited night baseball, we would be forced to consider moving to another municipality where we could operate under more reasonable conditions" (Spielman 1988).

February 1988 marked a period of intense political maneuvering. Alderman Rush pressed the Sawyer administration to strengthen the agreement's neighborhood protections, for example, by introducing local permit-parking regulations and declaring an 11 P.M. curfew for Wrigley Field contests. For his part, 44th Ward Alderman Bernard Hansen, closely aligned with CUBS, worked to line up votes in opposition to the compromise agreement (Spielman and Hanania 1988b; Strong 1988). Then, on February 10, the *Chicago Tribune* published an editorial that seemed to strengthen the hand of lights opponents. The *Tribune's* editorial, which predictably urged approval of the Wrigley Field settlement, within the space of two sentences referred to City Council members as "boneheads" and "political manipulators" (*Chicago Tribune* 1988a). In a matter of hours, several aldermen who had previously expressed support for the lights compromise threatened to swing to the opposition. As a consequence, the Sawyer administration was forced to devote great energy to holding onto a majority of the fifty-member City Council. On February 23 Alderman Rush's committee, with the chair in opposition, approved the Wrigley Field agreement, which was passed by the full City Council on February 25. The council vote was twenty-nine in favor, nineteen opposed. Hansen's minority bloc included north-lakefront aldermen sympathetic to local residents' concerns, loyalists of the late mayor Washington (and therefore Sawyer opponents), and one or two aldermen who remained incensed by the February 10 *Tribune* editorial, such as Edward Burke of the Southwest Side's 14th Ward (Spielman and Hanania 1988a).

The leaders of CUBS and the Lake View Citizens Council were disconsolate, and in the short term they turned their attention to an upcoming advisory referendum on the lights. By a ratio of approximately three-to-one, residents of twenty-one precincts in the 44th and 46th wards would vote in opposition to nighttime baseball at Wrigley Field (Braden 1988). The CUBS leadership also threatened a suit to overturn the agreement between the City and the Cubs. Ultimately, local activists did not file suit; instead, in the succeeding months they entered into negotiations with the City and the Cubs organization over the pragmatics of crowd control, parking, and litter. The ball club, having pledged to remain in Wrigley Field through the 2002 baseball season, hosted the Philadelphia Phillies in the ballpark's first evening contest on August 8, 1988. Undoubtedly some CUBS activists smiled when a torrential rainstorm halted the game in the fourth inning.

The Tribune Company: Franchise Owner, Media Conglomerate . . . Local Political Power?

Chicago Cubs executives were prone to claim that the ball club's success in 1984, by producing postseason competition and therefore eliciting pressure from television executives and the baseball commissioner's office

(Grenesko 1987), had forced the Wrigley Field lights issue. But the real turning point in this tale had occurred early on, when the baseball franchise passed from Wrigley family into corporate hands. The Wrigleys had had no interest in ratcheting up the Cubs as a sports/entertainment commodity, and Philip Wrigley in particular had developed a paternalistic sense of obligation to the Wrigleyville neighborhood. When the Tribune Company purchased the Cubs, neither of these conditions was sustained. For the Cubs' new ownership, the ball club's principal attraction was its status as an underutilized resource. Nor was it at all likely that any of the Tribune Company executives had developed an appreciation for the subtle ballpark/neighborhood symbiosis that had resulted from the Cubs' long-standing daytime playing schedule.

Having taken over the Cubs, the Tribune Company did not hesitate to use its corporate power to advance its Wrigley Field agenda. Tribune Company and Cubs executives repeatedly emphasized the consequences of the City's failure to rescind its ordinance restricting evening baseball at Wrigley Field. Nor did the *Chicago Tribune* hesitate to weigh in on behalf of its corporate sibling. Indeed, because the newspaper is a local emblem, possibly as renowned as the baseball club, its editorial writers and reporters were comfortable in chastising the city's politicians for mishandling the Wrigley Field negotiations. In effect, the *Tribune* writers seized the moral high ground, determining with unchallengeable insight that the Cubs' and the City's interests converged, and from there condemning the small-minded machinations of the city's political operatives. However, as an institution whose identity is so closely bound up with the city's identity, as well as a corporate entity whose fortunes are linked at the hip to success in the Chicago market, the Tribune Company had limited policy options. For example, no one associated with either the newspaper or the Tribune Company ever proposed that the Cubs would move farther from Chicago than northwest suburban Schaumburg. Safely ensconced in such a locale, the ball club could still call itself the Chicago Cubs and prosper in nearly the same local market, and to the degree that there was grumbling within the city, its spokespersons could simply remind the world of the mendacity, backbiting, and indecisiveness of city politicians. But to move farther afield than Schaumburg, say to a beckoning Sunbelt community like St. Petersburg, Florida? This was a threat that the Tribune Company could not exercise.

Nevertheless, local politicians clearly sensed that bucking the *Tribune's* line on Wrigley Field posed risks. State Representative John Cullerton, a North Sider and a long-time opponent of modifying the ballpark, told a reporter following the first season of lights at Wrigley Field: "The perception is that if you oppose the Tribune Company on lights, their editorial writers will clobber you. You won't find a lot of people eager to take our side" (Joravsky 1989). For Cullerton and Alderman Bernard Hansen, whose constituencies included many Wrigley Field neighbors, the force of *Tribune* editorializing was muted by the antilights stance adopted by many local residents. However, for state legislators or aldermen whose constituents were relatively indifferent to the environmental consequences of bringing lights to Wrigley Field, facing up to criticism from the city's leading newspaper was much less palatable.

Still, by overplaying its dubious role as community conscience, the *Chicago Tribune* came close to killing the City-Cubs compromise agreement. The newspaper's notorious editorial of February 10, 1988, included the following characterization of several City Council members:

> Suddenly, some old Washington supporters who were for the lights compromise now are against it. Maybe it is just coincidence that they are the same boneheads who keep trying to thwart commercial and residential growth in the city and get criticized by the newspaper for it. But not likely, the only change from the Vrdolyak-Madigan days is that it is a different set of political manipulators who think they can silence or negate *Tribune* editorial criticism and undercut the mayor at the same time. (*Chicago Tribune* 1988a)

Not only did the *Tribune* editorial name names, but by seeming to honor the late mayor Harold Washington—whom many Washington supporters felt had been repeatedly, and often unfairly, attacked by the *Tribune*—the newspaper especially angered aldermen such as Bobby Rush, who was pressing for a lights compromise, but one that would require more commitments from the baseball club.

This *Tribune* editorial did not rest with its excoriation of lights opponents. The commentary then asserted that the views of the newspaper were perfectly independent of those of the Cubs management:

> And in case anyone still thinks Cub decisionmaking and editorial position-taking have any connection, consider this: If the *Tribune* editorial board had any say in Cubs policy, the team would long since have had enough of political rebuffs and runarounds, and be ready to move into a new Wrigley Field replica in the suburbs. And the opponents of the lights would be trying to figure out whether to pave over the hole in the ground left at Clark and Addison.

The most direct effect of the *Tribune's* salvo was to lead 14th Ward Alderman Edward Burke, formerly a lights-compromise supporter, to seek an immediate council vote in hopes of defeating the City-Cubs deal. Burke was unable to force the vote, but another alderman, Robert Shaw, undoubtedly expressed the view of many City Council members:

> The *Tribune* is trying to put a gun to the Council's head, to force us to do something they want and to ignore the democratic process of determining what the people want. I am for lights, but it sure doesn't make it easy for me to vote in favor of lights with this type of irresponsible writing. (Hanania and Spielman 1988, 14)

Two weeks later the Chicago City Council did approve the Wrigley Field compromise. The February 10 *Tribune* editorial probably added a few votes to the opposition total of nineteen. For many of City Council's supporters of the compromise, the sense of inevitability produced by council members' recognition of the Tribune Company's corporate power, which was in turn reinforced by several years of *Tribune* reporting and commentary, dictated their choice more than their admiration for the deal that had been crafted in negotiations between the City and the ball club.

Lights, Action, Neighborhood?

Lost in the hubbub that greeted the February 10 *Tribune* editorial was the curious alternative solution offered by the editorial staff, that the Cubs "move into a new Wrigley Field replica in the suburbs." Of course, one wonders just how the replica would duplicate the views of city and lake that constitute such a large part of Wrigley Field's charm. Even if architects and builders could produce a structure that would stand in for the old ballpark, did the *Tribune* writers really suppose that such a facility, located just off an expressway and girded by acres of parking, would retain the affection of fans accustomed to the old stadium? Or—to push the editorialists' fantasy in another direction—did the *Tribune* writers suppose that the new Wrigley Field could be located in one of Chicago's inner-ring suburbs, possibly Evanston or Oak Park, where something like the neighborhood environment of Wrigleyville could be recreated? This last scenario seems to us particularly interesting because it is quite obvious that residents of neither town would tolerate such a scheme. Indeed, the only reason that Wrigley Field is permitted in Lake View is because it is already there. Even the new Wrigley-like ballparks such as Oriole Park at Camden Yards, Coors Field, and Jacobs Field have been built in older nonresidential areas. To the extent that residential development has followed in the wake of these stadium projects, it has been aimed at a very specific market: younger urbanites attracted by the carnival-like ambiance of ballpark and neighborhood.

The *Tribune* editorialists, in their indignant scorn for the clash of perspectives on Wrigley Field's future, clearly misunderstood why the economic logic driving the move to upgrade the ballpark failed to persuade lights opponents on the City Council and in the neighborhood. Opponents were trying to protect a valued place and the social networks that had come to define that place. The economics of ball club and stadium have surely played their part in shaping Lake View, but other factors as well have structured local residents' appreciation of their neighborhood. As every opponent of lights at Wrigley Field seemed to recognize, altering the physical structure and use of the ballpark would inevitably alter the ballpark-neighborhood equilibrium that has made Wrigley Field's neighborhood such an evocative urban space. In the next chapter we explore the sense of place and equilibrium shared by many Lake View residents, how local activists sought to protect their neighborhood, how residents and merchants have variously responded to the upgrading of Wrigley Field, and finally, how the illuminated Wrigley Field has contributed to the reshaping of Lake View.

6

Lake View

From Complete City to

Port of Entry for All the Young People

In 1959, the executive director of Lake View's principal neighborhood organization, the Lake View Citizens Council (LVCC), described his community in this way: "We have all of the elements of a complete city. The range goes from luxury apartments to public housing, and everything in between" (Newman 1959). As the 1950s gave way to the 1960s, this was a useful way of characterizing Lake View. Stretching from Diversey Avenue on the south to Irving Park Road on the north, and from Lake Michigan on the east to Ravenswood Avenue on the west, the neighborhood's four square miles were home to over one hundred thousand residents. As suggested by the LVCC's director, local housing and resident characteristics varied dramatically from one part of Lake View to another. Along the area's eastern margin, overlooking Lincoln Park and Lake Michigan, scores of high-rise apartment towers had been built, first in the 1920s and then in greater numbers following World War II. Some of the wealthiest Chicagoans resided on Marine Drive and on the adjoining side streets within walking distance of park and lake. To the west, Lake View's housing stock was extremely heterogeneous. It included three-flat and six-flat buildings, larger courtyard apartment buildings, and single-family houses. As a rule, residents' affluence diminished as the view of Lake Michigan receded. And, as the neighborhood's African American and Latino populations increased during the 1950s and 1960s, the greatest concentrations of minority residents congregated on Lake View's western flank (Chicago Fact Book Consortium 1995, 50–51).

Lake View's heterogeneity was more than demographic and residential. Along Ravenswood Avenue could be found a busy industrial corridor comprising dozens of small manufacturing operations. Lake View also included several distinctive shopping districts. The neighborhood's southwestern quadrant radiated from a "little downtown," complete with a Wieboldt's department store, centered on the intersection of Lincoln, Belmont, and

Ashland Avenues. Nearer Lake Michigan, north-south-oriented Broadway, Clark, and Halsted Streets were bustling commercial spines for the adjoining residential blocks.

Lake View's status as complete city within the larger metropolis might have complicated its process of forging a local identity in the post–World War II era, when local residents began to perceive signs of neighborhood decay along some of its commercial streets and in several residential areas. However, in the early 1950s the LVCC emerged to give focus to neighborhood concerns, and during subsequent decades it mounted an impressive array of local campaigns and projects. In 1982, less than a year after the Tribune Company purchased the Cubs, a group of younger LVCC members spun off and formed Citizens United for Baseball in Sunshine (CUBS), which became the principal neighborhood voice in the debate that accompanied the franchise's efforts to add lights to Wrigley Field. In the first half of this chapter we discuss how local activists defined their neighborhood and sustained a highly effective campaign to counter the Tribune Company's plans for Wrigley Field. In the concluding sections of the chapter we examine the ironic outcomes of the Wrigley Field conflict and of the subsequent retooling of the ballpark. We consider how the new Wrigley Field has contributed to processes of neighborhood change already afoot in Lake View, which have in turn yielded a neighborhood environment not quite foreseen by either the forces supporting the lights or those opposing them in the 1980s.

And So the LVCC Begat CUBS

The LVCC was formed by a group of neighborhood women in 1952, and by the end of the decade the organization was strong enough to hire a paid executive director. A profile of Lake View that appeared in the *Chicago Daily News* in May 1959 describes an LVCC effort to win "conservation area" recognition by the city government (Newman 1959). As a conservation area, Lake View would be eligible for federally funded urban renewal assistance. In a later newspaper account, one of the LVCC's members characterizes the group as having been dominated by local businessmen until the mid-to-late 1960s. Some vestiges of the organization's early domestic concerns were retained as late as 1963, when the LVCC approved a resolution denouncing "steady dating" by local youths (Lowe 1973).

By the late 1960s, members of the LVCC were directing their energies at a local issue whose ramifications would occupy the organization for years to come. In the eastern end of Lake View, real estate developers were buying scores of old single-family homes and smaller apartment buildings, which they demolished and replaced with cheaply built "four-plus-one" apartment buildings. Four-plus-ones earned their name from their distinctive street profile, four floors of apartments set atop a slightly submerged concrete base given over to open-air parking and a small entrance foyer. At this time, the city's building code set more demanding construction and materials standards for residential complexes reaching five or more floors in height. Four-plus-ones just skirted the five-story building code provisions, but still managed to increase residential density quite substantially. Nor were the strictly utilitarian, blocklike four-plus-ones a joy to behold.

As four-plus-one projects proliferated in east Lake View, LVCC members initially picketed their construction sites. At one such demonstration in October 1969, LVCC member Herbert Lowinger proclaimed four-plus-ones to be "instant slums." Joining Lowinger at the construction site were several mothers pushing their babies in strollers. Another LVCC member commented to the reporter covering the demonstration: "They're driving our best families out of the neighborhood" (Goodyear 1969). In the years to come, LVCC and its offspring, CUBS, would frequently articulate variations of this theme. Each group characterized itself as a confederation of middle-class citizens striving to preserve a stable, family-friendly neighborhood.

In addition to staging public actions to bring attention to the neighborhood threat posed by four-plus-one construction, the LVCC worked with local aldermanic representatives to craft corrective legislation. In March 1971, the Chicago City Council passed zoning restrictions that effectively put an end to four-plus-one construction ("LVCC Race Called Friendly" 1971). Four years later, the LVCC worked with a coalition of North Side lakefront aldermen to promote and pass a city ordinance downzoning Lake View, a measure that limited the areas in which high-rise structures could be built (Hinz 1975).

By the early 1970s, the LVCC was a highly visible grassroots organization. Its board of directors included elected local representatives as well as delegates from ten smaller neighborhood groups, businesses, social service agencies, and churches. The LVCC claimed a membership of over two thousand individuals, and at a tightly contested election meeting in 1970 six hundred people turned out (Sussman 1970). During this period the LVCC also staked out an unusually liberal position on various neighborhood issues. For example, at a time of considerable racial tension in Chicago, the LVCC began discussions with an integrationist housing group, the Leadership Council for Metropolitan Open Communities, to establish an equal-housing center in Lake View ("Mayor Daley, Conlisk Invited to LVCC Forum" 1969). On another occasion, the LVCC supported a petition demanding the investigation of charges that Chicago police officers had harassed local Latino-owned businesses (Flaherty 1970).

In 1977, the LVCC celebrated its silver anniversary, marking an unusually long run for a community group. But as the LVCC slipped into organizational midlife, its affairs were not perfectly in order. Aside from the personal conflicts that often plague grassroots organizations, the LVCC was beginning to experience some stresses with its affiliate organizations. For years, the LVCC's principal concern had been the development pressures on the neighborhood's eastern end, and by the mid-1970s at least one of the its local affiliates, the West Lake View Association, was considering withdrawal from its parent organization. The West Lake View group's president voiced a familiar complaint: "They forgot all about the West Lake View Association" (Olson 1975). Nevertheless, as the LVCC celebrated its twenty-five-year anniversary, signs were emerging of a substantial neighborhood renaissance. Homeownership in Lake View increased substantially during the 1970s, and in various parts of the neighborhood's "other side," that is, the largely residential areas west of Clark Street, dozens of houses and smaller apartment buildings were undergoing renovation. During the LVCC's quarter-century of operations, Lake View had evolved from a community one journalist described as threatened by "decay . . . pressing in from outside" to a neighborhood on the upswing to which single persons and younger couples were rushing, often not just to settle for a year or two, but with the aim of purchasing property and starting new businesses.

CUBS was formed in the spring of 1982 after Cubs general manager Dallas Green made his statement that unless his baseball team was able to play night games, it would never break out of its cellar-dwelling morass. The core CUBS activists were younger LVCC members, many of whom had settled in Lake View in the preceding few years. Formally CUBS was an LVCC committee, but very quickly the new group established its own identity. Nonetheless, CUBS's claim to speak for a broad Lake View constituency turned on its continued affiliation with the LVCC, and in pursuing its campaign to prevent the modernization of Wrigley Field, CUBS regularly called on LVCC resources and political contacts.

Early in the fight to prevent the lighting of Wrigley Field, CUBS member Sue Hanselmann offered a concise summary of the group's stance:

> You know, we really do want to cooperate with the Cubs. We are all fans here. We love the Cubs. But we also love daytime baseball. This is a community that has existed amicably with the Cubs for 65 years. I think that they have a responsibility to Cubs fans and the community both. But nighttime baseball would destroy what we have here. We'd all have to move out. Who could live here? (Keegan 1982)

CUBS was looking out for the interests of a fragile urban neighborhood whose residents had for years coexisted with and demonstrated loyalty to the baseball club. Furthermore, it was incumbent upon the franchise's new corporate ownership to sustain the ball club–neighborhood pact that had been forged during the Wrigley-family years. And CUBS was intransigent on one point: there would be no lights.

During its period of peak activity, from 1982 to 1988, CUBS pursued a sophisticated, multiple-front political strategy. In 1982 and 1983, the group used its contacts in the Illinois state legislature and Chicago City Council to line up sponsors and win passage of the statutory prohibitions of nighttime baseball at Wrigley Field. At the same time, CUBS created an organizing team to canvass local residents and, when necessary, to deliver crowds of antilights activists to public events. Lake View businessman and CUBS member Sam Toia views this as the groups' most effective tactic: "The group could always muster fifty people for a meeting, even on short notice. And in front of the cameras, if you have forty people in the room it looks like four hundred" (interview, November 12, 1998). In provoking grassroots opposition to the ball club's plans, CUBS was ingenious. For example, Sue Hanselmann's husband, Mark, designed "No Lights" T-shirts and signs that became common features of the Lake View street scene (Heuer 1985, 30).

CUBS members also provided the group with technical resources not usually available to grassroots organizations. Between the 1984 and 1985 baseball seasons, when the Cubs ball club sought to overturn the municipal and state legislation prohibiting evening baseball at Wrigley Field, CUBS formed a legal committee that included eight attorneys to mount its side of the argument before the state circuit court judge hearing the case (Heuer 1985, 31). Not only did Judge Richard L. Curry rule in favor of CUBS on this occasion, over the coming years the group's ability to threaten legal action against the ball club undoubtedly contributed to the latter's inclination to negotiate a compromise settlement to the stadium-lights conflict.

In spite of the organization's varied efforts to block the illumination of Wrigley Field, the combined force of the Tribune Company's corporate power and citywide political realities following the surprising death of Mayor Harold Washington finally broke through the Wrigley Field deadlock in early 1988. At that time, many CUBS activists felt that the group had not been sufficiently involved in the preceding months' negotiations between the City and the ball club. Nevertheless, the staying power of CUBS, and ultimately of LVCC, is such that the organization has continued to play a visible role in regulating relations between the baseball club and the neighborhood in the period since the coming of nighttime baseball to Wrigley Field.

The Wrigley Field Traffic Operations Committee

At the behest of City Council members Bobby Rush, Bernard Hansen, and Helen Shiller—Hansen's 44th Ward and Shiller's 46th are the two council districts most affected by Wrigley Field—the lights settlement mandated the formation of the Wrigley Field Traffic Operations Committee (Orrick 1998). This group, which includes representatives of the Chicago Cubs, various City of Chicago agencies, the local aldermanic offices, and the Lake View neighborhood, has convened throughout the decade and a half since evening baseball came to Wrigley Field. Its principal function has been to maintain the lines of communication among the various parties operating Wrigley Field and living in its vicinity. On several occasions the Traffic Operations Committee has identified creative solutions to emergent traffic, parking, sanitation, and public-order problems.

On the neighborhood side, the vitality of the Traffic Operations Committee is largely due to the commitment of CUBS leader Charlotte Newfeld. While several other neighborhood residents have found it difficult to attend the committee's half-dozen or so meetings each year, which are scheduled during working hours and convened downtown, the self-employed Newfeld has made a point of sustaining a CUBS presence in discussions of ballpark/neighborhood issues. Newfeld, in turn, commends the work of Chester Kropidlowski, a Department of Transportation official who chaired the Traffic Operations Committee until his retirement in 1998. Kropidlowski prepared the committee's annual report, which summarizes the City's local policing activities and describes how traffic-management and parking-permit programs have fared. In a number of instances, the members of the Traffic Operations Committee have developed useful measures to deal with baseball-related neighborhood problems. For example, the committee suggested the creation of a telephone hotline to permit Lake View residents to report illegally parked cars. In another case, neighborhood residents began to complain that overzealous tow-truck drivers were carrying off legally parked cars. Having been alerted to this problem by Alderman Hansen, the Traffic Operations Committee identified a new method of parking-permit display, which enabled tow-truck drivers to more readily distinguish legally parked cars from illegally parked ones (Newfeld, interview, October 13 and December 9, 1998; Orrick 1998).

Charlotte Newfeld attributes the success of the Wrigley Field Traffic Operations Committee to Chester Kropidlowski's hard work and his gift for diplomacy, as well as the potential for CUBS to remobilize even a decade following the Wrigley Field lights conflict. It is also evident that Cubs management has learned some lessons in neighborhood public relations over the nearly twenty years since the Tribune Company purchased the baseball franchise from William Wrigley. And then there is that other often-neglected element that sustains the ongoing dialogue facilitated by the Traffic Operations Committee: the dogged determination of a particular activist, in this instance, Charlotte Newfeld.

The Social Context of the Wrigley Field Lights Conflict:
A Neighborhood Already in Motion

In the years before the Tribune Company won the Chicago City Council's approval to add lights to Wrigley Field, CUBS and the LVCC purported to speak for a quiet, family-anchored neighborhood that had for several generations coexisted with major-league baseball. And yet most CUBS leaders were relatively young adults, many with advanced professional training and substantial business interests, who had settled in Lake View in the 1960s or 1970s. Between 1960 and 1980 the prospects of the Lake View area changed dramatically, and these changes produced both the cadre of activists who sought to stabilize the relationship between the neighborhood and the baseball franchise, and the neighborhood environment that by the mid-1980s was ripe for a new wave of commercial investment.

In 1950, the U.S. Census count of Lake View's population was just below 125,000, a gain of a few thousand from 1940 and the neighborhood's historical peak. By 1970 the area's population fell below 115,000, and in the next decade Lake View lost another 17,000 residents. Post–World War II Lake View was experiencing the demographic shifts felt in many Chicago neighborhoods, as well as in central-city neighborhoods across the United States. In 1950, Lake View's population was over 99 percent white, but by 1980 the area's black and Latino population (6.9% and 18.8%, respectively) together exceeded one-quarter of the total. Between 1950 and 1970 home ownership dropped slightly, and residential vacancy increased substantially, from 1.8 percent to 7.3 percent of local properties (Chicago Fact Book Consortium 1984, 15).

The force of these trends provided much of the impetus for the formation and development of the LVCC in the 1950s and 1960s. It is ironic, therefore, to recall that much of the LVCC's energy in the 1960s was devoted to coping with new residential development, as embodied in the four-plus-one buildings. At that time lakefront and western Lake View appeared to be following distinctly separate paths. On the neighborhood's eastern flank, residential density was increasing, and commercial streets such as Broadway thrived. On the neighborhood's western side, that is, on the other side of Clark Street from Wrigley Field, inconspicuous blue-collar residential areas seemed to be going the way of comparable neighborhoods across urban America: older homeowners were moving out, residential and commercial property maintenance was on the wane, and a new, less affluent population was arriving.

During the 1970s the two Lake Views began to converge. Across the community, the value of owner-occupied dwellings tripled from just under $18,000 to slightly more than $52,000. In the wake of the small drop in homeowner occupancy during the 1960s, from 1970 to 1980 the proportion of dwellings that were owner-occupied nearly doubled, from 10.9 percent to 20.4 percent. The latter jump reflected the rental-to-condominium conversion both of several lakefront high-rise towers and of dozens of three-flats and six-flats in all parts of Lake View. Possibly the most striking shift in Lake View's demographic profile during the 1970s was reflected in its workforce composition. In 1970, just over one-third (35.2%) of Lake View residents held white-collar jobs. By 1980, this percentage had doubled to 69.8, and the upward swing in Lake View residents' job status was evident throughout the neighborhood (Chicago Fact Book Consortium 1984, 15–16).

The sources of Lake View's change in the 1970s are clear enough. By the middle of that decade, the gentrification of the Lincoln Park residential area to the south of Lake View was well under way. Indeed, many of Lake View's near-lakefront streets offer the same enticements to developers as Lincoln Park: access to lakefront beaches and parks, vintage properties amenable to rehabilitation, access to mass-transit lines. As Lincoln Park filled up, the residential investment stream flowing into that community began to spill over into Lake View. Moreover, although the clarion call of neighborhood decline had been sounded in the 1950s, twenty years later even the comparatively drab backyard of Lake View west of Wrigley Field, where many blocks featured solidly built stone and brick structures, had not experienced substantial physical decay. In this sense, even nonlakefront Lake View was ripe for upgrading.

An additional factor that may have helped to channel residential investment into Lake View was the shaky reputation of its lakefront neighbor to the north, Uptown, where during the 1970s physical decay advanced dramatically and well-organized tenants and low-income residents mobilized to block the efforts of gentrification-oriented developers (Bennett 1997, 75–96). Some smart money probably followed an investment path of lesser resistance into the promising nonlakefront areas of Lake View. Finally, one must not underestimate the neighborhood stabilization that resulted from the LVCC's efforts during the 1950s and 1960s. During this crucial period, a core of activist residents and merchants had founded an organization that on the one hand promoted local and City action aimed at preserving the neighborhood, and on the other hand highlighted Lake View's status as a neighborhood with a considerable store of institutional will and collective loyalty. At a time when many Chicago neighborhoods could claim neither attribute, this was the stuff of local stability.

Wrigley Field and the New Lake View

During the period of intense political debate and maneuvering preceding the decision to bring nighttime baseball to Wrigley Field, Lake View activists, the press, and many politicians routinely employed an interpretive framework that defined the lights conflict as a standoff between a corporation and neighborhood residents. But Wrigley Field's environs have long been more than a residential neighborhood, and the likely alternative resolutions to the conflict—maintenance of the lightless status quo, the modernizing of the stadium, the Cubs' withdrawal to a suburban sports palace—augured widely varying impacts on local businesses. On Wrigley Field's western flank, Clark Street had for many years been a busy commercial thoroughfare, and along Clark Street, Addison Street, and Sheffield Avenue, directly adjoining the ballpark, a cluster of taverns, restaurants, souvenir shops, and sports-apparel merchants thrived on the spending of baseball partisans. During the 1980s, the owners of several residential buildings beyond Wrigley Field's right- and left-field walls had built roof decks providing views of the playing field below. Soon, what was at first an amenity informally available to a handful of neighborhood residents was quite transformed when several deck owners expanded their facilities and began to rent them to groups of partying spectators. During the period of negotiations among CUBS/LVCC, the baseball franchise, and the City of Chicago in the mid-1980s, several local merchants sat in with the neighborhood representatives. At that time there were no evident divisions separating residents from merchants (Sam Toia, interview, November 12, 1998). However, some of the most striking neighborhood impacts of the decision to bring lights to Wrigley Field have centered on the fortunes of local businesses, which have not been uniform.

Since the commencement of nighttime baseball at Wrigley Field in August 1988, some local enterprises have experienced a boom, while others have seen business drop off substantially (McCracken 1989; Swanson 1994). The arrival of evening games has shifted temporal patterns around the ballpark, and increased automobile traffic as well as more elaborate parking restrictions have further restructured how local residents and visitors make their way through Lake View. On the one hand, many smaller enterprises such as bookstores, dry cleaners, pharmacies, video rental businesses, and even some restaurants that do not cater to the baseball market have found the new pattern of neighborhood use quite inhospitable. In contrast, the sports-bar enclave directly adjoining the ballpark has thrived both in season and out of season, as have other businesses that serve the crowds of young people flowing into Wrigley Field and its surrounding bars and nightspots.

Local activists, residents, and merchants are acutely sensitive to the changes in Lake View wrought by the Wrigley Field lights settlement. Noting the shift in her neighborhood's economic base that was evident at least a decade before lights appeared at Wrigley Field, Charlotte Newfeld of CUBS observed: "Remember that the small-industrial base in the community was disappearing. A local precision-tool plant was closing. What was growing were jazz clubs, theaters, retail, and other small businesses, . . . and the gay and lesbian community along Halsted . . . because of cheap rents" (interview, October 13 and December 9, 1998). This transformation of local economic activity was perfectly in step with the residential upgrading of Lake View that occurred in the 1970s and early 1980s and as such was welcomed by community leaders. However, with the arrival of nighttime baseball, some of the very enterprises that had thrived in the preceding decade began to suffer. Paul Kendall of CUBS attributed their pinched circumstances to the new neighborhood environment produced by evening baseball: "The businesses we tried to help and preserve were the restaurants, theaters. . . . I mean the real restaurants! As the Cubs play a night game, the real restaurants are not doing well. They have suffered because bars came to the area. Now everyone goes to the bars" (interview, September 28, 1998).

Small retail establishments and other businesses catering to specialized clienteles have similarly suffered. Joe Pinter, owner of a violin shop on Clark Street to the north of the ballpark, described for us the impact of the lights installation on his business:

> I have been here for 28 years, and things in recent years have changed tremendously. Parking has been helped around here for the better . . . I mean for the residents. There are more bars and restaurants in the area than ever before. My business has not gotten any help from all this. Actually, some customers are afraid to visit the area because of the parking restrictions. Bar and restaurant business is the type of business you want to get yourself into here. That's where the money is now. (Interview, August 22, 1995)

Likewise, an employee at Bookworks, a second-hand retailer south of Wrigley Field on Clark Street, reported at best a mixed impact:

> There has been definitely an increase in trendy stuff around here. Many young people are bar hopping. Often you have long lines outside these bars as people wait to get in. The lights have been good for those businesses, but they have not helped us. Our hours go from noon to 10 P.M. and noon to 11 P.M. Some of the people who come here to go to the game might stop by and pick up a baseball book. But you cannot rely on that. Many of the local residents are our customers. The long evening hours are mostly for them since you cannot rely on the crowds after the night games for business. (Jeffrey Frisone, interview, August 25, 1995)

In 1995, when we spoke to the owner of Damen Foods, a small grocery (since closed) at the corner of Damen Avenue and Addison Street about a mile west of Wrigley Field, he emphasized that nighttime baseball meant different things to different merchants:

> Right here where I am, they [night games] do not affect me. Business has not been good here because of the lights. But I'll tell you what, my buddy who is closer to Wrigley Field and runs a small bar has seen better business because of the lights. The people come at night and they stay outside longer. At night people will drink . . . eat. These businesses benefit from the night games.

As suggested by the Damen Foods proprietor, the local establishments that have benefited the most from the "expanded hours" of Wrigley Field are businesses that cater to baseball fans. Paul Kendall described to us how two Lake View taverns across the street from the ballpark have fared in the last decade: "Some bars have expanded after the lights. Like the Cubby Bear. It has expanded three times. The owner even wanted recently to add a beer garden on the street. Some residents behind the place found out, and we stopped his plans. Same thing with Murphy's Bleachers. He also expanded" (interview, September 28, 1998). Other businesses have shifted emphasis. For many restaurants, this has meant recreating themselves in the image of sports bars. According to Kendall, "There is no question that since the lights came to Lake View, the nature of restaurants has changed. They all put in TVs to give customers an opportunity to watch games. They want to compete with the sport bars" (interview, September 28, 1998). Another CUBS leader and former aide to Alderman Hansen, Mike Quigley, suggested that such changes may be good for business, but not so good for local customers: "Some of the restaurants in the community get killed because of the games. Fine dining restaurants are having a hard time making it. Many of these establishments are cutting down their menus and are placing TV sets in their premises. In reality they have been converted into bars" (interview, November 23, 1998).

Another factor that is recasting the neighborhood business environment is the baseball franchise's movement into new markets. Like other professional sports clubs, in recent years the Chicago Cubs have substantially expanded the array of services they offer fans. For example, the ball club operates three restaurants within Wrigley Field—The Stadium Club, the Friendly Confines Cafe, and the Sheffield Grill—with the aim of increasing its take of the spending of baseball fans who choose to make a day or evening of attending a sporting contest (Deacon 1996). Of course, by moving into the tavern and restaurant business, as well as by selling Cubs souvenirs and apparel on their premises, the ball club cuts into the spending stream available to sports-oriented neighborhood enterprises. However, unlike the immediate vicinity of the new Comiskey Park, whose absence of small merchants ensures that the bulk of fan expenditures will be collected by the White Sox franchise, the density of the commercial area around Wrigley Field results in a very substantial spillover of food, beverage, and memorabilia expenditures.

As several of the foregoing comments attest, for many local participants in the Wrigley Field lights conflict Lake View of the 1990s had become a less congenial neighborhood. Charlotte Newfeld, who feels that in many ways the lights compromise represented an unavoidable resolution to the Wrigley Field standoff, nonetheless has also told a local reporter: "It's not baseball in the tradition I know" (Swanson 1994). Since the coming of nighttime baseball, the range of cultural and entertainment venues in the near-vicinity of Wrigley Field has narrowed. For example, in the last few years one of the neighborhood's leading stage companies, the Organic Theatre, moved from Lake View, and its performance space just a few blocks south of Wrigley Field has been converted to residential condominiums. A few blocks west of Wrigley Field, along Southport Avenue, a distinctly cosmopolitan commercial revival has occurred. Two theatres—one specializing in international and art films, the second presenting live stage productions—anchor a strip of upscale restaurants and galleries. Without catapulting small-market businesses and arts groups clear out of Lake View, the recently more boisterous environs of Wrigley Field seem to have pushed such establishments into adjacent areas more amenable to the attraction of local and relatively sedate clienteles.

In another respect, the impact of nighttime baseball does not appear to have fulfilled anyone's expectations. Speaking at a neighborhood hearing in early 1988, a local residential developer predicted, "I believe lights would be a disaster to future real estate development" (Hurt 1988). During the 1990s, however, residential investment in Lake View accelerated. From 1994 to 1996, residential loans within Lake View totaled 1.4 billion dollars, a figure that was exceeded only by that of Lincoln Park among Chicago's seventy-seven community areas. Moreover, recent residential buyers in Lake View have been very affluent. From 1994 to 1996, the majority of local residential loans were directed to individuals and families with annual earnings in excess of $62,000 (Woodstock Institute 1996, 16 and 51; 1997, 16 and 51; 1998, 14 and 28). An outgrowth of this development boom is the emergence of a neighborhood issue reminiscent of the four-plus-one conflict of three decades ago. Across Lake View developers have been purchasing older single- and two-family homes, demolishing them, and replacing them with larger three-, four-, and five-unit condominium buildings. A 1996 article on local real estate trends noted, "In one four-square-block quadrant . . . at least 27 houses have been razed in the last 10 years to make way for new buildings, nine of them in the last two years" (Chanen 1996). In many instances, the neighbors of these new buildings have complained about their scale and incompatibility with older adjoining residences. Thus, even as the new entertainment environment around Wrigley Field brings floods of baseball fans and fun seekers to the neighborhood, the residential areas near the ballpark have experienced a parallel tide of new investment, and with it the growing pains associated with increased population density.

"The Port of Entry for All the Young People"

The emergence of the new Lake View that has coincided with the advent of nighttime baseball at Wrigley Field represents a strikingly ambiguous story of neighborhood transformation. The area immediately adjacent to the ballpark has become an entertainment center whose multitude of nightclubs, restaurants, sports bars, and souvenir shops attract customers throughout the year. While it is obvious that the modernizing of Wrigley Field contributed to the emergence of this wildly popular district, with each passing year it becomes equally evident that the allure of "Wrigleyville," a designation generally despised by local residents, transcends the allure of baseball. The crowds of club hoppers along Clark Street and Sheffield Avenue most of the time are brought to Lake View by the simple prospect of joining the big party—baseball game or no baseball game. Of course, the big party is itself a highly ambiguous feature of Lake View. For some fans an afternoon or evening spent at the ballpark is synonymous with the carnival-like atmosphere of Wrigley Field's environs. But for local residents the ballpark, which itself is usually viewed as an amenity, represents a threat to peace and local stability as the atmosphere of revelry spreads to adjoining areas. It is thus ironic that from the standpoint of stadium-driven urban development, Wrigley Field and its neighborhood have come to be viewed as a model for other cities to emulate.

The entertainment-driven economy of Lake View, which has been stimulated by the growing popularity of the Cubs and Wrigley Field, has contributed to a noticeable differentiation of neighborhood space. In the vicinity of Wrigley Field, most of the taverns and restaurants cater to a sports-oriented clientele. Directly across the Addison Street–Sheffield Avenue intersection from Wrigley Field, the TV monitors at Hi-Tops draw a rolling audience of Cubs, NFL football, NCAA basketball, and Olympic sports fans depending on the season and year. Several blocks to the west of Wrigley Field the theatres and restaurants along Southport Avenue are populated by an older crowd, and very few establishments, particularly those that have opened in the last five years, cater to sports fans. To the east of Wrigley Field along Halsted Street, the gay-oriented bars, restaurants, and retailers that began to appear in the 1970s continue to thrive; but again, like the Southport merchants', their fortunes are largely independent of baseball.

In his effort to define a "new urban sociology," Mark Gottdiener (1994, 15) observes that "One of the principle sources of symbolic life involves . . . the built environment." For many decades, the Cubs and Wrigley Field have been a part of Lake View, and yet for much of that time baseball and the ballpark were relatively inconspicuous elements of the larger neighborhood. As recently as the 1950s, many journalistic descriptions of Lake View failed to note the presence of Wrigley Field. It is since the 1960s that the designation "Wrigleyville" has emerged to describe the area immediately surrounding the ballpark, and it is only with the Tribune Company's acquisition of the Cubs in the 1980s that Lake View has become popularly understood as "the neighborhood of baseball."

Lake View's mushrooming entertainment economy is closely aligned with its symbolic identity, an identity that in recent years has been promoted by a legion of entrepreneurs both large and small. The unfolding of this new Lake View, in many respects, parallels the redefinition of Manhattan by what Sharon Zukin, perhaps slyly, has called the "artistic mode of production" (1995, 111). Though Zukin's work has mainly concentrated on the factors linking neighborhood development, artistic production and display, and shopping as a leisure activity, we propose that sports and entertainment are just as central to the new urban economies of leisure. Indeed, if we consider the long-standing interurban competition between New York City and Chicago, it might be contended that sports, far more than the arts, represent a field in which the "second city" can plausibly claim a comparative advantage over its larger East Coast rival.

In the two decades since the Tribune Company's acquisition of the Cubs, the ball club's owners have become acutely aware of the comparative advantage offered by their ballpark and its neighborhood. Occupying a ninety-year-old facility with the second smallest seating capacity in Major League Baseball might be viewed as an economic liability, as the Cubs' owners repeatedly asserted before nighttime games were permitted. In the last decade, however, Wrigley Field has not performed like an economic liability. The historic ballpark and its surroundings have proved to be powerful income generators. Though holding only 38,765 seats, the fewest among National League stadiums, the widely heralded "temple of baseball" has done wonders for the franchise's bottom line. By the mid-1990s, the Cubs' annual gate receipts and "venue revenues" (from suites, luxury seating, concessions, parking, and advertising) routinely stood near the top of National League rankings. From 1993 to 1996 the Cubs' gate receipts and venue revenues never fell below fourth among National League franchises (Ozanian 1994, 52; Ozanian 1995, 46; Atre et al. 1996, 56; Badenhausen and Nikolov 1997, 47).

Speaking to a journalist in 1996, Cubs president Andy MacPhail, unlike some of his predecessors, did not hesitate to link the ball club's positive financial position to the draw attributable to Wrigley Field and Lake View: "We are very happy at Wrigley Field and we have no plans to make changes. . . . While it is true Wrigley Field is not going to generate what new ballparks can generate (in revenue), there is a very special appeal to the place that we well recognize" (Deacon 1996). Indeed, Wrigley Field and the adjoining neighborhood have become pilgrimage sites for contemporary stadium builders. Before Denver began construction of Coors Field, municipal and Rockies franchise officials visited Lake View to explore how their project could approximate the neighborhood environment of Wrigley Field (Newfeld, interview, October 13 and December 9, 1998). According to MacPhail, "With any new park that's being built, they always come here first and try to capture some of what this ballpark is. I understand that the park that they're contemplating in San Francisco [Pacific Bell Park] is going to be sort of subtitled 'Wrigley Field meets Camden Yards'" (Deacon 1996).

Possibly the central irony of the Wrigley Field lights conflict is that once the traditional ballpark was upgraded, the theming of Lake View as the year-round neighborhood of baseball could shift into high gear. As a result, Wrigley Field's surroundings have become a much more integral part of the baseball club's drawing power. A few years ago, Cubs' vice president John McDonough underlined this relationship: "The 'Wrigleyville' area draws thousands of revelers for its night life, and buses and 'L' trains stop just outside the park. . . . We're kind of in an area that's an ultimate destination, too. It's like an entertainment mecca all its own. I am not sure you can improve upon it" (Deacon 1996). The Wrigley Field appeal encompasses both the ballpark and its neighborhood environment, and this atmosphere has become the foundation of fan support for the Cubs. In the words of Andy MacPhail: "Wrigley Field is just a special place. It provides you with some [financial] insulation when you have a lousy year" (Miles 1999).

The upgrading of Wrigley Field and the coming of evening baseball to Lake View illustrate in the most dramatic manner the subtle effects on a neighborhood's geographic structure, economic make-up, and cultural identity that can be produced by a physical development project. What is especially intriguing about the emergent Lake View is the curious relationship between the neighborhood that is and the neighborhood that was. As recently as the 1970s, Lake View was a relatively unassuming Chicago neighborhood that happened to possess an "antique" sporting facility whose main attraction, major-league baseball, for about half the year gave the neighborhood a very distinctive temporal pace: the mid-morning arrival of street vendors, stadium employees, and sports fans, the crescendo of mid-afternoon baseball competition, and the late-afternoon ebbing away of baseball partisans—some departing for home, others pausing in local taverns and restaurants. In the era of nighttime baseball, the Wrigleyville entertainment district has expanded and has contributed to a physical restructuring of Lake View well away from the ballpark. More generally, the Lake View neighborhood has become a key element in Chicago's drive to refashion itself as a metropolis rich in arts, entertainment, and sports venues. Local merchant Sam Toia aptly characterized Lake View's new role within the Chicago economy: "We've become the port of entry for all the young people" (interview, November 12, 1998).

7

Redeveloping
the Near West Side

From Conflict to Collaboration

During the 1980s, Chicago's Near West Side appeared to be a fertile ground for the city's professional sports franchises. Serious development initiatives sought first to place a mammoth football stadium for the Chicago Bears about two miles west of the Loop, then to rehouse the Chicago Bulls and Blackhawks, the city's major-league basketball and hockey teams, in the United Center. Only the latter project was completed, but along the way the Chicago press also picked up the occasional drumbeat heralding the West Side as the new home of the White Sox. In each of these instances, stadium proponents contended that their favored project would rejuvenate a derelict section of the central city whose main commercial thoroughfare, Madison Street, had been devastated by rioting in the wake of Martin Luther King Jr.'s assassination in April 1968 (Farber 1988, 139–42). Over the longer arc of the post–World War II period, as racial turnover and residential disinvestment spread west from central Chicago to the city's border with Oak Park, the Near West Side had lost a substantial portion of its residential population and housing stock (Chicago Fact Book Consortium 1995, 103–6).

Though the fact was only obliquely noted, for stadium proponents a primary attraction of the Near West Side was this physical devastation. Large tracts of land were vacant, and the presumption of many stadium project boosters was that local residents could be won over to the idea that a major sports facility project would inject new vitality into adjoining residential and commercial areas. However, the process of selling stadium-centered neighborhood development to Near West Siders turned out to be a contentious enterprise. There were prostadium as well as stadium-wary factions among Near West Side residents and merchants. The Interfaith Organizing Project (IOP), a movement that was led by a group of ministers serving local congregations, emerged as a creative and determined neighborhood advocate. In addition to having a major hand in blocking the

The United Center, set amid acres of parking and occasional remnants of the old neighborhood

Bears-stadium proposal, IOP won substantial concessions from the development group sponsoring the United Center. And over the past decade, one of IOP's leaders in the 1980s, Earnest Gates, has emerged as an influential neighborhood figure in his own right. Moreover, a variety of other forces, including residential gentrification fanning out from areas to the east of the United Center and from the University of Illinois at Chicago (UIC) complex to the south, as well as the redevelopment of nearby public housing complexes, have added fuel to the transformation of the Near West Side.

The Bears' Falling Out with Soldier Field

By the mid-1980s, the Chicago Bears football franchise had become disenchanted with its home ground, Soldier Field. The Bears had moved into the 1920s-era Soldier Field in the early 1970s and at various times had explored the prospects of finding a better home facility. Situated just southeast of the Loop near the shore of Lake Michigan, Soldier Field—especially in the late autumn and winter months—is subject to freakish weather conditions. However, the Bears' principal objections had to do with the physical features of

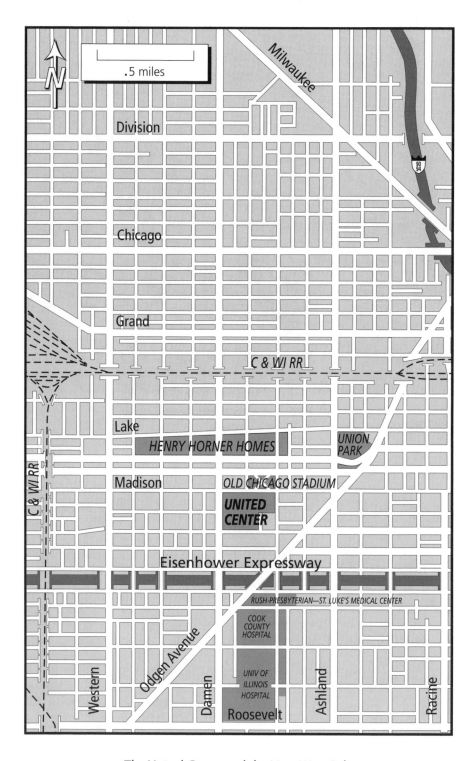

The United Center and the Near West Side

Soldier Field and their marriage of convenience to the stadium's public landlord, the Chicago Park District. A greater-than-typical share of the arena's seating was behind the end zone sections of the playing field, and beneath the structure's huge bowl, space for public lavatories, locker rooms, and commercial vendors was spartan. Moreover, and in spite of a modernization program carried out by the park district, Soldier Field did not offer the kind of skybox accommodations considered essential in contemporary sporting palaces. Finally, over the course of the 1970s and early 1980s, the Bears' owners had become increasingly frustrated by their dependence on the park district for day-to-day maintenance as well as more substantial renovation work (Baade and Sanderson 1997, 330–31).

These frustrations came to a head in the mid-1980s as a result of two circumstances. Newly selected Bears president Michael McCaskey, grandson of the franchise's legendary founder, George Halas, turned up the volume of the team's complaints about Soldier Field and the park district and began to explore the prospects of moving to a football facility outside the city of Chicago. Secondarily, the Bears experienced an on-the-field renaissance under Coach Mike Ditka which resulted in a Super Bowl championship in January 1986. At that moment, the Bears were the city's premier professional sports franchise, having brought a championship to a success-starved city and, unlike the Cubs and White Sox, not subject to the vagaries of North Side/South Side fan rivalry. In short, Bears executives believed that they were in a position to dictate the terms of a new stadium deal.

In early 1986, the Bears engaged in discussions with the Washington administration, which was attempting to cobble together the South Loop stadium development initiative whose presumed joint tenants would be the White Sox and the Bears. In the months following the breakdown of this plan, the Bears proceeded to investigate prospective stadium sites in west suburban DuPage County. However, by the end of the year the Bears had feinted back toward the Chicago lakefront. Members of the Chicago Central Area Committee (CCAC), an elite business network that often proposes major downtown development initiatives, and Bears officials joined forces to advocate the construction of a 75,000-seat open-air football stadium situated just to the south of the Soldier Field site. Perhaps mindful of his upcoming reelection campaign, Mayor Washington quickly endorsed the lakefront stadium proposal. The mayor's enthusiasm for the lakefront stadium was not, however, matched by a number of influential civic groups.

Development initiatives along Chicago's Lake Michigan shoreline, much of which is publicly held park land, and especially those on sites as prominent as the Near South Side vicinity of Soldier Field, inevitably generate substantial public and civic attention, and the CCAC/Bears proposal was no exception. A prominent parks-advocacy group, Friends of the Parks, immediately objected to the lakefront stadium proposal and was joined by four other civic groups, including the League of Women Voters and the Metropolitan Planning Council (MPC), the latter a civic voice with fully as much prestige and nearly as much corporate clout as the CCAC. Speaking for this alliance of lakefront stadium opponents, Erma Tranter of the Friends of the Parks commented "we're in total agreement that this is the wrong location" (McCarron 1986). Cook County assessor Thomas Hynes, who was gearing up his effort to challenge Mayor Washington and was certainly mindful of the upcoming election, labeled the CCAC/Bears plan a "lakefront land grab" (McCarron 1987c).

By late December 1986, Mayor Washington had tempered his initial enthusiasm for a football stadium south of Soldier Field, and in the face of intense debate regarding the wisdom of this siting preference, had appointed a three-member committee to evaluate alternative stadium proposals and sites. The committee included Mary Decker, executive director of the MPC; Walter Netsch, president of the Chicago Park District; and mayoral advisor Al Johnson. The stadium siting committee anticipated convening for up to six months, which, as numerous political commentators noted, would place the conclusion of its deliberations long past the date of the mayoral election (McCarron 1987c). During the next half-year a surprising variety of alternative stadium proposals emerged, but when the dust settled in June 1987, the Bears appeared to be committed to a Near West Side stadium project that had significant institutional and corporate backing.

The Near West Side Bears Stadium Proposal

In the early months of 1987, prospective Bears stadium sites began to pop up like mushrooms on a rainy forest floor. The CCAC, led by financier Franklin Cole, continued to tout the lakefront site that had briefly won the admiration of Mayor Washington. However, in the face of environmental concerns regarding this site, the CCAC also suggested that a football stadium could be fit onto abandoned railroad property to the west of Soldier Field beyond Lake Shore Drive. On June 8, several weeks before the site-selection committee made its recommendation, developers William Spatz and Dan Shannon proposed a stadium/shopping complex to be built just northwest of the Loop, again on property that had once been devoted to railway uses. The site-selection committee also considered the Near South Side site on the eastern side of the Chicago River's south branch, where a two-sport stadium had been contemplated the year before (Spielman and Golden 1987a).

Yet another stadium proposal, this one targeting the Near West Side, had become the frontrunner by mid-April. One day before the second of two public hearings on stadium sites scheduled by the site-selection committee, a consortium headed by developer Marshall Bennett unveiled an elaborate plan for an area centered by a football stadium set between Paulina Street on the east and Damen Avenue on the west, with Madison Street and Jackson Boulevard the north and south boundaries, respectively—that is, in the heart of the Near West Side (Spielman and Golden 1987b). Bennett's development partners included William Wirtz, owner of the Chicago Blackhawks and of their home arena, the Chicago Stadium, which would be just north of the new stadium and would be renovated in conjunction with the football facility's construction (Spielman 1987d). Another, somewhat curious, participant in this development proposal was Rush-Presbyterian-St. Luke's Medical Center, one of the region's largest medical complexes and a neighbor on the southern flank of the prospective football stadium site. Rush-Presbyterian-St. Luke's contribution to the project was to be a "sports medicine complex" located just across the street from the football field, and accessible from the stadium, according to one description, via an underground passageway to allow the speedy evacuation of injured football players (Spielman and Golden 1987b). Though it may have been but a coincidence, Rush-Presbyterian-St. Luke's legal counsel was Oscar D'Angelo, an attorney with close ties to the city's Democratic Party leadership and a prominent player in West Side real estate activity.

Apart from auxiliary development, the football stadium would be a huge structure, seating 75,000 fans. A week following their initial announcement, the project's sponsors produced a development plan setting the total price tag for the stadium, auxiliary structures such as the sports medicine complex, and replacement housing for displaced neighborhood residents at $170 million (Spielman 1987e). From the outset, many Near West Side community leaders were wary of the project sponsors' displacement estimates and commitment to rehouse local people. Anticipating just this reaction, the development consortium had hired a Northwestern University professor, Louis Masotti, to present their proposal to local residents. Masotti, in turn, sought local support for the developers' pledge to found a community development corporation that would oversee the construction of replacement housing and other neighborhood projects. Unfortunately for developer Bennett and his associates, Masotti, a political scientist by training who had moved to the graduate business college at Northwestern, never seems to have won the confidence of Near West Side community leaders (Spielman 1987a).

In any event, following months of deliberation that included two public hearings dealing with the array of proposed sites, as well as a series of neighborhood meetings at Malcolm X College on the West Side, in early June 1987 the mayor's site-selection committee announced that the best location for the new Chicago Bears stadium was on the Near West Side. No doubt influenced by several public demonstrations led by IOP, in the following months city officials, most notably Washington advisors Al Johnson and Robert Mier, devoted considerable effort to defining a local planning process that would address neighborhood concerns over issues such as residential displacement (Mier 1987). At this time, the City and the development consortium estimated that 1,500 residents would be displaced by the project. During the summer of 1987, a community coordinating committee, with mainly local community leaders present, met to discuss stadium plans, but this group's discussions were marked by considerable acrimony (Butler 1987; West Side and Community Development Community Coordinating Committee 1987). In September 1987, Mayor Washington appointed a West Side Development Committee, whose co-chairs included his chief of staff, Ernest Barefield; two business leaders, Franklin Cole and Barry Sullivan; Al Johnson; and Nancy Jefferson, a long-time West Side activist and leading figure in the Midwest Community Council. In an April memo to Mayor Washington, Mier and Johnson had described Jefferson as "walking a fine (and fair) line on the West Side site" (Mier and Johnson 1987). In other words, unlike the combatively hostile IOP, Nancy Jefferson and the Midwest Community Council were cautiously supportive of the stadium project. Other than Jefferson and the area's City Council representatives, the fifteen-member West Side Development Committee included only two neighborhood residents.

Even as the city of Chicago churned with political uncertainty during late 1987 and early 1988 following Mayor Washington's death, the West Side Development Committee stayed its course. By June of 1988, the City, the Bears, and developer Bernard Weissbourd, president of Metropolitan Structures, announced their agreement to go ahead with the Near West Side stadium project. (The hospital-linked development consortium had dropped out of the proceedings.) At the press conference announcing the revamped stadium plan, which would place the Bears in their new home in time for the 1992 NFL season, Mayor Eugene Sawyer committed $35 million in city funds to the project. The City's contribution would be derived from a tax increment finance (TIF) district that would include the site of the new sports facility. Mayor Sawyer also pledged that residential relocation would precede construction of the new football arena. The parties to the development agreement also sought State of Illinois funding for $30 million of neighborhood infrastructure improvements (Devall and Franklin 1988). Representatives of the Bears and the Sawyer administration rushed to Springfield, where the General Assembly's spring session was nearing its close. They carried legislation intended to effect this commitment of state funds, and also including provisions that would enable the Bears to claim properties owned by William Wirtz and used for Chicago Stadium parking. Wirtz, who has been described as Chicago's "ranking sportsman," also owns of one of Illinois's largest liquor distributors, and therefore maintains a formidable lobbying team at the state capitol. Once he was apprised of the condemnation powers attached to the funding bill—neither Bears nor City of Chicago officials had cleared their draft legislation with him—Wirtz did not hesitate to take retaliatory action. In Wirtz's view, it was like someone "who buys the house next door, informs you he is taking your swimming pool, then tells you that you can still use it . . . for a price" (McCarron 1988c).

Wirtz's men in Springfield, including former Cook County assessor Thomas Tully and Governor James Thompson's one-time chief of staff James Fletcher, blitzed the City of Chicago and Bears forces in the state legislature. One account of the Wirtz ambush described it this way: "It was something to see. Fletcher had Xerox machines, a telephone bank, secretaries, even a reception area with free food" (McCarron 1988c, 22). In the face of Wirtz's concerted opposition, the state legislature tabled the Bears stadium infrastructure bill. Over the next several months, city officials attempted to patch up the relationship between William Wirtz and Michael McCaskey, but these efforts were never to succeed. As late as the spring of 1989, there was still press speculation that a rapprochement between the Blackhawks owner and the Bears president could yield a reinvigorated Near West Side football stadium proposal, but months earlier Wirtz had begun to explore another possibility. Instead of planning for the renovation of the Chicago Stadium, Wirtz began to contemplate building a new home for his Blackhawks and Jerry Reinsdorf's Chicago Bulls. This entrepreneurial seed would, a few years later, emerge fully developed as the United Center.

The Interfaith Organizing Project

The Interfaith Organizing Project (IOP) was founded by a group of Chicago area ministers in late 1985. Its original organizing staff, Ed Shurna and Karen Nielson, were recruited from the National Training and Information Center, a long-standing advocacy group for grassroots initiatives and a trainer of community organizers. IOP came to Chicago's Near West Side more or less by accident. One of its sponsoring ministers, Arthur Griffin of First Baptist Congregational Church on West Washington Boulevard, offered to house IOP in some office space adjoining his church building. IOP began an organizing effort in the far West Side Austin neighborhood, but that initiative was subsequently dropped in favor of focusing the group's attention on the Near West Side. As Ed Shurna recalled, in early 1987, when the West Side Bears stadium proposal emerged, "we probably weren't ready to deal with it, but then again, if we hadn't been around who knows what would have happened" (interview, August 2, 2000).

IOP had already begun to develop a visible presence on the Near West Side, as evidenced by the role it played in a peculiar warmup to the larger game of West Side stadium politics. In the spring of 1986, John Cullerton, a state legislator representing a district on the Northwest Side of Chicago, had introduced a bill that would have expanded the boundaries of the Illinois Medical Center Commission, a quasigovernmental board with development authority in the West Side area around the Rush-Presbyterian-St. Luke's, University of Illinois, and Cook County hospitals. Cullerton's legislation would have extended the eminent domain authority of the renamed West Side Development Commission to the Near West Side quadrant where, soon enough, officials would propose to build a new Bears stadium. Cullerton's bill had not been approved in the spring legislative session, but IOP was instrumental in bringing out a crowd of eight hundred to one thousand local residents to a public meeting to discuss the matter in September 1986. At this meeting, State Representative Cullerton, who claimed to have introduced his bill at the behest of one of the commission's board members, an individual he supposed "had the best interest of the community in mind," offered the remarkable comment: "I still haven't read the bill—all I know is it's got everyone upset" (Wilson 1986). Chastened by having made so many people visibly upset, Cullerton pledged to no longer promote his unread initiative. As for IOP and many Near West Side residents, the Cullerton imbroglio served as a heads up; it fixed their resolve to begin making their own plans for the future of the neighborhood.

Before local planning for a new neighborhood could proceed very far, the Near West Side Bears stadium proposal emerged in early 1987. From the outset, and undoubtedly linking the stadium plan to the recently scuttled Cullerton bill, IOP adopted a skeptical attitude toward every proponent of the West Side Bears stadium, including Mayor Washington. At this time, the main IOP spokesperson was Reverend Griffin, who in many press accounts was portrayed as an extremist opponent of any stadium-anchored neighborhood development initiative. Reverend Griffin was but one of a number of participants in a week-long "Peoples Development Seminar" organized by the Midwest Community Council in April 1987. Among the principles adopted by the participants in these meetings was the following, under the subheading "Respect":

> Many residents expressed the feeling that stadium developers were proceeding without the input and involvement of the community. Outsiders were viewed with suspicion regarding their plans and proposals. The community called for all stadium developers and supporters to respect the west side community, and to make public all plans and documents. (Midwest Community Council 1987)

Whether or not Reverend Griffin's—and by extension, IOP's—hostility to the Bears stadium proposal was unyielding, his sense that neighborhood interests could well be shortchanged in the rush to reach a West Side stadium deal does not appear to have been out of line with prevailing neighborhood sentiment.

In the coming months, IOP would win notoriety for its aggressive tactics. On Sunday, May 3, 1987, several busloads of IOP supporters visited the north suburban home of Bears president Michael McCaskey on a "site-finding mission," seeking a direct meeting with McCaskey (Siewers 1987). Over the next year, IOP would twice more seek out McCaskey, once traveling all the way to the Bears' preseason training camp in Platteville, Wisconsin. In conjunction with a second visit to McCaskey's residence in April 1988, IOP supporters played a touch football game ("West Side Residents" versus the "Chicago Bares") in a nearby public park. Closer to home, at a January 1988 presentation of prospective stadium designs, Reverend Griffin led a walkout, then "residents encircled the drawings and models, prayed, and, in an action straight from the Old Testament, walked around the 'walls of Jericho' seven times and destroyed the models" (Interfaith Organizing Project 1992, 11–16).

Ed Shurna recalls that he, Earnest Gates, and another IOP member, Wilma Ward, were always talking about means of projecting IOP's message, but that the group's decision making in general "was collective. No one person called the shots" (interview, August 2, 2000). One of the core principles of IOP was consultative decision making. Each Thursday morning its ministerial board met to discuss the group's activities, and later in the evening of every Thursday, IOP held a community-wide meeting. Shurna estimates that the typical turnout for these public discussions was about twenty-five, but on occasion the meetings drew much larger crowds. Out of this intensive community dialogue, IOP not only shaped its direct action protests, but also developed a community plan for what it called the "Better Alternative Area," which included some of the blocks coveted by stadium development interests, and initiated a Near West Side Community Development Corporation as the vehicle for implementing local improvements (Interfaith Organizing Project 1992, 21). Later, when IOP found itself in a deadlock with the developers of the United Center, the group's ties to rank-and-file residents of the neighborhood were crucial to its maintenance of a firm bargaining position.

In spite of IOP's strong neighborhood base, the organization was regularly excoriated in the local press, most notably the *Chicago Tribune*. The *Tribune*'s most sustained attack occurred in its August 29, 1988, issue by way of an article entitled "Slum Owner's Brother Tries to Sack Bears Stadium," which was part of the "Chicago On Hold: The New Politics of Poverty" series that purported to reveal the unsavory sources and aims of much grassroots activism across the city. The bulk of the August 29 article was devoted to highlighting the presumably clay feet of IOP leaders Reverend Arthur Griffin and Earnest Gates. Griffin, it was noted, lived thirty-three blocks from his church and owned a Lincoln Continental. Gates was singled out for driving a Mercedes Benz 450SL. The "slum owner" of the title was Arthur Griffin's brother Burdett, who was identified as being "among the major landowners in the area," though the extent of his local property holdings was not documented (McCarron 1988b). The essence of this article's claim regarding Reverend Griffin was that his effort to block the Bears stadium project may have been due to his brother's ownership of rundown, tax-delinquent buildings in the vicinity of the proposed stadium site.

Apart from this direct volley at IOP, in the *Tribune*'s day-to-day reportage of West Side stadium matters, the paper consistently found ways to drop insinuating comments into its descriptions of IOP. For example, an April 23, 1987, article, for no evident reason (two other individuals were discussed in the article; in neither instance was a place of residence identified), noted that Reverend Griffin lived in the Austin neighborhood rather than the Near West Side (Wilson 1987). A month later, on May 26, a second *Tribune* reporter quoted a neighborhood resident who labeled IOP ministers "a bunch of upstarts," a point that was then underlined by the article's writer: "many of them commute to their churches on Sunday in luxury cars from wealthier parts of the city" (McCarron 1987d). In the latter instance, reporter John McCarron did not quote his source; he seems to have added his own inflection to his source's more general assertion. Furthermore, if McCarron had the "upstart" Reverend Arthur Griffin in mind, fact checking would have revealed that Griffin had pastored the First Baptist Congregational Church since 1957 and that although his residence was some distance from his church (thirty-three blocks, evidently), the Austin neighborhood is not, in any familiar sense of the expression, one of the "wealthier parts of the city." At the time, IOP was well aware of its status, at least in some influential quarters, as a vilified upstart organization. This does not seem to have inhibited the group. The organization's authorized record of its activities in the late 1980s, *The New "West Side Story,"* asserts that its membership's collective sense of unfair treatment only recharged their commitment to press on with their campaign to reshape the stadium development process.

The unraveling of the Bears stadium proposal was not, in the first instance, the handiwork of IOP. What killed the drive to build a football stadium on the Near West Side was the land dispute brought to a head by the City of Chicago's and the Bears' state legislative initiative of June 1988. Nevertheless, IOP's skillfully articulated and concerted opposition to the football stadium project surely dampened the resolve of the Bears to follow through on their plans, and just as certainly communicated to William Wirtz that any kind of major stadium development project on the Near West Side would have to come to terms with the Interfaith Organizing Project.

If Not Football, Then Why Not Hockey and Basketball?

In the original rendition of the Bears stadium–anchored Near West Side redevelopment plan, the Chicago Stadium, the aging indoor arena that was home to the Chicago Blackhawks and Bulls, would be renovated. Like Chicago's other early-twentieth-century sporting facilities, the stadium was marred by cramped public spaces, the absence of up-market seating and private entertainment facilities, and inadequate locker room accommodations for the athletes. Then, during the trying years of 1987 and 1988, as the Chicago Bears' ability to anchor the West Side project was challenged by skeptical community leaders and William Wirtz's relationship with Michael McCaskey of the Bears soured, Wirtz came around to the view that constructing a new facility to house the Blackhawks and Bulls was his preferred course of action. Evidently, Wirtz was deeply impressed by the economic performance of the Palace, the recently opened professional sports arena outside Detroit, whose construction cost was substantially underwritten by skybox-derived revenues. According to a late-1988 press account, "Wirtz is now transfixed by the way Detroit corporations have snapped up skyboxes at the Palace, the new home of the basketball Pistons in suburban Auburn Hills" (McCarron 1988c).

The Bears had insisted on a privately financed stadium for precisely this reason. Yet as the prospects of a Near West Side football stadium dimmed, Wirtz was able to find an agreeable sporting partner in Jerry Reinsdorf, principal owner of the Chicago Bulls, whose on-the-court product was becoming an increasingly bankable asset. By the late 1980s, the Bulls, led by the incomparable Michael Jordan, were beginning their move into the upper echelon of National Basketball Association teams. The remarkably agile Jordan's various steals, fadeaway jump shots, and resounding dunks were making him the most visible athlete in the world. And unlike a National Football League stadium, which hosts between ten and twelve contests per year, an indoor arena featuring major-league hockey and basketball franchises can offer as many as one hundred events between October and June. Thus, even before the embers of the Bears project had thoroughly cooled, William Wirtz, Jerry Reinsdorf, and their staffs were planning a new indoor sports arena directly across the street from the Chicago Stadium.

The arena that would emerge from their architectural and accounting software, the United Center, was indeed a sporting palace, seating 22,000 fans and including 216 luxury boxes whose original annual rents were set between $70,000 and $175,000. As one journalist breathlessly described the new edifice while it was still in its planning phase, "the new stadium will contain restaurants and private dining clubs. All seats will be padded and have unobstructed views. Seats near the ice will be on a steeper incline than in any other stadium, making for a clear view of the hockey rink" (Bessone 1992, 91). Nor did Wirtz and Reinsdorf experience significant difficulty in their quest for private financing. A twelve-firm consortium headed by Japan's Fuji Bank offered a $140 million loan. Though only three U.S. banks participated in this syndicate, these were minority-owned institutions based in Chicago (Spielman 1992).

From a physical planning and land acquisition standpoint, the development of the United Center represented a much more manageable operation than the Bears stadium. In the first place, most of the site south of the Chicago Stadium—previously at the edge of the football stadium "footprint" and now the proposed location for the new indoor arena—was already owned by William Wirtz. Secondarily, only eight buildings stood directly on the prospective United Center site. Another three dozen houses would have to be demolished to make way for expanded parking to serve the new facility. Nevertheless, in spring of 1989 Chicago's newly elected mayor, Richard M. Daley, communicated to Wirtz and Reinsdorf that it was their responsibility to reach an understanding with the property owners over appropriate compensation, and if they were resident homeowners, over relocation support (Bessone 1992, 92–93). The new mayor would be delighted at the prospect of a new sporting facility rising on the Near West Side, but unlike the previous stadium proposal, the United Center would not be a City project in the strict sense. Ultimately, the City of Chicago and State of Illinois did contribute approximately $20 million in infrastructure improvements in the vicinity of the new arena.

A substantial portion of the property owners in the vicinity of the new indoor stadium were in contact with IOP, and from mid-1989 to mid-1991, when the Wirtz/Reinsdorf development entity, the Metropolitan Chicago Stadium Joint Venture, reached an agreement with these local residents, IOP functioned as their agent. By this time, IOP had worked up a sixteen-point plan for community improvement. The main items covered by the sixteen points were compensation for property owners, including relocation of resident owners and tenants; financial support for additional for-sale housing to be developed by IOP; investment in a new park and neighborhood public library, as well as in a then-shuttered neighborhood health clinic; churchgoers' access to arena parking areas; and support for the creation of a construction-trades program at nearby Malcolm X College (Interfaith Organizing Project 1992, 33–34).

During the initial encounters between the joint venture and IOP, negotiations were not especially cordial. Referring to Jerry Reinsdorf and his advisor Howard Pizer, Earnest Gates has recalled:

> At that first meeting, Jerry started right out by saying he wasn't here to rebuild the west side. Then Howard started in on all of the things they weren't going to do. . . . I thought they were the biggest jerks in the world. They thought they could just walk in here, throw a few dollars on the table, and take our land. (Joravsky 1996, 23)

Indeed, by the end of 1989 the Wirtz/Reinsdorf team broke off talks. Over the next several months the joint venture, evidently unsettled by IOP's demands, attempted to buy out the eight most proximate homeowners (Joravsky 1996). However, several of these individuals kept IOP informed of the joint venture's gambit, and by the late spring of 1990 only two of the eight homeowners had agreed to sell. The remaining individuals came to be known in IOP lore as the "Solid Six." In the words of one of the Solid Six, Irene Johnson: "I wanted to stand by IOP. They stood by the community all those years, fighting the Bears stadium" (Interfaith Organizing Project 1992, 25).

Forced to resume negotiations with IOP, the Wirtz/Reinsdorf representatives ultimately acceded to the entirety of the sixteen-point community improvement plan. At the time, the development team's assessment of the situation was largely instrumental. In the words of Howard Pizer,

> After a while a light bulb went off in our heads and we realized we weren't going to get the land without dealing with Earnest, and Wilma [Ward], and the seniors. And without the land the deal's dead and there is no United Center. It's tough to pay $225,000 for land that's only worth $50,000 or so. But you have to ask yourself, "Even if we're going to get ripped off, do you want to go ahead with the deal?" We decided yes. We ended up giving them almost everything they wanted. (Joravsky 1996, 23)

In marked contrast to events following the new Comiskey Park neighborhood settlement, after the joint venture and IOP reached agreement in March 1991, all parties found reason for satisfaction. By the following March, the Solid Six homeowners were moving into their new two-flats, and there were no Near West Side constituencies objecting to the results of the negotiations. Also in March 1992, William Wirtz and Jerry Reinsdorf nailed down the financial package for their new arena. The United Center opened in the fall of 1994. Though the Chicago Blackhawks have not excelled in the subsequent years, with the return of Michael Jordan (who had quixotically retired from basketball to pursue a baseball career), to the

Replacement housing for the families whose homes had been on the United Center site

Chicago Bulls in 1995, Jerry Reinsdorf's "other franchise" would go on to win its second hat trick of NBA championships within the decade.

The New Near West Side

From the standpoint of various city officials and downtown Chicago business and civic leaders, one of the principal frustrations associated with the effort to plant the Chicago Bears on the Near West Side was the attitude of Michael McCaskey, who never seemed to be altogether enthusiastic about his team's prospective new address. McCaskey's reservations concerning the Near West Side were encapsulated by this comment offered to local reporters in February 1987: "Right now, unfortunately, the perception on the part of many season ticket holders who drive in from the suburbs is that that's a dangerous area. . . . I'm not saying it's impossible, but we have to have some picture of how . . . the West Side might develop over time" (Spielman 1987c).

A decade and one-half later, McCaskey and many suburban Bears fans may still view the Near West Side as dangerous, but in a variety of ways the United Center's environs have been markedly transformed. Not only has the warehouse district east of the new arena, across Ashland Avenue, become a center of residential conversion, along major east-west gateways to the United Center, including Madison and Randolph streets, dozens of new restaurants and other commercial establishments have appeared. Table 9 (in the appendix) offers striking testimony to the takeoff of the residential market in the Near West Side. Clearly, the area has shed its reputation as a dangerous location for residential investment.

Just as surely, there is little that is intrinsic to the design or siting of the United Center that accounts for these and other signs of neighborhood transformation. Although HOK Sports Facilities, once more favored with a major arena project in Chicago, produced a sports palace whose facade nods to the art deco flourishes that graced the now-demolished Chicago Stadium, the United Center—just like the new Comiskey Park—is as urbanistically sympathetic as a spaceship parked in a sea of asphalt. Moreover, the owners of the United Center have taken care to limit outdoor vending in the vicinity of their property. Thus, although the United Center may have been, as Mayor Richard M. Daley phrased it, "the first step in the rebirth" of the Near West Side, the subsequent regeneration of the area has been the consequence of several additional developments, not the least of which has been the Daley administration's concerted effort to redefine and expand Chicago's downtown core (Reardon 1991, 1; Bennett 1999).

At the heart of Mayor Daley's downtown development and expansion effort is a huge program of public works improvements, some of which

A recently opened outdoor café on Randolph Street east of the United Center

have aimed to restore the magnificence of venerable Chicago amenities, such as Grant Park, the Loop's front yard facing onto Lake Michigan. Other projects, including the rebuilding of the Roosevelt Road bridge just south of the Loop, have framed pedestrian and automobile approaches to the downtown while creating a commodious backdrop for new residential development (Kamin 1996; Washburn 1998). Probably the most striking recent change in Chicago's central-area real estate profile has been the upsurge in residential construction, involving both new projects and the conversion of properties previously devoted to commercial and manufacturing uses. More than five thousand units of new or newly renovated housing were sold in the vicinity of the Loop in 1997 and 1998. New housing development on the city's Near South and West Sides in particular has tended to expand the geographic reach of the Loop, which two analysts redubbed the "Super Loop" as early as the mid-1980s (Ludgin and Masotti 1985; 1986). This explosion of residential building has also brought the return of commercial enterprises, notably supermarkets and chain pharmacies, whose presence can be expected to enlarge the entrepreneurial vision and attract the financial backing necessary for even more housing construction. As a policy priority, this chain of investment is "one of the main reasons that downtown Chicago has remained vital despite the inexorable move of businesses to the suburbs. It not only adds excitement but acts as a shield in an economic slump" (Allen and Richards 1999).

During the 1990s, the United Center played a significant part in the Daley administration's effort to expand the Loop, beautify it, and convert what had once been a central business district into the mixed-use hub of a world city. Although the day-to-day economic purpose of the United Center is to bring rank-and-file sports fans into central Chicago, during one week in August 1996, the week of the Democratic National Convention, the new arena brought government leaders, political activists, economic royalty, and journalists from across the United States into the Near West Side. In preparation for the Democratic Convention, decorative planters and ornamental street lighting were installed to dignify Madison and Randolph Streets, the main links between the Loop and the convention site (Kamin 1996). On the Loop flank of the Near West Side, the City made substantial sidewalk and landscaping improvements along Halsted Street's Greektown commercial corridor. In subsequent years, the commercial gentrification of Randolph Street, at one time a food wholesalers' strip, has continued. As for Madison Street, on a walk between Halsted Street and Ashland Avenue in July 2000, a three-quarters-of-a-mile stretch to the east of the United Center, we counted eleven residential projects in the works. In the run-up to the Democratic Convention, the Daley administration also exerted considerable pressure on property owners in the area to bound parking lots and other open spaces with black ornamental fencing, this evidently an aesthetic preference the mayor had carried back among the souvenirs of his tours of European cities.

Beyond public works beautification and aesthetic jawboning, the Daley administration has also pursued institutional initiatives that promise to work additional great changes on the Near West Side. To the southeast of the United Center, the City has assisted the University of Illinois at Chicago's plans to push its campus south of its long-standing boundary along Roosevelt Road (Marx 1997). The UIC South Campus expansion already has resulted in the relocation of the century-old Maxwell Street outdoor market and has fueled local concerns over residential gentrification in the adjoining working-class, largely Mexican American neighborhood of Pilsen (Pollack 1998; Lutton 1998; Ahmed-Ullah 2000). Even more ambitiously, the Daley administration has prodded the massive restructuring program of the Chicago Housing Authority (CHA), which in the fall of 1999 committed to demolishing the agency's entire stock of "family" high-rise buildings (Garza 2000). On the Near West Side, if the CHA's "Plan for Transformation" is implemented in full, this will result in the thoroughgoing redevelopment of the ABLA and Henry Horner residential complexes, which at one time held over five thousand units of public housing. The CHA's intention with respect to both of these developments is to reduce the number of public housing units and "deconcentrate" the remainder in low-rise residential enclaves (Bennett 1999).

The changing face of the Near West Side, as well as the city government's approach to shaping new development in this area, were illuminated by a land-use conflict that emerged in late 1999 along Fulton Street northeast of the United Center. Incumbent merchants, for the most part food wholesalers, had petitioned the local alderman to take steps to slow the pace of commercial-to-residential building conversions, which, in the view of the merchants, threatened to thin their ranks to the point of undermining the viability of their market district. Pitted against the food wholesalers were new loft purchasers and residential developers complaining about local traffic and parking congestion, "overflowing dumpsters," and "pre-sunrise commotion on delivery docks as workers shout to one another and trucks move in and out." Caught between the merchants and the residential interests was Alderman Walter Burnett, who was inclined to back the wholesale food vendors:

> I am here to protect those who are here now. . . . Speculators and residential redevelopers try to build as many units as they can, don't soundproof their buildings, and don't put in sufficient parking. I am trying to get the Planning Department to come up with a plan so I can get everyone to live in harmony. But in the meantime, I have to put a halt to development. (Washburn and Mendell 1999, 1)

Burnett intended to introduce an ordinance that would prohibit residential conversions along Fulton Street and several adjoining streets. However, at the last moment the Daley administration advanced its own amendment to the local zoning regulations, which used density restrictions to limit residential conversions. As a result, residential developers, though subject to stricter controls, could continue to acquire and convert commercial and industrial properties in the Fulton market area (Washburn 1999).

The emergence of the new Near West Side is thus a complicated process within which the United Center's part has been significant but not necessarily pivotal. Indeed, the United Center's grounds, a huge parking area subdivided by access streets and chain link fencing, are an eyesore from any vantage point. Moreover, the isolation of the sports complex ensures that virtually no street-level economic or security benefits accrue to adjoining areas. Indeed, apart from the quick pregame and postgame stops for food and drinks that bring business to merchants on Randolph Street and elsewhere on the Near West Side, the United Center's principal economic function, if one thinks of the arena as a neighborhood institution, may be a curious showcasing effect. As Bulls, Blackhawks, or Bruce Springsteen fans drive into and out of the neighborhood, or catch Loop-originating shuttle buses to and from the arena, they may be impressed, at a distance, by the visible signs of regeneration on their left and right. In the long run, the attention of this transitory captive audience may yield local commercial investments or contribute to the market for residential lofts in the Near West Side. At present, this showcasing of the neighborhood, far more than any more direct contribution to street vitality or commerce, constitutes the United Center's main impact on its immediate environs.

From the standpoint of the Daley administration and its drive to beautify and thus contribute to the cosmopolitanization of central Chicago, the United Center represents a blunt but useful instrument. This, however, is not an agenda without complications. Until a decade ago, the Near West Side's population was overwhelmingly African American and poor. The commercial and residential gentrification that has accompanied the success of the United Center as a sports and entertainment venue has begun to push up property values and bring new, upscale residents to the neighborhood. Correspondingly, the downsizing of public housing projects such the ABLA and Henry Horner developments will reduce the number of affordable housing units and push some long-standing residents out of the Near West Side. This restructuring of the neighborhood has already produced some outbursts of local discord, given that many poorer Near West Siders view themselves as suddenly superfluous, threatened with the loss of their homes just as their neighborhood has begun to rebound from decades of decline. One of the most visible contemporary neighborhood leaders is Earnest Gates, whose Near West Side Community Development

Corporation (NWSCDC) has become a key player in reshaping the areas adjoining the United Center. By looking at Gates and the NWSCDC, we can explore the vexing community development puzzles that still confront the residents, both new and old, of the Near West Side.

Earnest Gates and the Near West Side Community Development Corporation

Earnest Gates is a lifelong Near West Side resident who as a young man watched his neighborhood convulse in the days following the shooting of Martin Luther King Jr.:

> After King was assassinated I was standing at the corner of Madison and Western, watching it go up in flames. Prior to King's assassination, Madison Avenue was thriving. The nightlife was jumping. The Near West Side was like a little village. You didn't have to leave the community to do anything. But after King's death our innocence was lost. I didn't feel like a happy-go-lucky teenager. I felt violated. I could see that the neighborhood was gone, and I didn't think it would ever be the same. (*Working Assets* 1998)

Unlike many other Near West Siders, Gates did not flee his neighborhood, and by the mid-1980s he had built a thriving trucking business a few blocks from his home. In the spring of 1987 he attended a hearing devoted to discussing the Bears stadium proposal and encountered Reverend Griffin for the first time; within weeks he had become one of the leading figures in IOP (McCullom 1992).

For most of the past decade, Gates served as president of the Near West Side Community Development Corporation, a group launched by IOP in 1988 with the mandate to implement community development projects within the neighborhood. During the 1990s, the NWSCDC emerged as a powerful neighborhood force: collaborating with the Wirtz/Reinsdorf joint venture in building sixteen new two-flats for families displaced by the United Center; working with the City of Chicago on a Strategic Neighborhood Action Plan in 1992, which yielded a variety of physical improvements in the neighborhood; receiving over $500,000 in Community Development Block Grant funds (again, by way of the city government) in the first half of the 1990s; collaborating with a private developer in building low-rise public housing in conjunction with the redevelopment of the Henry Horner Homes complex; and building three groups of properties for New Homes for Chicago (a City-sponsored program that recycles vacant lots for the construction of affordable owner-occupied housing) (Davis 1992; McRoberts 1996; Simpson 1996; *Working Assets* 2000). By the mid-1990s, the NWSCDC and IOP had parted ways, leaders of the latter group contending that Gates's organization had become insufficiently attentive to the needs of the neighborhood's poorest residents (Simpson 1996, 8). In reference to his perception of the NWSCDC's change of course, IOP president Reverend George W. Daniels told us:

> In 1996 a decision was made to put on the board members from the Chicago Bulls . . . team VPs and other officials. This was not the vision. IOP stood in opposition to the Bulls. How can we be part of this organization? Since then, the two organizations have gone in their own directions. (Interview, October 10, 2000)

In the wake of the 1991 agreement between the Wirtz/Reinsdorf joint venture and IOP, and even more so given the NWSCDC's ascendance to neighborhood prominence, Earnest Gates's reputation has experienced a notable resurrection, especially via coverage in the *Chicago Tribune*. In the *Tribune's* much-discussed "Chicago On Hold" series of 1988, Gates had won attention in two articles. In the first, appearing on August 28, he was described as someone whose organization "hopes to replace [Nancy] Jefferson's Midwest Council as the main force to be dealt with on the West Side" (McCarron 1988a). The following day, Gates was identified as an owner of a fancy car (the scandalous Mercedes), who "frequently rails against 'speculators'" but "has himself bought up five houses and/or lots near his home on the 300 block of South Leavitt Street" (McCarron 1988b). Yet within a few years the *Tribune* recast Gates as a principled community spokesperson and frequently approached him as an authoritative source on Near West Side events. Shortly before the Democratic National Convention brought worldwide coverage to his neighborhood in August 1996, a *Tribune* article profiled Gates in this manner:

> Gates speaks for the middle class, the homeowners, the elderly residents. He is the strategic community planner who can leave the 'hood, put on a blue suit and hobnob with Daley, Bulls and White Sox owner Jerry Reinsdorf and Blackhawks owner William Wirtz. He also can spend an afternoon shooting hoops with his employees. He usually wears T-shirts and jeans to work. (Poe 1996)

Thus, from this influential press perspective, within the span of a half-decade Gates was transformed from conniving troublemaker to invaluable neighborhood intermediary.

Nor has the transformation of Earnest Gates been just a matter of media coverage. As a link connecting the city's governmental and business leadership with a strategically located upgrading neighborhood, Gates has won access to powerful people in Chicago and, in turn, has been endowed with a considerable degree of decision-making clout. Jerry Reinsdorf has referred to Gates as a "very close advisor" (Poe 1996). In 1993, Mayor Daley appointed

Gates to the board of the Metropolitan Pier and Exposition Authority, the agency that oversees the huge McCormick Place exposition facility and the popular Navy Pier festival marketplace (Simpson 1996, 9). When the CHA's board was reorganized in the fall of 1999, Gates was one of Mayor Daley's new appointees (Garza 1999). One of the components of the Henry Horner Homes redevelopment process has been the formation of a six-member screening committee to vet Horner residents seeking to move into newly constructed low-rise buildings. Two seats on the screening committee (of three appointed by the CHA) were awarded to the NWSCDC (Simpson 1996). In effect, Earnest Gates and the NWSCDC have become the designated agents of neighborhood improvement in the Near West Side.

There is, however, an ambiguous side to this surprising turn of events. The upgrading of the United Center area, now frequently called West Haven, is very much a matter of governmental and corporate patronage. We have already noted the substantial governmental investment that has scrubbed and polished the Near West Side's public spaces. For their part, Jerry Reinsdorf and William Wirtz did not stop with the financing of replacement housing for United Center displacees. As part of its agreement with IOP, their joint venture bankrolled the NWSCDC with $600,000 for additional housing construction and, shortly thereafter, established a $1 million fund in support of local business ventures. The Bulls, through a charitable subsidiary, also financed the construction of the James Jordan Boys and Girls Club in the vicinity of the NWSCDC's first group of replacement dwellings. Just to the north of the Boys and Girls Club, the joint venture underwrote the purchase of computers in the newly built Mabel Manning branch library (Poe 1995; Joravsky 1996, 23). In December 1996, the Bulls transferred an NBA-exacted fine of $105,000, which had been deducted from the salary of the flamboyant Dennis Rodman, to the coffers of the NWSCDC (Simpson 1996, 9).

The details of the neighborhood vision that drives the joint venture are unclear, but Earnest Gates has offered this interpretation:

> I'd never say Jerry [Reinsdorf] and Howard [Pizer] got in this from the goodness of their hearts. We never talked about the morality of the matter with them. We never said, "It's sinful the way society let this community fall apart." These are businessmen, not social workers—and we appealed to them as businessmen. We told them it only makes sense to protect your investment by investing in the neighborhood and by working with the residents. They went along with us and then something happened. They saw how their money made a difference and they wanted to do more. (Joravsky 1996, 23)

Gates has described his own approach to the neighborhood in the following fashion: "I'm more sticks and bricks. I tend to try to connect things" (Poe 1996). Thus, what might be called Gates's pragmatic communalism converges quite comfortably with the pragmatic philanthropy that seems to have animated Jerry Reinsdorf, William Wirtz, and their associates, such as Howard Pizer.

Nevertheless, there is the unmistakable accent of conventional wisdom—a conventional wisdom emanating from outside the Near West Side—driving the approach of the Daley administration, the joint venture, and NWSCDC to neighborhood uplift. In order for the Near West Side to be turned around, decayed properties must be demolished even as the anticipated influx of affluent homeowners can be counted on to deliver business to local merchants, buttress community organizations, and bring a modicum of order to neighborhood street life. Poor residents, including displaced public housing tenants, ought not to be forgotten, but as a practical matter their numbers in the community should be reduced. As Earnest Gates said in reaction to a court ruling concerning replacement housing for Henry Horner residents: "Our whole objective has been to break it up and spread it out, rather than break it up and concentrate it in one place" (White 1996).

An inherent feature of the emerging consensus on Near West Side redevelopment is that the poorer residents of the neighborhood require the tutelage of community leaders, such as Gates, but also of the successful entrepreneurs who own and work for enterprises such as the Bulls and Blackhawks, and even of incoming middle-class homebuyers. There is, to say the least, a considerable degree of condescension at the root of this view; furthermore, its grounding in a realistic assessment of how the poor residents of the Near West Side live is dubious. The unexamined proposition that the Near West Side's new middle class and old working and lower classes will effortlessly meld on the streets of the new neighborhood and in the public meetings of its various organizations is also questionable. Finally, the presumption that the Near West Side's poor and public housing population requires uplift through the good offices of outsiders and a core of successful local leaders yields an unavoidable political corollary: that the bulk of the neighborhood's incumbent residents cannot exercise responsible judgment in shaping the Near West Side of tomorrow. Viewed in this light, the evidently well-intentioned efforts of city government officials, sports moguls Reinsdorf and Wirtz, and commanding local figures such as Earnest Gates appear to be built on a weak foundation that mixes preconceived social analysis with a narrowly construed model of neighborhood development. Only with time, possibly ten to fifteen years, will observers and residents of the Near West Side be able to determine whether a new, inclusive community can be forged from these raw materials.

8

Stadium Development, Three Neighborhoods, and Urban Revitalization

Near the beginning of his provocative study of post–World War II local economic development, *Remaking Chicago*, political scientist Joel Rast poses this question: "what if public policy, along with market forces, plays a significant role in determining which kinds of economic activities will survive in . . . the city?" (1999, 20). The core of Rast's subsequent investigation of the apparel and printing industries and of the emergence of a "local producer strategy" of economic development in the 1980s affirms this proposition. Over the course of the quarter-century following World War II, during which an array of macroeconomic forces tended to undermine various components of Chicago's manufacturing-based economy, municipally devised and implemented policies accelerated the decline, or at least the spatial relocation, of several otherwise productive industrial sectors. Rast's analysis thus challenges the often-articulated perspective, most closely identified with Paul Peterson, author of *City Limits* (1981), that the economic fates of cities are essentially in the hands of agents operating beyond the boundaries of particular municipalities. Looking outward from the local arena to the encompassing terrain of global capitalism, Rast argues that municipally directed economic development policy making can play a significant role in guiding local economic growth within the parameters defined by broader economic trends.

In our five preceding chapters we have examined the decision making patterns that yielded three major sports development projects in Chicago within just a few years in the late 1980s and early 1990s. At a more general level of analysis, we contend that the city's focus on such development initiatives is reflective both of broad social and economic trends and of new, public policy–anchored perspectives on economic development that have become widely accepted among municipal officials, planners, and business leaders. With Rast's argument in mind, we contend that there are also specifically local sources of Chicago's recent embrace of the city-of-leisure mode of economic development. After briefly outlining the local political and public policy factors that have given rise to Chicago's version of the city of leisure, we will return to the series of questions that initially animated our exploration of stadium development projects in this city: Why and how did municipal officials become agents of these private development initiatives? Who wins and who loses at the neighborhood level? Can professional sports franchises serve as reliable municipal icons?

The Local Sources of Chicago's City of Leisure

To understand the specifically local ingredients of Chicago's current ascendance as a place in which "business travellers patronize . . . hotels, restaurants, high end shops and museums" and where "suburbanites once again visit, and . . . perhaps even acquire a pied-à-terre" (Lorinc 2000, 75), we must return to the dark old days of the mid-1970s. At that time, Chicago was suffering from a pair of intertwining political economic breakdowns. On the one hand, signs of Chicago's declining industrial might were everywhere apparent (Longworth 1981; Squires, Bennett, McCourt, and Nyden 1987, 25–31). After years of diminishing activity, the Union Stockyards at last closed its gates in 1971. Within a few years a far greater economic fatality struck the local economy as the huge complex of steel mills in South Chicago was shut down. Chicago, whose industrial economy had from the start been anchored by "large firms and long production lines" (Warner 1972, 92), was especially prey to the decentralizing tendencies of the emerging national and international economies. On the other hand, the city's municipal leadership was exhausted. Mayor Richard J. Daley, then in his seventies, remained the city's undisputed boss, but the elderly mayor was no longer capable of envisioning, much less shepherding the execution of, creative policy initiatives. Furthermore, Mayor Daley's long-standing monopolization of political power meant that following his death in late 1976 there were few capable leaders-in-waiting among the city's political, corporate, and civic elites. In the aftermath of Daley's demise, a handful of political subchieftains busied themselves with wrestling for control of the Democratic Party apparatus (Ungar 1977). On the civic and corporate sides, imaginative thinking, at that point approximately a quarter-century behind the times, supposed that the city might jump-start its economy by hosting a World's Fair in 1992 (Shlay and Giloth 1987).

Richard J. Daley's immediate successors were Michael Bilandic and Jane Byrne, the former a caretaker mayor who was defeated by the upstart Byrne in the Democratic mayoral primary of 1979. Most accounts of Jane Byrne's single four-year term as mayor emphasize her "revolving door" shuffling of top advisors and municipal bureaucrats, or, more consequentially, her maladroit efforts to manipulate Chicago's deep racial divisions for personal political advantage (Grimshaw 1992, 143–66; Kleppner 1985, 118–50; Rivlin 1993, 62–79). However, Mayor Byrne was also prepared, in the words of one commentator, to "think the unthinkable" (Holli 1995, 177), which included some of the earliest local articulations of the city-of-leisure model of economic development. Not only did Byrne throw her support behind the group of corporate executives seeking to bring a World's Fair to Chicago, her administration also sponsored a series of downtown-sited "bread and circus" events, including ChicagoFest, a week of musical performances on Navy Pier to the northeast of the Loop, and Taste of Chicago, an outdoor showcase for local restaurateurs. The latter has been retained by subsequent mayoral administrations. Though Jane Byrne's advocacy of such events was evidently animated by a desperate political hucksterism, there was a kernel of the future inhabiting these schemes: the notion that the central city could serve as a compelling backdrop for orchestrated entertainments and that the crowds drawn by these entertainments could serve as the fulcrum for substantial new private investment.

In 1983, Harold Washington, Chicago's first African American mayor, whose candidacy was backed by an assertive coalition of grassroots organizations, replaced Jane Byrne on the fifth floor of Chicago's City Hall. In the wake of the inert Bilandic administration and the operatic four years of Jane Byrne, Washington took office committed to a populist vision of participatory municipal decision making and "balanced growth" across the city's neighborhoods and economic sectors (City of Chicago 1984). In the words of Washington's Commissioner of Economic Development and chief stadium-project advisor, Robert Mier, the approach of the new administration:

> directly confronts the mainstream capital formation strategy by emphasizing job creation. A job focus strategy which targets the special needs of minorities and women must assess a method of capital formation by its ability not only to generate jobs, but to generate jobs that provide a significant improvement in the quality of life of the people most in need. While this certainly involves job training, it also requires balancing manufacturing and service sector growth. This principle has been central to Chicago's efforts to revitalize the steel industry and other basic manufacturing industries. (Stanback and Mier 1986–1987, 13–14)

Most of the negotiations between the City and sports franchises that we have discussed took place during the Washington years. In part, this was a matter of circumstances. Not only did the City of Chicago possess an unusually aged inventory of major sports facilities—the old Comiskey Park, Wrigley Field, Soldier Field, and the Chicago Stadium—but within the span of a few years new and more aggressive owners took over the Chicago White Sox, Cubs, and Bulls. These circumstances forced Washington administration officials to look at sports, as a component of the local service economy, in a new light. The Washington aide who likened the loss of a sports franchise to the closing of a steel mill was not simply spinning out an exaggerated comparison. The Washington administration pursued state fiscal support, agreements between franchises and neighborhoods, and private investment for the purpose of franchise retention ultimately because it sensed that the maintenance of civic pride dictated this course of action. As Robert Mier later intimated, Harold Washington was convinced that his own political future would be jeopardized by the emigration of the White Sox or Bears. But beyond the mayor's concern about his political fortunes, for an administration striving to recharge the public's sense of civic allegiance in the face of a decade-long period of political and economic turmoil, holding on to professional sports franchises and shoring up the city's sporting infrastructure became a central policy objective.

Since 1989 Chicago's mayoralty has been held by Richard M. Daley, the late boss's son and by the early 1990s a commanding figure in his own right. It is during the last decade that Chicago's whole-hearted embrace of the city-of-leisure model has been consummated. On the one hand, Mayor Daley and his wife, Maggie, are seasoned world travelers, and press accounts of their returns from Europe routinely note which cities and what varieties of municipal beautification along the way have drawn the attention of the City's first couple. On the other hand, a generally healthy economic environment has blessed the mayor with a deep pool of fiscal resources, and the early returns from initiatives mounted in the 1980s—such as the ongoing success of Taste of Chicago and the neighborhood boom pursuant to the modernization of Wrigley Field—seem to have made a deep impression on the second Daley's administration. Against this backdrop, Richard M. Daley's city government has pursued its macrogentrification strategy of massive downtown-focused public works improvements; streetscape and parks beautification; support for arts, entertainment, and university development; targeted neighborhood investment, frequently underwritten by tax increment financing; and streamlining of regulatory processes bearing on private residential development.

In political terms, Mayor Daley has used his macrogentrification program to forge what analysts such as Alan DiGaetano and John Klemanski (1999) characterize as a progrowth regime. Daley and his inner core of advisors exercise mastery over the municipality's bureaucratic apparatus and have won a high degree of cooperation and admiration from the broader field of local real estate and development interests, as well as the city's civic leadership and media. Within the electoral realm, the mayor and his program are unchallenged. Since his initial mayoral victory in 1989,

Richard M. Daley has won reelection three times with increasingly lopsided margins and on the shoulders of an increasingly encompassing voting coalition. Within City Council, Mayor Daley faces no cohesive oppositional faction. In short, political skill, a plausible vision for the city's economic future, and favorable national circumstances have, for the time being at least, centralized political power in Chicago in a fashion last observed during the heyday of Richard J. Daley in the early 1960s.

The Political Economy of Municipal Support for Professional Sports Franchises: Some Additional Chicago Themes

In broad outline, our accounts of sports facilities development in Bridgeport and South Armour Square, Lake View, and the Near West Side conform to the principal themes that have emerged from the flurry of research on sports and urban revitalization that has appeared during the last fifteen years. Most evidently, four of the five principal professional franchises in Chicago—the White Sox, Cubs, Blackhawks, and Bulls—have, respectively, been able to reach advantageous agreements with local officials to finance a new sporting facility, restructure municipal and state regulatory controls that had inhibited the modernization of an older baseball park, and provide public infrastructure improvements in the vicinity of a new, privately financed indoor arena. This bargaining power, grounded in the major professional sports leagues' ability to limit the supply of franchises, probably has been most succinctly stated by political scientist Charles Euchner: "The teams hold all of the advantages in negotiations with cities, chief among them being a highly desirable product in artificially short supply" (1993, 50). And lest the failure of the Chicago Bears to win a new stadium seem to point to at least one exception to this rule, since the late 1980s several rounds of stadium negotiations between the Bears and the City of Chicago have ensued (Baade and Sanderson 1997). As this book goes to press, a $600 million renovation of Soldier Field, largely funded by public sources, appears to represent the final chapter in this saga (Long and Holt 2000).

From the standpoint of cities, the willingness of municipal officials to meet the demands of professional sports franchise owners is well documented and is reflected in these Chicago case studies. Michael Danielson, in *Home Team* (1997), has catalogued the local political forces pushing mayors into the arms of grasping franchise executives:

> Politicians . . . are drawn to sports endeavors by a desire to enhance their jurisdiction's prestige, boost the local economy, reap the political benefits of large-scale public works, advance development goals, and appeal to voters who want big league sports. Concern about the possible consequences of losing a team

> reinforces the predisposition of elected officials, particularly highly visible
> mayors and governors, to support professional sports. (263–64)

Each of these forces promoting alliances between cities and sports franchises has been at work in Chicago, though our narratives also highlight
two significant local elements in the Chicago's rush to upgrade its professional sports stadiums in the 1980s and 1990s.

The first of these local circumstances is the perilous political situation
encountered by Harold Washington during the mid-1980s. Having won the
mayoralty by virtue of African American voter dissatisfaction with the incumbent, Jane Byrne, and espousing a populist program of neighborhood-
oriented economic development, Washington presided over a city whose
established power centers viewed his leadership with trepidation. Corporate and civic leaders, long accustomed to City Hall access and priority in
defining Chicago's public agenda, were forced to share the mayor's attention with a new class of civil rights and grassroots activists (Ferman 1996,
95–97). A City Council majority made up of Democratic Party loyalists
sought to wreck the mayor's program through a strategy of obstruction—
for example, holding up mayoral appointments and provoking municipal
budget crises—ultimately aimed at defining Washington's administration
as inept (Grimshaw 1992, 184–86; Rivlin 1993, 207–344).

Amidst this vexing political atmosphere, the Washington administration committed itself to a public funding scheme for the new Comiskey
Park, sought to mediate negotiations between the Cubs and Lake View
over Wrigley Field, and tried to advance the Bears' Near West Side stadium
plan (McCarron 1987a). A crucial political motivation for these endeavors
was Harold Washington's determination not to be held captive by his Democratic Party opponents or by the perception that he was a mayor unable to deliver major policy initiatives. As mayoral aide Robert Mier recalled, in reference to the new Comiskey Park deal making:

> He did not want to be the mayor that lost a major sports team for the city. He
> knew the public would perceive it not as a team relocating—a metropolitan
> area team relocating within a metropolitan area. It would be viewed as
> Chicago losing a team and he the mayor of Chicago being the one that was
> unable to prevent that from happening. (*Laramore v. ISFA*, 1989b)

Such thinking undoubtedly has driven the action of municipal leaders in
other cities. Nevertheless, the degree of City Hall attention devoted to
meeting the demands of franchise owners—especially given the Washington administration's otherwise divergent policy priorities—cannot be understood without emphasizing the local political environment within
which Harold Washington maneuvered.

We can illustrate the peculiar pressures on Harold Washington by recounting some pertinent details of a major economic loss for Chicago that occurred just a few years after the end of the Washington administration and that did not become a local cause célèbre. Over the late summer and early autumn of 1992, Spiegel, Inc., which operated a large mail-order warehouse in Bridgeport, decided to close this facility and shift its operations to a suburban complex outside of Columbus, Ohio. Given that Spiegel's Bridgeport warehouse employed 2,200 persons at an average wage of $12 an hour (Rylaw 1992), the direct loss to the Chicago economy was nearly $53 million per year, a figure that does not include nonsalary income or multipliers. Though Joel Rast (1999, 145) has characterized the relocation of Spiegel's warehouse as a "major embarrassment" for the administration of Mayor Richard M. Daley, press coverage of the affair was not extensive. From the time the possibility of the Spiegel relocation was reported in the *Chicago Tribune* (August 17) to the time the corporation's decision to move was confirmed (September 24), the *Tribune* carried six articles on Spiegel's plans and the City's efforts to retain the warehousing operation somewhere in Chicago. Conversely, in the first two weeks of June 1988, as the state legislature put together its stadium development package for the new Comiskey Park, the *Tribune* printed 16 articles discussing the proceedings. From a strictly economic standpoint, many other businesses and policy areas may exceed the importance of professional sports, but as a news item, the attraction and retention of professional sports franchises represents a central consideration for any big city mayor.

Of course, the exaggerated visibility of professional sports as a symbol of local economic vitality is, to a very large degree, a function of press coverage. While we have not attempted to gauge the volume and orientation of the Chicago press's coverage of sports-related economic development in comparison to press activity in other cities, our cases do suggest that the framing of sports-related economic development in local reporting does follow a characteristic path. This is not to say that the coverage of such decision making is uniformly one-sided. Local media in Chicago have not hesitated to document the decision-making foibles of certain sports moguls, notably White Sox owner Jerry Reinsdorf and former Bears president Michael McCaskey, and quite a bit of newspaper space has been devoted to reporting White Sox–fan dissatisfaction since the early 1990s. Nevertheless, the city's dominant press voice, the *Chicago Tribune*, has tended to script its overall coverage in the following manner: although the city's professional sports franchises may use the threat of relocation to hold out for sizable public subsidies (and, as in the case of the White Sox, may even renege on the terms of a new stadium package after it has been fixed), the villains in the city's efforts to maintain a high professional sports profile have been politicians, who are typically too weak and vacillating to offer sufficient incentives to the team owners, and neighborhood activists, whose particularistic agendas prevent them from understanding the greater good advanced by professional sports-franchise subsidies. Clearly the most remarkable news scripting of this sort that we have documented is the *Tribune's* sanctimonious and self-interested interpretation of the Wrigley Field lights conflict. Whether press coverage of sports-related economic development decision making is more biased or simplistic in Chicago than in other major cities is beyond the scope of this analysis. Unquestionably, however, in this city, public officials who do not cater to the expressed needs of professional sports franchises will be skewered by the local media.

The View from the Neighborhood: Who Wins, Who Loses

Since the outbreak in the 1950s of the interpretive war between "elitist" and "pluralist" analysts of urban power structures (Dahl 1961; Hunter 1953; Polsby 1980), social scientists have devoted considerable attention to examining how and when neighborhood, grassroots, or other "outsider" groups can exercise substantial influence over public policies affecting their constituencies. In reaction to some crucial blind spots in the pluralist model of decision making via intergroup competition and compromise, notably the problem of "nondecisionmaking" first articulated by political scientists Peter Bachrach and Morton Baratz (1962), a distinguished group of observers (Crenson 1971; Fainstein and Fainstein 1974; Lipsky 1970; Stone 1982) has wrestled with the paradox posed by Frances Fox Piven and Richard Cloward: "People cannot defy institutions to which they have no access, and to which they make no contribution" (1979, 23).

Piven and Cloward, focusing on efforts of "poor people's movements" to win concessions from government and large-scale economic powers, surely were correct in this generalization. However, as our case studies demonstrate, neighborhood-based organizations vary dramatically in their ability to mobilize local resources, and moreover, they possess widely varying capacities to define and pursue agendas that can be accommodated by powerful outside-the-neighborhood institutions. More specifically, both the social and economic status of particular neighborhoods and the availability and effective deployment of community resources represent critical ingredients influencing how stadium development initiatives will affect adjoining areas.

Of our case-study neighborhoods, Lake View possessed and was able to mobilize the greatest human and material capital in its effort to resist the installation of lights at Wrigley Field. Indeed, more than a decade after the installation of lights, neighborhood activists in this North Side community continue to participate in a dialogue with the sports franchise and the City about local-area protection. At the other end of the neighborhood resource continuum, South Armour Square organizations were unable to sustain a neighborhood-centered opposition movement, forge coalitional action capable of resisting the south-of-35th-Street siting of the new Comiskey Park, or negotiate a comprehensive compensation package for local residents. The Near West Side falls somewhere between the extremes represented by Lake View and South Armour Square. As a direct outgrowth of determined negotiation with the developers of the United Center, Near West Side community leaders were able to wrest from them replacement housing for local homeowners and a variety of other neighborhood investments; however, given the subsequent gentrification of their neighborhood and adjoining areas, their victory has been, at best, ambiguous.

The starting point of community mobilization in Lake View was a commitment to blocking the installation of lights at Wrigley Field. Due to the persistence of the local antilights forces, the Chicago Cubs settled for a compromise arrangement permitting the modernization of the ballpark but limiting the annual number of night games and mandating a followup neighborhood improvement plan involving the franchise, the City of Chicago, and local residents. In large measure, the Cubs' willingness to deal with their Lake View opponents was a function of the latter's resource base and tactical skills. As the forces that were lined up for and against lights sought to reach a Wrigley Field settlement, local activists conducted well-attended meetings featuring printed agendas and press releases. Regularly attending and often addressing these events were government representatives, including local aldermen, state representatives and senators, and City Hall officials. As they sought to preserve their treasured, antique neighborhood facility, the Lake View antilights activists could also count on the rapt attention of local Chicago media.

In the face of the Chicago White Sox franchise's push to win public funding for a new ballpark adjoining the original Comiskey Park, the character and outcomes of neighborhood mobilization in South Armour Square could not be more strikingly different. Local activists fighting the new Comiskey Park proposal lacked the sort of political contacts, financial resources, and legal expertise that fueled the antilights organizing in Lake View, a point given concreteness by the following account:

> We went over to meet with Bobby Rush [alderman in an adjoining ward]. . . .
> He said there's not much he can do because it's not his ward. . . . Our own alderman, Patrick Huels, came to a meeting, but he didn't know nothing about the deal either. . . . It was all done in Springfield. . . . John Daley, our state representative, came out. He promised to get back to us. But one man can only do so much. (Joravsky 1987, 17)

In spite of the indifference expressed by various political representatives, the South Armour Square residents did put up a fight to protect their neighborhood, but in marked contrast to that of their North Side counterparts in Lake View, their mobilization drew on a very narrow local resource base.

The South Armour Square residents, divided by race and social class from crucial prospective allies, were unable to make common cause with residents in adjoining Bridgeport or with the membership of the Save Our Sox organization. In particular, the advancement of Armour Square Park as a preferable stadium location was unworkable because many Bridgeporters and residents of the area north of the small city park believed that a baseball stadium on that site would destabilize their own areas. Negotiators representing the White Sox and the Illinois Sports Facilities Authority (ISFA) were able to divide the South Armour Square Neighborhood Coalition (SASNC) by offering a settlement favoring the more prosperous leadership of the SASNC, but leaving behind an angry and uncompensated majority of renters and public housing residents.

On the Near West Side, community organizers helped block the Bears stadium proposal, then a few years later, when confronted with the politically and fiscally more viable United Center proposal, shifted tactics in order to capture a portion of the redevelopment benefit generated by the latter project. Although the Near West Side, like South Armour Square, was an impoverished community, the presence of long-standing community organizations, including the Midwest Community Council, combined with extremely effective oppositional organizing conducted by the Interfaith Organizing Project (IOP), gave the Near West Side considerable negotiating leverage. Ultimately, representatives of the Bulls and Blackhawks were forced to ask themselves: "Even if we're going to get ripped off, do you want to go ahead with the deal?" Answering this question in the affirmative, Bulls executive Howard Pizer recalled, meant that the United Center's backers had to come to terms with IOP (Joravsky 1996, 23).

In one sense, nothing startling is revealed by this assessment of our case studies: neighborhoods of higher status and possessing more internal resources deal with outside interests—corporate or municipal—more effectively. In the words of planning scholars Susan Fainstein and Clifford Hirst, "Some neighborhoods simply lack the leadership cadre and institutions necessary to articulate the interests of residents" (1996, 110). These case studies also point to a lesson that is often neglected in analyses of confrontation and negotiation between communities and external agents: while local organizing strength is a necessary, though not sufficient, factor in achieving desirable community outcomes, local activists themselves possess only an imperfect sense of how alternative development scenarios will play out over the long run.

This latter point is most directly illustrated by the disparate fortunes of IOP and the Near West Side Community Development Corporation (NWSCDC) in the mid- to late 1990s. While the former group has attempted to maintain a critical posture in reference to the activities of the United Center's owners, as well as to the broader trend in neighborhood residential upgrading—and concurrently has witnessed the erosion of its local prominence—the latter has emerged as the leading community organization on the Near West Side. In large part, the NWSCDC's ascendancy can be attributed to the convergence between its agenda and the interests of the United Center's owners and of Chicago's municipal leadership. What this alliance does not seem to cement is a continued neighborhood equilibrium through which incumbent, low-income Near West Siders will be assured a share of the economic boom brought to the their community by the last decade's municipal and private investment surges. Our point is not to condemn the NWSCDC for selling out what ought to be its primary constituency. Rather, it appears to be the case that the pragmatic community development strategy adopted by the NWSCDC is likely, contrary to the expressed wishes of its leadership, to speed a one-sided gentrification of the Near West Side.

The proposition that community activists may not always have a firm hold on just what their proposals will yield is even more provocatively illustrated by that curious subplot to the new Comiskey Park negotiations, architect Philip Bess's Armour Field proposal. To this day, advocates for the South Armour Square residents, such as their attorney, James Chapman, view the South Armour Square siting of the new ballpark as a "gentrification strategy" aimed at driving out a poor, racial minority population from a desirable inner-city location. However, virtually every aspect of the new stadium's design and operation has worked at cross purposes to any such spillover gentrification. The sea of surface parking that surrounds the new baseball stadium is not conducive to upscale development—residential or otherwise—on adjoining properties; by demolishing McCuddy's and every other nearby commercial establishment, the developers of the new stadium destroyed what little local character might have been retained in the immediate vicinity of the new facility.

In contrast, architect Bess's proposal to build a small-scale, traditional ballpark set within an urbanistically attractive district featuring new commercial and residential structures amid off-street parking might have turned the 35th Street area into a South Side version of Wrigleyville. This scenario, indeed, could have seeded subsequent rounds of residential investment in South Armour Square and Bridgeport—and, one can imagine, upward pressure on local real estate values. Bess's plan to build a facility more suited to fan-friendly baseball and incorporating "neighborhood sensitive" urban design principles could have produced a version of the local economic boom that the White Sox/ISFA project has so clearly failed to engender. There is no evidence that Philip Bess sought to sneak a gentrification strategy past White Sox and municipal officials or, for that matter, the residents of South Armour Square. Rather, just as in the case of the Near West Side, the ultimate consequences of alternative development schemes may elude local activists and their allies even as real, on-the-ground consequences typically defy the prognostications of conventional development advocates.

The Mixed Blessing of Corporate/Community Partnerships

While the advocates of sports development projects invariably sell their schemes by pointing to the potential for community benefit to be derived from new and upgraded stadiums, our three cases demonstrate that corporate/community partnerships are typically one-sided affairs. The objectives that drive these projects are defined in corporate office suites, not in local taverns, meeting rooms, or church basements. On the occasions when substantial values must be compromised in the quest to find solutions to physical development, transportation access, or fan behavior problems, the values that will be recalculated inevitably center on the neighborhood partner: housing clearance is necessitated by parking needs, interruption of conventional traffic patterns is required to permit sports fans' prompt entrance to and exit from the neighborhood, or a higher threshold of tolerance is required before signaling that street behavior is unacceptable. It is true that some corporate/community partnerships appear to mesh smoothly, but this is attributable to either a more formidable local negotiating stance (thus forcing franchise concessions) or the sports franchise's success in winning over local leaders to its view of the neighborhood interest.

At first glance, the Chicago Cubs' relationship with their Lake View neighbors appears to represent an ideal corporate/community partnership. The baseball franchise and its corporate owner, the Tribune Company, devoted years to developing the modernization scheme for Wrigley Field, and in the end, the franchise accepted a compromise arrangement that retained Wrigley Field as primarily a daytime ballpark. Moreover, since the achievement of the Wrigley Field compromise, negotiations between the franchise, the City of Chicago, and the neighborhood have continued. From the standpoint of the local activist who has been most involved in the ongoing Cubs/Lake View dialogue, Charlotte Newfeld, the neverending challenge for Lake View residents has been to ensure that the Cubs continue to uphold their end of the bargain (interview, October 13 and December 9, 1998). Apart from the details of the 1988 Wrigley Field agreement, the arrival of nighttime baseball in Lake View has induced a variety of changes in the ballpark's immediate vicinity, as well as the larger neighborhood, many of which were unanticipated either by Cubs officials or local activists. The most profound of these changes, the pumping up of Wrigley Field's environs as an entertainment haven, was recently addressed by no less than Mayor Daley: "It's a great party atmosphere. Go out there, relax, get the sun, have a few cool ones, you know, a few beers, and enjoy yourself. It's become more of a happening. It's a different setting" (Patterson 2000). Although we cannot predict how smoothly or roughly the Cubs/Lake View partnership will work in ten years, we are quite confident in anticipating that the neighborhood adjustments most likely to occur in the coming decade will mainly work in the interest of the Chicago Cubs as a for-profit, professional sports franchise.

Aside from the new Comiskey Park's indifferent economic performance and the lack of ancillary economic development in South Armour Square and Bridgeport, the White Sox franchise's dealings with its neighbors defies any conventional understanding of the term *partnership*. Running back to the planning of the new facility, the White Sox owners were unwilling to even acknowledge alternative proposals such as the Philip Bess's urban ballpark scheme or the Save Our Sox–advanced renovation plan for the original Comiskey Park. Likewise, the Senese family's efforts to relocate McCuddy's, a proposal that could have yielded dividends both for the White Sox and the neighborhood, from the outset faced a coldly unequivocal rejection from Jerry Reinsdorf and Eddie Einhorn, which, over the subsequent decade, has not been reconsidered. Much to the evident dismay of the White Sox franchise, its indifference to its neighbors in South Armour Square and Bridgeport has been returned in kind. Not only is there little love lost between local merchants and the White Sox, on several occasions in recent years visiting sports fans have been physically assaulted by neighborhood youths, certainly not a testament to franchise/community harmony (Washburn and McRoberts 2000). At its core, the unhappy tenure of the White Sox in the unfriendly confines of the new Comiskey Park demonstrates that corporate/community partnership has no meaning whatsoever in the absence of sustained dialogue and concrete cooperative ventures linking the sports franchise and neighborhood residents.

The trend of recent events on the Near West Side reveals a particularly telling complication to the concept of corporate/community partnership. Earnest Gates and the NWSCDC's philosophy of homeownership-centered community development fits perfectly with the United Center owners' neighborhood interest. Therefore, the NWSCDC's businesslike approach to local development has won both the endorsement and the financial backing of Jerry Reinsdorf and William Wirtz. However, the transformation of the Near West Side, which has been driven by upscale residential development, has already begun to reveal the local specter of intense real estate speculation accompanied by the pricing out of low-income renters and property owners. At some point in the coming years one can expect the emergence of neighborhood voices contending that a stronger grassroots tilt and less corporate oversight ought to define the program of the NWSCDC, or perhaps that a new organizational vehicle for neighborhood improvement should emerge on the Near West Side. At such a time, the terms of the Near West Side's corporate/community partnership will be sorely tested. For example, will the United Center's owners be willing to work with neighborhood organizations whose agendas do not conform to the NWSCDC's? Or alternatively, is the NWSCDC capable of embarking on an intra-organizational transformation in response to new movements in its own backyard? Either scenario points to the same conclusion regarding the present terms of corporate/community partnership on the Near West Side: a corporate-endorsed deal with a single local organization that is presumed to speak for an entire neighborhood bears a greater resemblance to a marriage of convenience than to an abiding commitment linking equal partners.

Given the stadium construction boom of the last decade, professional sports franchises across America increasingly find themselves dealing with the non-sports-related concerns of their neighboring communities. This trend is the result of more than just physical proximity. Municipal leaders' advocacy of sports development projects routinely rationalizes public subsidy for stadiums as an indirect source of neighborhood investment, as well as, more speculatively, the grounding for future franchise/neighborhood cooperation. In this rendition of corporate/community partnership, the inherent divide between corporate and neighborhood history, concerns, and objectives is downplayed. Moreover, the fundamental reality that typically stamps this relationship, the asymmetrical distribution of economic and political resources between corporation and community, vastly complicates efforts to hitch neighborhood improvement to the cart of professional sports. As a rule, the corporate partner's interest in profit enhancement defines the outer parameters of acceptable local action. Correspondingly, the commitment to building responsible and effective neighborhood-based organizations, which is at the heart of community building, is not central to the aims of the corporate partner. Indeed, at that point when local mobilization begins to challenge past accords reached by the prevailing corporate/community partnership, indigenous grassroots action is very likely to be defined, possibly by both the corporation and the established neighborhood organization, as illegitimate.

Reasonably successful corporate/community partnerships can emerge, as demonstrated by the Chicago Cubs/Lake View relationship, but the critical factor in cementing this kind of durable, mutually acceptable partnership is the stock of political capital that the neighborhood brings to the table before the terms of partnership are settled. Fundamentally, professional sports franchises are not neighborhood institutions, and the degree to which their actions can be shaped to provide community benefit depends, ultimately, on the independent political leverage marshaled by their neighborhood partners.

Sports Franchises as Municipal Icons

Historically, any number of professional sports franchises have developed powerful symbolic connections with their home cities. In such instances—when a sizable share of the local population closely follows the home team's triumphs and tragedies—the sporting franchise truly has become a municipal icon. The team's performance and identity can be expected to play a role in defining its fans' sense of civic loyalty and participation in a community transcending the confines of family, ethnicity, or neighborhood. Public officials often point to this desired, perceived, or attained status as the justification for pouring hundreds of millions of dollars into franchise-directed stadium development projects. Our case studies speak volumes on the slipperiness of the perceptual slope that must be negotiated by the aspiring or reigning municipal sports icon, but first we discuss in more general terms how sports clubs and their facilities seem to achieve and sustain this status.

The most durable municipal sporting icons are franchises that have stayed put, such as baseball's New York Yankees (since 1903), or the Boston Celtics (since 1946), of the comparatively youthful National Basketball Association (NBA). The local standing of such franchises is further strengthened if their longevity has brought on-the-field acclaim. Both the Yankees, major league baseball's most titled team with twenty-six "world championships," and the Celtics, with sixteen NBA championships, have come to be viewed as key emblems of their home cities' national and even international prominence. But a beloved home team's on-the-field success need not rise to the level of the Yankees or Celtics. A franchise that manages to remain a steady contender and experiences occasional on-the-field supremacy can also become a focus of local pride. The Denver Broncos and the Miami Dolphins of the National Football League (NFL), the Utah Jazz and the Indiana Pacers of the NBA, the Baltimore Orioles of Major League Baseball—each of these franchises plays a significant role in defining its home city's civic identity.

Sometimes longevity and a variety of failure can win a sports franchise a special form of local loyalty. Baseball's Boston Red Sox are another longstanding franchise (since 1901), but they have not won a World Series since 1918. Nevertheless, the last eight decades have not been an unmitigated disaster for the Red Sox; they have played in four World Series

(1946, 1967, 1975, and 1986), losing each by the narrowest of margins, four games to three. Given this record, the Red Sox ball club's appeal to Bostonians is, in part, defined by its star-crossed quality—which, incidentally, is akin to the warm feelings the Chicago Cubs evoke in their long-suffering fans.

Though the instances of a second form of civic identification, affection for the beloved playing field, may be on the decline in an era of widespread modernization of sports facilities, some franchises continue to exercise a hold on the local public imagination because of the grandeur, the legacy, or simply the peculiarities of their home facilities. The Cubs' role in Chicago's history and in the formation of the city's broader identify has, quite obviously, derived from the storied record of Wrigley Field. And the potency of fan loyalty to the Boston Red Sox is, in part, attributable to the eccentric layout of their home field, Fenway Park—including the thirty-seven-foot tall "Green Monster" left-field wall, a permanent temptation for right-handed sluggers—and the myriad famous events that have transpired there. Likewise, no testimonial to Brooklyn's lost baseball franchise, the Dodgers, fails to recall the intimacy of Ebbets Field. In journalist Roger Kahn's recollection, this physical intimacy had a profound psychological effect on many of the Dodgers' fans:

> Ebbets Field was always in reach. There were obstacles—money, the policeman's shoe, a leap, the greasy garageman—but a boy could contend with them and triumph, if he had wit and persistence and a touch of courage. It was easy and absolutely irrational to relate getting to *see* a Dodger game with getting to *be* a Dodger. Which, in the fine irrationality of boyhood, is what generations of Brooklyn children did. (1971, 22, italics in original)

On rare occasions, the good works of a sports franchise owner can win a public approval that transcends on-the-field performance. The flamboyant, populist former owner of the Chicago White Sox, Bill Veeck, is still affectionately recalled by Bridgeport merchants and residents. Veeck was a regular patron of local restaurants and taverns, and during his two stints as White Sox owner, the ball club frequently sponsored eccentric, crowd-pleasing special promotions (Hayner 1990, 4–5; Joravsky 1987, 16; Lou Knox, interview, August 11, 1999).

More characteristically, and often aided by the imaginative power of sports journalism, successful professional teams become identified with character traits presumed to define a city and its residents. During their renaissance of the 1980s, the Chicago Bears, led by straight-talking coach Mike Ditka and featuring a stout defensive unit, were widely viewed as embodying the city's no-nonsense working-class identity. At about the same time, the glamorous, fast-paced *Angeleno* lifestyle, by many accounts, was mirrored in the up-tempo basketball played by the Los Angeles Lakers. During the 1999–2000 NFL season, the Super Bowl champion St. Louis Rams, a recently arrived football franchise in a city that has suffered decades of economic decline and population loss, were led by a previously unknown quarterback, Kurt Warner. Warner's rise from obscurity and the Rams' sudden achievement of NFL dominance were often linked metaphorically to a presumed turnaround in St. Louis's fortunes (Fleming 2000; Levins 2000; Pierson 1999).

As numerous as the foregoing examples seem to be, the presumption that sporting-derived loyalties can be turned to civic purposes, or even that fan loyalties ensure that sports development projects will generate substantial economic payoffs, often fails to pass the muster of hard reality. The increasingly corporatized shape of professional sports has not been lost on either sports fans or the public at large. More directly, as franchises seek to win municipal or state government support for projects by manipulating revenue figures or engineering reports, or most typically, by threatening to relocate to more welcoming communities, the good will of the local public and the loyalty of fans may fall away.

An inventory of professional franchises in contemporary Chicago, with the question of their civic pull in mind, reveals an extremely mixed picture. Throughout the 1990s, the Chicago Bulls were easily the city's most prominent professional sports franchise, six-time champions of the NBA and led by the sport's leading performer, Michael Jordan. The Bulls' collective success and the marvelous individual exploits of Michael Jordan, without question, represented the most effective accidental public relations campaign ever mounted on behalf of the city of Chicago. During the same period, the city's other bellwether franchise was the Cubs, usually mediocre on the field but still occupying one of the last old-time ballparks. Neither the addition of lights in 1988 nor the controversy that preceded the ballpark's makeover undermined the lure of the Cubs. Indeed, the prospect that Wrigley Field might one day be abandoned in favor of a more modern facility, a scenario voiced many times during the debate over the Cubs' plan to upgrade their stadium, may have given greater resonance to Wrigley Field's status as a baseball fan's pilgrimage destination.

In contrast, the public's regard for Chicago's other two leading professional franchises, the White Sox and the Bears, waned during the 1990s, and to a considerable degree these clubs' loss of public favor can be attributed to their managements' grasping efforts to win governmental aid for new stadiums. Although Chicago's local press characteristically indicted city and state officials for holding up the approval of the new Comiskey Park, the self-serving actions of the White Sox ownership were unmistakable. And once the second new Comiskey Park deal was done, from the public's vantage point the White Sox owners' malefactions only multiplied: a new but unlovable physical facility took shape south of 35th Street; all vestiges of the old ballpark's environs, such as McCuddy's, were excised; and high-handed customer relations emerged as the hallmark of the franchise's public face. The predictable consequences, declining attendance and revenues, have followed, and more saliently, by building a new stadium for the White Sox, the City of Chicago and the State of Illinois have not managed to preserve a municipal emblem of any great luster. The White Sox ball club's on-the-field revival in 2000 brought an upturn in attendance at Comiskey Park, but it will be many years before the White Sox franchise reemerges as a much-admired local institution.

A similar fate struck the Chicago Bears during the 1990s, though in this case team president Michael McCaskey seems to have served as principal lightning rod for the public's disapproval. Constantly on the stump to advocate public subsidization of a new Bears stadium, McCaskey never managed to establish a congenial bargaining relationship with local government officials even as he unsuccessfully cast about for out-of-town suitors. Coincidentally, the dominant Bears football team of the 1980s returned to the NFL's middling ranks in the next decade. Like the White Sox, the Bears retain a base of loyal fans—undoubtedly numbering in the hundreds of thousands—but the Bears franchise, revealed through its actions as a corporate entity first and foremost, has lost its hold for some years to come on the imaginations of most Chicagoans.

Contrary to widely expressed and seldom examined conventional wisdom, sports franchises are not automatic municipal icons. Their role in the lives of a city and its residents varies depending on team performance and a constellation of other factors that are peripheral to on-the-field success or failure. This truth means that when public officials choose to subsidize professional teams, they can have no assurance that they are building their communities' collective harmony or sense of pride, much less bringing substantial economic benefit to their cities. There is no reason to suppose that professional franchises possess a sure hand at constructing themselves as beloved icons. Most obviously, success on the court or playing field is uncertain. Furthermore, as our case studies demonstrate, franchise owners driven by the urge to increase revenues routinely threaten to relocate their teams unless their demands for public fiscal support are met, encourage land-acquisition policies that shut down popular neighborhood businesses and force the relocation of residential populations, and seek to monopolize the food and souvenir expenditures of their fans. To the degree that a sports franchise's hold on the hearts of its local fans is due to its behavior beyond the playing field, the contemporary era of professional sports may be most tellingly marked by the emotional gap that separates it from a time of individually and family-owned franchises with enduring ties to local communities.

Sports Development Projects and the Prospect of Surprising Outcomes

When municipalities sponsor or offer support for stadium development projects, the neighborhood impacts are very likely to be negative. The requisites for profitably mounting professional sports events—local traffic infrastructure permitting the periodic arrival and departure of thousands of fans, acres of parking, and the modern franchise's inclination to corral as much auxiliary fan spending as possible—yield facilities that do not, as a rule, fit comfortably within surrounding physical environments and may generate only inconsequential economic spillovers. Thus, it is far from surprising that of the three cases examined in this book, the Wrigley Field modernization, easily the least physically ambitious of these developments, has produced the most satisfactory neighborhood impacts. Yet even in the case of Wrigley Field, the equilibrium that seems to have been achieved in the last decade between the stadium and the neighborhood has rested, in large part, on the vigor of the ongoing dialogue between the franchise and the community and on the various measures taken by the City of Chicago and the Cubs organization to manage traffic, fans' street behavior, and so on. As a consequence, nighttime baseball in Lake View has not brought, as some predicted, declining property values or a blighting of the commercial and residential areas nearest the ballpark. Even as Lake View has absorbed an increasing volume of baseball-generated tourism, its local geographic structure and commercial make-up have shifted, so far producing an updated neighborhood ambiance that still serves local residents and merchants reasonably well while accommodating the rush of visitors during the warmer months, and now most evenings year-round.

But—as some local activists continue to fear—could Wrigley Field come to be too much of a good thing for Lake View? We cannot rule out that prospect. In recent seasons fan behavior inside Wrigley Field has become rowdier, and if such unruliness begins to spill out onto local streets, Lake View could lose its reputation as a spirited yet secure neighborhood. Or in coming years the Cubs franchise, anxious to accommodate larger numbers of automobile-borne fans, could attempt to increase parking adjacent to Wrigley Field and begin to erode the density of activity that makes the ballpark's immediate environment so vibrant.

Considered in light of the Wrigley Field/Lake View experience, the neighborhood impact of the United Center and the new Comiskey Park has been far less salutary. The United Center stands near the heart of a section of Chicago that is undergoing rapid transformation, but there is little evidence that the new sporting facility is the main source of the adjoining area's renaissance. From an architectural and urban planning standpoint, the United Center adds nothing to the Near West Side, and the Bulls and

Blackhawks owners have linked their local patronage to the agenda of a single neighborhood organization. It remains far from certain that the emergent, gentrifying Near West Side will have much room for its longstanding, largely minority population. If affordable-housing activists can apply sufficient pressure on the Chicago Housing Authority and private developers to ensure that presently low-income West Siders can maintain a foothold in the neighborhood, and if new commercial and holdover light-industrial concerns provide a reasonable level of job opportunity, then the new Near West Side may indeed become a stable mixed-income community. However, the latter prospect has little or nothing to do with the ongoing operations of the United Center and its home sports franchises. Ultimately, the fortunes of the Near West Side and its poorest residents will rest in the hands of dozens of commercial and residential investors, local activists, and city planners and other administrators who have the wherewithal to direct municipal resources into the neighborhood.

Viewed as a neighborhood investment, the new Comiskey Park has been an outright failure. Cut off by transportation infrastructure from the residential areas to its east and west, and having been built directly on the site of the small commercial district that once served the old White Sox home field, the new Comiskey Park contributes nothing to the neighborhood environment of Bridgeport and South Armour Square; nor has it provided a measurable economic stimulus to either area. And yet there are signs of life to be discerned near Comiskey Park. In the last decade some new residential investment has come to Bridgeport, in part because the growing Asian population is spilling over from the Chinatown area on its northern margin. To the east, across the Dan Ryan Expressway, the Chicago Housing Authority plans to raze the huge Robert Taylor Homes public housing complex, and the City of Chicago has built a new police headquarters just south of 35th Street. In short, new development is filling in some of the holes in this long-neglected section of the city, and if a sensible redevelopment plan can be devised, the Robert Taylor complex could become a far more humane residential environment than it has been in recent decades.

There is little likelihood that the new Comiskey Park will ever become a beloved neighborhood institution in the fashion of its predecessor. In the future, few if any Bill Veecks will run any major league sports franchises, and there is little reason to suppose that any future Chicago White Sox management will strive for the congenial franchise/neighborhood relations that marked the Veeck era. Nor is it likely that any future White Sox owners will come to their senses and lease out for commercial development a portion of the parking area north of the new Comiskey Park. Consequently, there is no way that Comiskey Park's physical isolation will be substantially reduced. Nevertheless, if recent trends in Comiskey Park–area private and public investment continue and bear the fruit of population increases, business start-ups, and reinvigorated street life, the rebirth of the ballpark's surroundings might enliven even the home of the White Sox.

Even in the face of the disturbing patterns we have documented—franchise-driven stadium development proposals that muster very little sensitivity for their neighborhood environments and decision-making processes that rarely take into account the interests of marginalized neighborhood populations—we do have cause to express a sliver of optimism. Sports development projects rarely save cities, or even their immediate neighborhoods, but vital neighborhoods and cities hold the promise of transforming even unremarkable sports palaces into places of wonder and excitement.

Appendix

Table I—Selected Corporate Ownership of Professional Sports Teams

Anaheim Angels (MLB)	Disney Corporation
Anaheim Mighty Ducks (NHL)	Disney Corporation
Atlanta Braves (MLB)	AOL Time Warner
Atlanta Hawks (NBA)	AOL Time Warner
Atlanta Thrashers (NHL)	AOL Time Warner
Chicago Cubs (MLB)	Tribune Company
Colorado Avalanche (NHL)	COMSAT Corporation
Colorado Rockies (MLB)	Coors
Denver Nuggets (NBA)	COMSAT Corporation
Detroit Red Wings (NHL)	Little Caesar Enterprises
Los Angeles Dodgers (MLB)	NewsCorp
Montreal Canadiens (NHL)	Molson
New York Knicks (NBA)	Cablevision Systems
New York Rangers (NHL)	Cablevision Systems
Philadelphia 76ers (NBA)	Comcast Corporation
Philadelphia Flyers (NHL)	Comcast Corporation
Phoenix Suns (NBA)	Pinnacle West Capital
Portland Trailblazers (NBA)	Microsoft
Orlando Magic (NBA)	Amway
St. Louis Blues (NHL)	Anheuser-Busch
Seattle Supersonics (NBA)	Ackerley Communications
Toronto Blue Jays (MLB)	Interbrew

Table 2—Team Relocations in the NFL, 1982–1997

1982	Oakland Raiders move to Los Angeles
1984	Baltimore Colts move to Indianapolis
1988	St. Louis Cardinals move to Phoenix
1995	Los Angeles Rams move to St. Louis
1995	Los Angeles Raiders move back to Oakland
1996	Cleveland Browns move to Baltimore
1997	Houston Oilers move to Nashville (after a two-year stopover in Memphis)

Table 3—Stadium Construction and Major Renovations in the NFL, 1992–2001

1992	Georgia Dome opened in Atlanta
1995	Jacksonville Municipal Stadium opened
1995	TransWorld Dome opened in St. Louis
1996	Ericsson Stadium opened in Charlotte
1996	Oakland Coliseum undergoes major expansion
1996	Louisiana Superdome expanded in New Orleans
1997	FedEx Field opened in suburban Maryland
1998	Qualcomm Stadium undergoes major renovations in San Diego
1998	PSINet Stadium opened in Baltimore
1998	Raymond James Stadium opened in Tampa
1999	Adelphia Coliseum opened in Nashville
1999	Cleveland Browns Stadium opened
2000	Paul Brown Stadium opened in Cincinnati
2001	Heinz Field opened in Pittsburgh
2001	Invesco Field at Mile High opened in Denver

Table 4—Population, Housing, and Economic Trends in Pontiac, Michigan

	Population	Housing Units	Median Home Value	Jobs in City	Jobless Rate
1970	85,279	26,810	15,000	63,910	11.2%
1976	79,778	——	——	——	12.8%
1990	71,166	26,593	36,000	56,308	14.9%
1996	——	——	——	55,246	9.6%

Sources: Southeast Michigan Council of Governments, Michigan Employment Security Commission, Accurate Appraisals & Realty, Inc.

Table 5—Job Trends Near Comiskey Park, 1991–1997

	ZIP CODE 60609		ZIP CODE 60616	
	Retail	Misc./All Other Services	Retail	Misc./All Other Services
3/91	2989	2108	3171	4330
3/92	3708	1947	2606	4611
3/93	3065	1882	3060	4808
3/94	2717	1831	2684	4225
3/95	2447	1996	2701	3815
3/96	2481	2136	3270	3849
3/97	2570	2419	3447	3499

Source: Illinois Dept. of Employment Security, *Where Workers Work*, April 1995, June 1996, and August 1998.

Table 6—Chicago White Sox Home Attendance and Won/Lost Records, 1989–1998

	Attendance	Won/Lost
1989	1,045,651	69-92
1990	2,002,359	94-68
1991	2,934,154	87-75
1992	2,681,156	86-76
1993	2,581,091	94-68[a]
1994	1,697,398	67-46[b]
1995	1,609,773	68-76[c]
1996	1,676,416	85-77
1997	1,865,222	80-81
1998	1,391,146	80-82

[a]won division championship

[b]season interrupted by players' strike

[c]players' strike delayed beginning of season

Source: <http://www.chicagosportsweekly.com>, accessed on August 25, 1999.

Table 7—White Sox Fiscal Performance, 1990–1993 (in millions of dollars)

	Gate Revenues[a]	Media Revenues	Stadium Revenues	Total Revenues
1990	16.2	24.2	6.4	49.0
1991	27.5	25.7	19.3	78.0
1992	28.3	26.2	18.0	77.9
1993	28.1	26.2	21.8	78.8

[a] both home and away

Source: *Financial World*, "Valuation of Professional Sports Franchises," July 9, 1991; July 7, 1992; May 25, 1993; May 10, 1994.

Table 8—Reactions to the Prospect of the Cubs Installing Lights at Wrigley Field

Residents' Distance from Ballpark	In Favor	Opposed	No Opinion
Less than one-half mile	32	52	16
One-half mile to one mile	33	36	31
More than one mile (but within city)	49	22	29

Source: Economic Development Commission of the City of Chicago, *Public Opinion Poll on the Installation of Lights at Wrigley Field*, September 1987.

Table 9—Near West Side Residential Lending

	Number of Loans	Dollar Value
1985	224	12,119,000
1986	186	13,503,000
1987	198	14,123,000
1988	236	23,083,000
1989	266	27,659,000
1990	233	26,405,000
1991	244	36,503,000
1992	380	67,909,000
1993	508	67,998,000
1994	387	57,404,000
1995	341	36,766,000
1996	647	89,023,000
1997	812	119,618,000
1998	1,309	202,583,000

Source: The Woodstock Institute, *Community Lending Fact Books,* 1987–2000.

Bibliography

Abbot, Elizabeth. 1997. "New Luster in Providence Jewelry District." *New York Times,* January 26.

Ahmed-Ullah, Noreen S. 2000. "Protesters Decry UIC's Plans for Maxwell St. Area." *Chicago Tribune,* February 28.

Allen, J. Linn, and Cindy Richards. 1999. "Making No Plans." *Chicago Tribune,* February 9.

Associated Press. 1995a. "Proposal for New Denver Stadium Likely to Hinge on Sales-Tax Extension," Denver, Col., November 7.

———. 1995b. "Silverdome Negotiations Take a Nasty Turn," Pontiac, Mich., May 15.

Atlas, James. 1996. "The Daleys of Chicago." *New York Times Magazine,* August 25, pp. 37–39, 52–58.

Atre, Tushar, Kristine Auns, Kurt Badenhausen, Kevin McAulliffe, Christopher Nikolov, and Michael K. Ozanian. 1996. "The High Stakes Game of Team Ownership." *Financial World,* May 20, pp. 49–64.

Baade, Robert, A. 1987. "Is There an Economic Rationale for Subsidizing Sport Stadiums?" Heartland Policy Study No. 13. Chicago, Ill.: The Heartland Institute.

———. 1996a. "Professional Sports as Catalysts for Metropolitan Economic Development." *Journal of Urban Affairs* 18 (no. 1):1–17.

———. 1996b. "Stadium Subsidies Make Little Economic Sense for Cities: A Rejoinder." *Journal of Urban Affairs* 18 (no. 1):33–38.

Baade, Robert A., and Richard F. Dye. 1990. "The Impact of Stadiums and Professional Sports on Metropolitan Area Development." *Growth and Change* 21 (no. 2): 1–14.

Baade, Robert A., and Allen R. Sanderson. 1997. "Bearing Down in Chicago." Pp. 324–54 in *Sports, Jobs, and Taxes: The Economic Impact of Sports Teams and Stadiums,* ed. Roger G. Noll and Andrew Zimbalist. Washington, D.C.: Brookings Institution Press.

Bachrach, Peter, and Morton S. Baratz. 1962. "The Two Faces of Power." *American Political Science Review* 56 (no. 4):947–52.

Badenhausen, Kurt, and Christopher Nikolov. 1997. "More Than a Game." *Financial World,* June 17, pp. 40–50.

Baim, Dean V. 1990. "Sports Stadiums as 'Wise Investments': An Evaluation." Heartland Policy Study No. 32. Chicago, Ill.: The Heartland Institute.

———. 1994. *The Sports Stadium as a Municipal Investment.* Westport, Conn.: Greenwood Press.

Bartlett, Sarah. 1992. "A Tax Boon, Or Boondoggle?" *New York Times,* March 1.

Beauregard, Robert A. 1993. *Voices of Decline: The Postwar Fate of U.S. Cities.* Cambridge, Mass.: Blackwell.

———. 1998. "Tourism and Economic Development Policy in U.S. Urban Areas." Pp. 220–34 in *The Economic Geography of the Tourist Industry,* ed. Dimitri Ioannides and Keith G. Debbage. London: Routledge.

Becker, T. J. 1994. "All in Fun." *Chicago Tribune,* January 2.

Bennett, Larry. 1993. "Harold Washington and the Black Urban Regime." *Urban Affairs Quarterly* 28 (March):423–40.

———. 1997. *Neighborhood Politics: Chicago and Sheffield.* New York: Garland.

———. 1999. "Restructuring the Neighborhood: Public Housing Redevelopment and Neighborhood Dynamics in Chicago." Paper presented at the annual meeting of the Urban Affairs Association, Louisville, Ky.

Bess, Philip. 1988a. Letter to Ronald Labinski, HOK Sports Facilities Group, April 7. Authors' collection.

———. 1988b. Letter to Jerry Reinsdorf and Eddie Einhorn, June 28. Authors' collection.

———. 1989. *City Baseball Magic: Plain Talk and Uncommon Sense about Cities and Baseball Parks.* Madison, Wis.: Minneapolis Review of Baseball.

Bessone, Lisa Twyman. 1992. "Power Play." *Chicago,* January, pp. 89–93, 122–24.

Bissinger, Buzz. 1997. *A Prayer for the City.* New York: Random House.

Botts, Paul. 1988. "A New Old Ballpark." *The Reader,* June 3, pp. 8–9, 35–38.

Braccidiferro, Gail. 1994. "For Providence, a New Convention Center." *New York Times,* February 20.

Braden, Bill. 1988. "Day-by-Day Account of Night Lights Battle." *Chicago Sun-Times,* August 8.

Bremner, Brian. 1986. "Money and Market Will Keep Sox in Area." *Crain's Chicago Business,* July 14, pp. 1, 78

Briggs, Michael, and Charles N. Wheeler III. 1986. "Sox, Arlington Win a Twin Bill." *Chicago Sun-Times,* December 6.

Bukowski, Douglas. 1987. "A Real National Monument to Baseball: Comiskey Park." *Chicago Tribune,* July 29.

Bukowski, Douglas, Mary O'Connell, and John Aranza. 1987. *Comiskey Park: A Landmark Proposal.* Chicago: Save Our Sox. Authors' collection.

Butler, Sheneather Y. 1987. Letter to the Honorable Harold Washington, July 9. Neighborhood and Economic Development Policy Papers, 1982–1989, Chicago Historical Society.

Buursma, Bruce. 1989. "Giants Ballpark Vote Goes Extra Innings." *Chicago Tribune,* November 8.

Cappo, Joe. 1985. "Trib Facing No-Winner: Lights in Wrigley Field." *Crain's Chicago Business,* April 1.

Caraley, Demetrios. 1992. "Washington Abandons the Cities." *Political Science Quarterly* 107 (no. 1):1–30.

Cattau, Daniel. 1991. "Baseball Strikes Out with Black Fans." *The Chicago Reporter,* April, pp. 1, 6–9, 13.

Challos, Courtney. 2001. "Parks Group Urging City to Ax Plan for Soldier Field." *Chicago Tribune,* February 9.

Chanen, Jill Schachner. 1996. "Preserving Wrigley Field's Neighborhood." *New York Times,* July 28.

Chernick, Howard, and Andrew Reschovsky. 1997. "Urban Fiscal Problems: Coordinating Actions among Governments." Pp. 131–76 in *The Urban Crisis: Linking Research to Action,* ed. Burton Weisbrod and James Worthy. Evanston, Ill.: Northwestern University Press, pp. 131–76.

Chicago Cubs. 1985a. *Chicago Cubs, General Public Survey.* Chicago: Market Facts. Authors' collection.

———. 1985b. *Chicago Cubs, Neighborhood Residents Survey.* Chicago: Market Facts. Authors' collection.

Chicago Fact Book Consortium. 1984. *Local Community Fact Book, Chicago Metropolitan Area, 1980.* Chicago: Chicago Review Press.

———. 1995. *Local Community Fact Book, Chicago Metropolitan Area, 1990.* Chicago: Academy Chicago Publishers.

Chicago Sun-Times. 2000. "Bring Back McCuddy's." April 17.

Chicago Tribune. 1986. "Indiana Is Making a Wild Pitch." November 4.

———. 1987a. "Cubs' Lights Approved in House." June 18.

———. 1987b. "Wrigley Field Lights." June 30.

———. 1988a. "Cubs Lights, Political Lightweights." February 10.

———. 1988b. "A Puzzling Rebuff to the White Sox." May 11.

———. 1988c. "Wrigley Lights Chronology." August 8.

———. 1991. "Comiskey II: No Walk in the Park." April 17.

———. 2001. "A Smarter Stadium for the Bears." August 22.

Christian, Shirley. 1996. "Kansas City Rediscovers Its Downtown." *New York Times,* October 6.

City of Chicago. 1984. *"Chicago Works Together" 1984 Chicago Economic Development Plan.* Chicago: City of Chicago.

Clarke, Susan E., and Gary L. Gaile. 1992. "The Next Wave: Postfederal Local Economic Development Strategies." *Economic Development Quarterly* 6 (May):187–98.

———. 1998. *The Work of Cities.* Minneapolis: University of Minnesota Press.

Clavel, Pierre, and Wim Wiewel, eds. 1991. *Harold Washington and the Neighborhoods: Progressive City Government in Chicago, 1983–1987.* New Brunswick, N.J.: Rutgers University Press.

Colclough, William G., Lawrence A. Daellenbach, and Keith Sherony, 1994. "Estimating the Economic Impact of a Minor League Baseball Stadium." *Managerial and Decision Economics* 15 (no. 5):497–502.

"Constitutional Law: Cubs Lose on Justice Ward's Error." 1987. *Loyola Entertainment Law Journal* 7:371–84.

Conway, William G. 1977. "The Case against Urban Dinosaurs." *Saturday Review,* May 14, pp. 12–14.

Coopers and Lybrand. 1995. "New Multi-Purpose Minor League Baseball Stadium Study." Commissioned by the City of Austin, Tex. Authors' collection.

Crain's Chicago Business. 1985. "Yes, Lights at Wrigley Field." June 24, p. 10.

Crenson, Matthew A. 1971. *The Un-Politics of Air Pollution.* Baltimore: Johns Hopkins Press.

Cronon, William. 1991. *Nature's Metropolis: Chicago and the Great West*. New York: Norton.

Dahl, Robert A. 1961. *Who Governs?* New Haven, Conn.: Yale University Press.

Danielson, Michael N. 1997. *Home Team: Professional Sports and the American Metropolis*. Princeton, N.J.: Princeton University Press.

Davidson, Joe. 1992. "An Enterprise Zone Just Grows and Grows around Louisville, Ky." *Wall Street Journal*, August 26.

Davis, John Emmeus. 1991. *Contested Ground: Collective Action and the Urban Neighborhood*. Ithaca, N.Y.: Cornell University Press.

Davis, Robert. 1989. "Wreckers Leave McCuddy's Down and Out on 35th St." *Chicago Tribune*, March 28.

———. 1992. "$2 Million Seed Money Behind 'Holistic' Rebirth of West Side." *Chicago Tribune*, June 10.

Deacon, Mike. 1996. "Friendly Confines Forever?" *Daily Southtown*, August 18.

Department of Economic Development, City of Chicago. 1986. *The Impact of a Major League Baseball Team on the Local Economy*. Chicago: City of Chicago.

Devall, Cheryl. 1988. "Sox, Residents Not Ready to Play Ball." *Chicago Tribune*, July 11.

Devall, Cheryl, and Tim Franklin. 1988. "Bears Plan Gets Cool Reception." *Chicago Tribune*, June 15.

Diesenhouse, Susan. 1990. "Boston's North Station: Neighborhood in Transition." *New York Times*, February 11.

———. 1991. "Boston and Builders: The Shoe Is on the Other Foot." *New York Times*, February 10.

———. 1995. "Office Buildings Revive on Boston Harbor." *New York Times*, March 12.

DiGaetano, Alan, and John S. Klemanski. 1999. *Power and City Governance: Comparative Perspectives on Urban Development*. Minneapolis: University of Minnesota Press.

Donato, Marla. 2001. "Wrigley Neighbors Have Say." *Chicago Tribune*, July 12.

Dreier, Peter. 1997. "The New Politics of Housing: How to Rebuild the Constituency for a Progressive Federal Housing Policy." *Journal of the American Planning Association* 63 (Winter):5–27.

Economic Development Commission of the City of Chicago. 1987. *Public Opinion Poll on the Installation of Lights at Wrigley Field*. Report prepared for the commission by Elrick and Lavidge. Authors' collection.

Eisinger, Peter K. 1988. *The Rise of the Entrepreneurial State*. Madison: University of Wisconsin Press.

———. 1998. "City Politics in an Era of Federal Devolution." *Urban Affairs Review* 33 (January):308–25.

Elie, Steven J. 1986. "Joy in Wrigleyville? The Mighty Cubs Strike Out in Court." *Comm/Ent, Hastings Journal of Communications and Entertainment Law* 8:289–300.

Euchner, Charles C. 1993. *Playing the Field: Why Sport Teams Move and Cities Fight to Keep Them*. Baltimore: Johns Hopkins University Press.

Fainstein, Norman I., and Susan S. Fainstein. 1974. *Urban Political Movements: The Search for Power by Minority Groups in American Cities*. Englewood Cliffs, N.J.: Prentice-Hall.

Fainstein, Susan S. 1991. "Promoting Economic Development: Urban Planning in the United States and Great Britain." *Journal of the American Planning Association* 57 (Winter):22–33.

Fainstein, Susan S., and Clifford Hirst. 1997. "Neighborhood Organizations and Community Planning: The Minneapolis Neighborhood Revitalization Program." Pp. 96–111 in *Revitalizing Urban Neighborhoods*, ed. W. Dennis Keating, Norman Krumholz, and Philip Star. Lawrence: University Press of Kansas.

Farber, David. 1988. *Chicago '68.* Chicago: University of Chicago Press.

Ferman, Barbara. 1996. *Challenging the Growth Machine: Neighborhood Politics in Chicago and Pittsburgh.* Lawrence: University Press of Kansas.

Fishman, Robert. 1998. "Philadelphia Tries Everything." *New York Times Book Review,* January 11, pp. 9–10.

Fitzpatrick, Tom. 1986. "Reinsdorf Takes His Pitch to Addison." *Chicago Sun-Times,* July 11.

Flaherty, Roger. 1970. "LVCC Asks Police Probe." *The Booster,* November 11.

Fleming, Richard C. D. 2000. "The Rams, Like the St. Louis Region, Took a While to Turn Around." *St. Louis Post-Dispatch,* February 28.

Ford, Liam. 2001a. "2nd Suit Filed over Soldier Field Plan." *Chicago Tribune,* August 14.

———. 2001b. "Soldier Field Revamp Leaps onto Fast Track." *Chicago Tribune,* July 12.

Frieden, Bernard J., and Lynne B. Sagalyn. 1989. *Downtown, Inc.: How America Rebuilds Cities.* Cambridge, Mass.: MIT Press.

Garza, Melita Marie. 1999. "Daley Looks to Experience for New CHA Board." *Chicago Tribune,* June 23.

———. 2000. "CHA To Be Torn Up, Rebuilt." *Chicago Tribune,* February 6.

Gelfand, Mark I. 1975. *A Nation of Cities: The Federal Government and Urban America, 1933–1965.* New York: Oxford University Press.

George, John. 1989. "Assessing Sports Teams' Financial Impact." *Philadelphia Business Journal* 8 (no. 31):5.

Gershman, Michael. 1993. *Diamonds: The Evolution of the Ballpark.* Boston: Houghton-Mifflin.

Gibbons, Tom. 1986. "Other Cities Eye Sox." *Chicago Sun-Times,* July 9.

Gibson, Ray. 1985. "3-Stadium Plan Being Studied," *Chicago Tribune,* July 3.

———. 1995. "Daley Campaign Fund Towers over Burris'." *Chicago Tribune,* March 21.

Gierzynski, Anthony, Paul Kleppner, and James Lewis. 1996. "The Price of Democracy: Financing Chicago's 1995 City Elections." Chicago Urban League and Office for Social Policy Research, Northern Illinois University.

Gittell, Ross J. 1992. *Renewing Cities.* Princeton, N.J.: Princeton University Press.

Goetz, Edward G. 1993. *Shelter Burden: Local Politics and Progressive Housing Policy.* Philadelphia: Temple University Press.

Goldberger, Paul. 1990. "Comiskey: No Field of Dreams, But a Real Park in a Gritty City." *New York Times,* September 30.

Golden, Harry, Jr. 1986. "Mayor Pushes Sports Palace." *Chicago Sun-Times,* April 24, 1986, pp. 1, 4.

Goodyear, Sara Jane. 1969. "Pickets Hit Construction of Buildings." *Chicago Tribune,* October 5.

Goozner, Merrill. 1986. "In Play: Why Sox Future Rests with Pols." *Crain's Chicago Business,* July 14, pp. 1, 80.

Gottdiener, Mark. 1994. *The New Urban Sociology.* New York: McGraw-Hill.

Greenstein, Teddy. 2001. "'Viable' Park Vital to Team." *Chicago Tribune,* September 11.

Grenesko, Donald. 1987. Letter to the Honorable Harold Washington, January 21. Neighborhood and Economic Development Policy Papers, 1982–1989, Chicago Historical Society.

Grimshaw, William. 1992. *Bitter Fruit: Black Politics and the Chicago Machine, 1931–1991.* Chicago: University of Chicago Press.

Gunther, Marc. 1997. "They All Want to Be Like Mike." *Fortune,* July 21, pp. 51–53.

Hanania, Ray, and Fran Spielman. 1988. "Lights Out?" *Chicago Sun-Times,* February 11.

Hardcastle, James. 1994. "For Norfolk, a Downtown Regional Mall." *New York Times,* September 18.

———. 1997. "A New Life for an Old Richmond District." *New York Times,* May 18.

Harmon, Brian, and Gary Heinlein. 1996. "Silverdome: Sell Stadium or Raze It, Some Say." *Detroit News,* August 22.

Hayner, Don. 1990. "Memories, by the Decade." *Chicago Sun-Times,* September 28, Comiskey Park 1910–1990 supplement.

Heinlein, Gary. 1996. "New Lions Stadium Scores Big with Voters." *Detroit News,* November 6.

Hersh, Phil. 1986. "Comiskey Park Bears Skid Mark of White Flight." *Chicago Tribune,* July 13.

Heuer, Robert. 1985. "Neighbors." *The Reader,* April 12, pp. 11, 24–32.

Hinz, Greg. 1975. "Lakefront Downzoning Passed by City Council." *The Booster,* May 10.

Hirsley, Michael, and Gary Washburn. 2001. "Team Wants More Night Games, Bleacher Seats." *Chicago Tribune,* June 19.

Holcomb, Briavel. 1993. "Revisioning Place: De- and Re-constructing the Image of the Industrial City," Pp. 133–43 in *Selling Places: The City as Cultural Capital, Past and Present,* ed. Gerry Kearns and Chris Philo. Oxford: Pergamon Press, pp. 133–43.

Holli, Melvin G. 1995. "Jane M. Byrne: To Think the Unthinkable and Do the Undoable." Pp. 168–78 in *The Mayors: The Chicago Political Tradition,* ed. Paul M. Green and Melvin G. Holli. Carbondale: Southern Illinois University Press.

Hornung, Mark. 1987. "What's Behind the Fight over Sox Park: Minority Contracts." *Crain's Chicago Business,* August 17, pp. 1, 46.

———. 1988. "What's Behind Advisers' Stadium Bickering." *Crain's Chicago Business,* December 5, pp. 3, 48.

Hudnut, William. 1995. "It's the Economy, Not Just the Game." *Chicago Tribune,* September 3.

Hunter, Floyd. 1953. *Community Power Structure.* Chapel Hill: University of North Carolina Press.

Hunter, William, J. 1989. "Economic Impact Studies: Inaccurate, Misleading and Unnecessary." *Site Selection and Industrial Development* 34 (August):10–16.

Hurt, Suzanne E. 1988. "Wrigley Lights Hearings to Be Continued." *Inside Lincoln Park,* January 27.

Huxtable, Ada Louise. 1992. "Inventing American Reality." *New York Review of Books,* December 3, pp. 24–29.

Interfaith Organizing Project. 1992. *The New "Westside Story".* Report prepared by the Interfaith Organizing Project, Chicago, Ill. Authors' collection.

Iverson, Doug. 1992. "Courting Conventions." *Pioneer Press* (St. Paul, Minn.), October 12, pp. 1E, 3E.

Jacobs, Jane. 1961. *The Death and Life of Great American Cities.* New York: Vintage.

Jamison, Pat. 1987. "Don't Build, Just Fix Comiskey, Group Says." *Chicago Tribune,* November 20.

Jenkins, Jerome R., and Richard W. Lewis. 1982. "Queensgate II and 'the Movement': A View from the Community." Pp. 105–21 in *The Planning Partnership: Participants' View of Urban Renewal,* ed. Zane L. Miller and Thomas H. Jenkins. Beverly Hills, Calif.: Sage, pp. 105–21.

Johnson, Arthur T. 1993. *Minor League Baseball and Local Economic Development.* Urbana, Ill.: University of Illinois Press.

Johnson, Arthur T., and James H. Frey. 1986. *Government and Sport: The Public Policy Issues.* Totowa, N.J.: Rowman and Allenheld.

Johnson, Bill. 1996. "Stadium Deal Speaks Loudly about Team Commitment." *Detroit News,* August 23.

Johnson, Roy S. 1997. "Take Me Out to the Boardroom." *Fortune,* July 21, pp. 42–47.

Jones, Tim. 1996. "No Silver Lining for Pontiac's Dome." *Chicago Tribune,* November 24.

Joravsky, Ben. 1987. "Comiskey Neighbors Organize for Survival." *The Neighborhood Works,* November/December, pp. 1, 15–17.

———. 1988. "The Stadium Game: Who Loses if the White Sox Win?" *The Reader,* April 22, pp. 3, 43.

———. 1989. "Lights and Liquor: Wrigleyville Residents Are Losing the Power of the Beer Ban." *The Reader,* July 14, p. 3.

———. 1991. "The McCuddy's Mess: Big Jim Opens Big Mouth, Tavern Owners Get Big Shaft." *The Reader,* May 3, pp. 3, 40.

———. 1995. "Working for Peanuts." *The Reader,* October 13, pp. 5–6.

———. 1996. "Reinsdorf's Secret Weapon." *The Reader,* September 20, pp. 1, 18–23.

———. 2001. "Soldiering On." *The Reader,* July 20, pp. 5–9.

Judd, Dennis R., and Susan S. Fainstein, eds. 1999. *The Tourist City.* New Haven, Conn.: Yale University Press.

Judd, Dennis R., and Todd Swanstrom. 1998. *City Politics: Private Power and Public Policy.* New York: Longman.

Kahn, Roger. 1971. *The Boys of Summer.* New York: Harper & Row.

Kallenberg, Gregory. 1995. "Creating an Urban Dallas Neighborhood." *New York Times,* July 16.

———. 1996. "For Downtown Ft. Worth, A Family Affair." *New York Times,* May 19.

Kamin, Blair. 1994. "Context Sport." *Chicago Tribune,* May 8, s. 13, pp. 20–21.

———. 1996. "The Big Fix." *Chicago Tribune Magazine,* August 4, pp. 13–18.

———. 2001a. "The Monstrosity of the Midway." *Chicago Tribune,* June 11.

———. 2001b. "Soldier Field Plan: On Further Review, the Play Stinks." *Chicago Tribune,* April 5.

Kaplan, David A., and Patricia King. 1996. "City Slickers." *Newsweek*, November 11, pp. 28–35.

Karwath, Rob, and Katherine Seigenthaler. 1988. "Mayor Says Sox Bond Request Will Be Met." *Chicago Tribune*, December 14.

Kass, John. 1988a. "City Facing a Final At-Bat." *Chicago Tribune*, May 1.

———. 1988b. "Despite Agreement, White Sox Aren't Safe at Home Just Yet." *Chicago Tribune*, July 3.

———. 1988c. "Plea from McCuddy's Strikes Out." *Chicago Tribune*, October 8.

———. 1988d. "Sox May Pick Up Some Heavy Hitters." *Chicago Tribune*, June 10.

———. 1988e. "Sox Stadium Foes Offered Homes, Jobs." *Chicago Tribune*, July 7.

———. 1988f. "Thompson Jumps into Sox Stadium Fray." *Chicago Tribune*, May 3.

Kass, John, and Kerry Luft. 1988. "Sox Neighbors Agree to Stadium Deal." *Chicago Tribune*, August 4.

Keegan, Anne. 1982. "Residents Going to Bat for Wrigleyville." *Chicago Tribune*, April 23.

Keyes, Langley Carleton, Jr. 1969. *The Rehabilitation Planning Game: A Study in the Diversity of Neighborhood.* Cambridge, Mass.: MIT Press.

Kirk, Margaret O. 1995. "Putting Pizazz in Downtown Philadelphia." *New York Times*, November 26.

Klein, Frederick C. 1987. "On Sports: One Man's Model Ballpark." *The Wall Street Journal*, July 24.

Kleppner, Paul. 1985. *Chicago Divided: The Making of a Black Mayor.* DeKalb: Northern Illinois University Press.

Kopytoff, Verne G. 1996. "A New, Dazzling Las Vegas Downtown." *New York Times*, January 28.

Kotler, Philip, Donald H. Haider, and Irving Rein. 1993. *Marketing Places: Attracting Investment, Industry, and Tourism to Cities, States, and Nations.* New York: The Free Press.

Krallitsch, Peter. 1986. Letter to Jerry Reinsdorf, March 21. Authors' collection.

Kramer, Staci. D. 1995. "Spirit of St. Louis Takes Off with the Rams." *Chicago Tribune*, September 24.

Lake View Task Force. 1987. "Interim Report to Mayor Washington," September 11. Neighborhood and Economic Development Policy Papers, 1982–1989, Chicago Historical Society.

Laramore, Dorothy, et al. v. *Illinois Sports Facilities Authority et al.* 1989a. Complaint for Declaratory Judgment, February 9.

———. 1989b. Deposition of Robert Mier. November 6.

———. 1992a. Deposition of Maria Choca. March 26.

———. 1992b. Deposition of Thomas A. Reynolds. March 27.

———. 1992c. Deposition of Timothy W. Wright III. January 22.

———. 1996. Memorandum Opinion and Order, April 1, 1996. WL 153672 (N.D.Ill.).

Lash, Scott, and John Urry. 1994. *Economies of Signs and Space.* London: Sage.

Lefebvre, Henri. 1995. *Writings on Cities.* Oxford: Blackwell.

Levine, Marc V. 1987. "Downtown Redevelopment as an Urban Growth Strategy: A Critical Appraisal of the Baltimore Renaissance." *Journal of Urban Affairs* 9 (no. 2):103–23.

Levins, Harry. 2000. "St. Louis Shares in the Celebrity and Bounty of an Uncertain World." *St. Louis Post-Dispatch,* January 1.

Lipsky, Michael. 1970. *Protest in City Politics.* Chicago: Rand McNally.

"Living in Greater Chicago: The Buyers and Renters Guide!" 1997. Spring/Summer Edition. Chicago: GAMS Publishing, p. A5.

Long, Ray, and Douglas Holt. 2000. "Bears Win the Big One." *Chicago Tribune,* December 1.

Longworth, R. C. 1981. "Fewer Firms, Fewer Jobs, Less Revenue." *Chicago Tribune,* May 11.

———. 1994. "Maxwell Street Teardown Begins." *Chicago Tribune,* August 16.

Lorinc, John. 2000. "The City That Really Works." *Toronto Life,* September, pp. 72–84.

Lowe, Frederick. 1973. "Lake View Council to Mark Birthday." *Chicago Tribune,* May 17.

Ludgin, Mary K., and Louis H. Masotti. 1985. *Downtown Development: Chicago, 1979–1984.* Center for Urban Affairs and Policy Research, Northwestern University, Evanston, Ill.

———. 1986. *Downtown Development: Chicago, 1985–1986.* Center for Urban Affairs and Policy Research, Northwestern University, Evanston, Ill.

Lutton, Linda. 1998. "Will Development Bury the Barrio?" *The Reader,* April 24, pp. 1, 18–30.

"LVCC Race Called Friendly." 1971. *The Booster,* May 19.

Mahtesian, Charles. 1994. "Major Problems for Minor League Towns." *Governing,* April, pp. 18–19.

Markus, Robert. 1981. "Sox Board OKs Reinsdorf, Einhorn Bid; Sale a Formality." *Chicago Tribune,* January 30.

Marx, Gary. 1997. "Opposition Brewing to UIC Expansion." *Chicago Tribune,* March 12.

"Mayor Daley, Conlisk Invited to LVCC Forum." 1969. *The Booster,* January 12.

McCarron, John. 1985a. "Mayor Gives Nod to Sox-Only Stadium Plan." *Chicago Tribune,* December 21.

———. 1985b. "Washington Goes to Bat for a Dome." *Chicago Tribune,* October 2.

———. 1986. "Bears Closing In on Lakefront Site." *Chicago Tribune,* December 19.

———. 1987a. "City 'Stadium Wars' Rage on 3 Fronts." *Chicago Tribune,* May 17.

———. 1987b. "Expert Offers His Dream Sox Stadium." *Chicago Tribune,* July 26.

———. 1987c. "Mayor's Stadium Hunters Won't Make Play Till after Election." *Chicago Tribune,* January 29.

———. 1987d. "Stadium Partnership Suggested." *Chicago Tribune,* May 26.

———. 1988a. "It Works: 'Maybe It's Time We Learned How to Get Cut In.'" *Chicago Tribune,* August 28.

———. 1988b. "Slum Owner's Brother Tries to Sack Bears Stadium." *Chicago Tribune,* August 29.

———. 1988c. "Stadium Moguls Go One-on-One." *Chicago Tribune,* October 16.

———. 1990a. "Cost Overruns for Sox Stadium at $10.5 Million." *Chicago Tribune,* December 14.

———. 1990b. "No One Beats Thompson in His Ballpark." *Chicago Tribune,* July 11.

McCarron, John, and Thomas M. Burton. 1986. "Are Teams Dealing in Bluffs to Up

City's Ante?" *Chicago Tribune*, March 23.

McCarron, John, and Daniel Egler. 1986. "Mayor Covered All Bases to Swing Sox Deal." *Chicago Tribune*, December 6.

———. 1987. "Thompson, Mayor End Feud over Sox Stadium." *Chicago Tribune*, October 23.

McCartney, Jim. 1996. "The Right Stadium Can Revitalize Area but Cleveland, Denver Examples Show Success Isn't Guaranteed." *Pioneer Press* (St. Paul, Minn.), November 17.

McCloud, John. 1996. "Berkeley Hopes Plant Erases Image." *New York Times*, September 29.

McCracken, David. 1989. "Joy in Cubville?" *Chicago Sun-Times*, September 29.

McCullom, Rod. 1992. "Playing Ball: West-Siders and Stadium Developers Make Up a New Set of Rules." *The Reader*, April 10, pp. 3, 34–35.

McNamee, Tom. 1988. "Sox Bosses' Losses . . ." *Chicago Sun-Times*, March 27.

McQuade, Walter. 1973. "Urban Renewal in Boston," in James Q. Wilson (ed.), *Urban Renewal: The Record and the Controversy*. Cambridge, Mass.: MIT Press, pp. 259–77.

McRoberts, Flynn. 1996. "Horner Housing Plan Has a Developer." *Chicago Tribune*, April 12.

Medoff, Peter, and Holly Sklar. 1994. *Streets of Hope: The Fall and Rise of an Urban Neighborhood*. Boston: South End Press.

Melaniphy and Associates. 1986. *Chicago Cubs Economic Impact Analysis*. Chicago: Melaniphy and Associates.

Mendell, David. 2001. "Landmark Panel Offers Bears Plan." *Chicago Tribune*, August 22.

Midwest Community Council. 1987. *Peoples Development Seminar Consensus Report*. Chicago, April 24. Neighborhood and Economic Development Policy Papers, 1982–1989, Chicago Historical Society.

Mier, Robert. 1987. Memo to Paul Karas, Brenda Gaines, Elizabeth Hollander et al., June 22. Neighborhood and Economic Development Policy Papers, 1982–1989, Chicago Historical Society.

Mier, Robert, and Al Johnson. 1987. Memo to Mayor Washington, April 14. Neighborhood and Economic Development Policy Papers, 1982–1989, Chicago Historical Society.

Mier, Robert, and Kari J. Moe. 1991. "Decentralized Development: From Theory to Practice." Pp. 64–99 in *Harold Washington and the Neighborhoods*, ed. Pierre Clavel and Wim Wiewel. New Brunswick, N.J.: Rutgers University Press.

Miles, Bruce. 1999. "MacPhail: Cubs a 'Middle' Team in Revenue Terms." *The Daily Herald*, March 1.

Mollenkopf, John Hull. 1983. *The Contested City*. Princeton, N.J.: Princeton University Press.

———. 1992. *A Phoenix in the Ashes: The Rise and Fall of the Koch Coalition in New York City Politics*. Princeton, N.J.: Princeton University Press.

Muschamp, Herbert. 1993. "42d Street Plan: Be Bold or Begone!" *New York Times*, September 19.

———. 1995. "A Wonder World in the Mile High City." *New York Times*, May 7.

———. 1998. "With the Spare, Sinewy Grace of the Athlete." *New York Times*, June 21.

Newman, M. L. 1959. "Sturdy Lake View Girds to Hold Own." *Chicago Daily News,* May 5.

Newman, Morris. 1996. "Hollywood Staging Its Rehabilitation." *New York Times,* April 28.

New York Times. 1997. "10 Residents Under Siege by Proposal for Big Mall." May 18.

Noll, Roger G., and Andrew Zimbalist, eds. 1997. *Sports, Jobs, and Taxes: The Economic Impact of Sports Teams and Stadiums.* Washington, D.C.: Brookings Institution Press.

Olson, Jim. 1975. "West LV Group May Quit LVCC." *The Booster,* February 12.

Orrick, Dave. 1998. "Decade Later, Wrigley Shines On." *Skyline,* July 2.

Osnos, Evan, and Rick Pearson. 2000. "Bears, City Say This May Be Real Deal for Soldier Field." *Chicago Tribune,* August 15.

Ozanian, Michael K. 1994. "The $11 Billion Pastime." *Financial World,* May 10, pp. 50–59.

———. 1995. "Suite Deals." *Financial World,* May 9, pp. 42–56.

Pagano, Michael A., and Ann O. Bowman. 1995. *Cityscapes and Capital: The Politics of Urban Development.* Baltimore: Johns Hopkins University Press.

Papajohn, George. 1986. "Sox Attract a Crowd of Naysayers in Addison." *Chicago Tribune,* July 16.

———. 1995. "No Bears? We'd be a City on the Fake." *Chicago Tribune,* August 13.

Pastier, John. 1989. "The Business of Baseball." *Inland Architect,* January/February, pp. 56–62.

Patterson, John. 2000. "Daley into Sox Hype, Can't Resist Cubs Swipe." *Daily Herald,* September 27.

Pelissero, John P., Beth M. Henschen, and Edward I. Sidlow. 1992. "The New Politics of Sports Policy Innovation in Chicago." Pp. 57–78 in *Politics of Policy Innovation in Chicago,* ed. Kenneth K. Wong. Greenwich, Conn.: JAI Press.

Pepper, John. 1996. "A 'Miraculous' Deal Gets Done." *Detroit News,* September 1.

Peterman, William. 2000. *Neighborhood Planning and Community-Based Development.* Thousand Oaks, Calif.: Sage.

Peterson, Paul E. 1981. *City Limits.* Chicago: University of Chicago Press.

Pierson, Don. 1999. "Warner Grasps Life, Opportunity." *Chicago Tribune,* December 22.

Pietrusza, David. 1993. *Lights On!* South Bend, Ind.: Diamond Communications.

Piven, Frances Fox. 1974. "The Great Society as Political Strategy." Pp. 271–83 in *The Politics of Turmoil,* Richard A. Cloward and Frances Fox Piven. New York: Pantheon, pp. 271–83.

Piven, Frances Fox, and Richard A. Cloward. 1979. *Poor People's Movements.* New York: Vintage.

Poe, Janita. 1995. "It's a 'United' Effort." *Chicago Tribune,* February 27.

———. 1996. "Might of 2 Men Helps Area Rebound." *Chicago Tribune,* August 9.

Pollack, Neal. 1998. "Wrecking Ball Blues." *The Reader,* April 10, pp. 12–15.

Polsby, Nelson W. 1980. *Community Power and Political Theory.* New Haven: Yale University Press.

Presecky, William, and Gabe Fuentes. 1985. "Sox Dome Is No Wild Pitch." *Chicago Tribune,* November 29.

Puls, Mark. 1998. "Lions Must Pay to Leave Dome." *Detroit News,* January 23.

Purdum, Todd S. 1997. "Sunny Forecast for Los Angeles Mayor." *New York Times,* March 9.

Quirk, James, and Rodney Fort. 1992. *Pay Dirt: The Business of Professional Team Sports.* Princeton, N.J.: Princeton University Press.

Rapoport, Ron. 1987. "Architect Socks Stadium Planners." *Chicago Sun-Times,* July 26.

Rast, Joel. 1999. *Remaking Chicago: The Political Origins of Urban Industrial Change.* DeKalb: Northern Illinois University Press.

Reardon, Patrick. 1991. "Stadium Agreement Has a Winning Look." *Chicago Tribune,* May 10.

———. 1993. "Daley Pushes Mixed-Income Housing with $228 Million Pledge." *Chicago Tribune,* October 12.

Redburn, Tom. 1994. "Increasingly, Derelict Factories Are Being Returned to Productive Use." *New York Times,* April 17.

Reed, J. D. 1974. "Louisiana Purchase: Superdome in New Orleans." *Sports Illustrated,* July 22, pp. 66–80.

Reich, Kenneth. 1989. "Pro Teams: A Big Value for Small Cities." *Los Angeles Times,* December 3.

Reichl, Alexander J. 1999. *Reconstructing Times Square: Politics and Culture in Urban Development.* Lawrence: University Press of Kansas.

Reidenbaugh, Lowell. 1987. *Take Me Out to the Ballgame.* St. Louis: Sporting News Publishing.

Ribadeneira, Tatiana W. 1997. "Moooove Over, Folks: Pubs, Parks, Art Changing Denver's Cow Town Image." *Chicago Tribune,* August 31.

Rivlin, Gary. 1993. *Fire on the Prairie: Harold Washington and the Politics of Race.* New York: Henry Holt.

Roberts, Edwin, Jr. 1995. "The Major Reason for Keeping the Bucs." *The Tampa Tribune,* January 8.

Rosen, George. 1980. *Decision-Making Chicago-Style: The Genesis of a University of Illinois Campus.* Urbana: University of Illinois Press.

Rosentraub, Mark S. 1988. "Public Investment in Private Business: The Professional Sports Mania." Pp. 71–96 in *Business Elites and Urban Development: Case Studies and Critical Perspectives,* ed. Scott Cummings. Albany: State University of New York Press.

———. 1997. *Major League Losers: The Real Cost of Sports and Who's Paying for It.* New York: HarperCollins.

Rosentraub, Mark S., David Swindell, Michael Przybylski, and Daniel Mullins. 1994. "Sport and Downtown Development Strategy: If You Build It, Will Jobs Come?" *Journal of Urban Affairs* 16 (no. 3):221–39.

Rylaw, Nancy. 1992: "Spiegel Picks Ohio Distribution Site." *Chicago Tribune,* September 24.

Scully, Gerald. 1989. *The Business of Major League Baseball.* Chicago: University of Chicago Press.

Shepherd, Richard F. 1996. "It Was the Pits. It'll Be Missed." *New York Times,* April 1.

Sherman, Ed. 1991a. "New Facility as Modern as Other Was Outdated." *Chicago Tribune,* April 17.

———. 1991b. "The Night the Bell Saved the Sox." *Chicago Tribune,* April 17.

Shlay, Ann B., and Robert P. Giloth. 1987. "The Social Organization of a Land-Based Elite: The Case of the Failed Chicago 1992 World's Fair." *Journal of Urban Affairs* 9 (no. 4):305–24.

Siewers, Alf. 1987. "Protesters Scout Winnetka." *Chicago Sun-Times,* May 4.

Simpson, Burney. 1996. "City Plots New West Side Story." *The Chicago Reporter,* December, pp. 1, 6–10.

Sites, William. 1994. "Public Action: New York City Policy and the Gentrification of the Lower East Side." Pp. 189–211 in *From Urban Village to East Village,* Janet L. Abu-Lughod et al. Cambridge, Mass.: Blackwell.

Skertic, Mark. 2000. "Raising a Glass for McCuddy's." *Chicago Sun-Times,* April 14.

Smith, Wes. 1986. "Comiskey Neighbors Have Own Game Plan." *Chicago Tribune,* December 7.

Smith, William. 1995. "Convention's Cash Impact Won't Be Huge, Pros Say." *Chicago Sun-Times,* December 31.

Sorkin, Michael, ed. 1992. *Variations on a Theme Park.* New York: Hill and Wang.

South Armour Square Focus Group. 1996. Transcript of resident discussion, recorded by researchers from the University of Illinois at Chicago, February 27. Authors' collection.

Spielman, Fran. 1987a. "Arena Backers Got Lesson From World's Fair Fiasco." *Chicago Sun-Times,* April 16.

———. 1987b. "Mayor on Lights: Somebody Has to 'Bleed.'" *Chicago Sun-Times,* November 5.

———. 1987c. "McCaskey Jabs Mayor on Stadium Site Retreat." *Chicago Sun-Times,* February 26.

———. 1987d. "Stadium Foes Boo Plans." *Chicago Sun-Times,* April 16.

———. 1987e. "West Siders Cool to Plan for Stadium." *Chicago Sun-Times,* April 22.

———. 1988. "Lights Ban May Force Move, Cubs Say Again." *Chicago Sun-Times,* January 26.

———. 1992. "W. Side Stadium Set," *Chicago Sun-Times,* March 5.

———. 2001. "Bleacher Bums Get Break at Wrigley." *Chicago Sun-Times,* June 19.

Spielman, Fran, and Harry Golden Jr. 1987a. "Big Problems Still Ahead for Bears Stadium." *Chicago Sun-Times,* June 9.

———. 1987b. "Residents Are Promised Role in Bears Plan." *Chicago Sun-Times,* April 15.

Spielman, Fran, and Ray Hanania. 1988a. "Electrifying!" *Chicago Sun-Times,* February 26.

———. 1988b. "Panel Lights Up Cubs." *Chicago Sun-Times,* February 24.

Squires, Gregory D., Larry Bennett, Kathleen McCourt, and Philip Nyden. 1987. *Chicago: Race, Class, and the Response to Urban Decline.* Philadelphia: Temple University Press.

Stanback, Howard, and Robert Mier. 1986–87. "Economic Development for Whom? The Chicago Model." *Review of Law and Social Change* 15 (no. 1):11–22.

Stoffel, Jennifer. 1991. "Countering Suburbs' Lure." *New York Times,* March 17.

Stone, Clarence N. 1982. "Social Stratification, Nondecisionmaking, and the Study of Community Power." *American Politics Quarterly* 10 (no. 3):275–302.

Strahler, Steve. 1986. "S. Side and DuPage: When Worlds Collide." *Crain's Chicago Business,* July 14, pp. 1, 79.

Strong, James. 1988. "Lights Pact for Wrigley Going Dim." *Chicago Tribune*, February 8.

Sussman, Lesley. 1970. "Board Race—A Close One." *The Booster*, May 20.

Swanson, Lorraine. 1994. "Neighbors Pining for Bygone Era." *Skyline*, April 4.

Tabak, Lawrence. 1994. "Wild about Convention Centers." *Atlantic Monthly*, April, pp. 28–34.

Teaford, Jon C. 1990. *The Rough Road to Renaissance*. Baltimore: Johns Hopkins University Press.

Ungar, Sanford J. 1977. "Chicago A. D. (After Daley)." *Atlantic Monthly*, March, pp. 4–18.

Vasquez, Beverly. 1997. "Bistros Complaint: Parking Pads Tabs." *The Denver Business Journal*, August 2, p. 3A.

Verdi, Bob. 1988. "Don't Blame Sox for Stadium Mess." *Chicago Tribune*, May 12.

Vidal, Avis C. 1992. *Rebuilding Communities: A National Study of Urban Community Development Corporations*. New York: Community Development Research Center, New School for Social Research.

Viuker, Steven J. 1992. "It's Boom Time for the Playing Fields across the Country." *New York Times*, October 25.

Voorhees Neighborhood Center. 1995. South Armour Square Neighborhood Coalition Redevelopment Project Report. Chicago: Nathalie P. Voorhees Neighborhood Center.

Wallace, David J. 1997a. "Hotel Projects Flourish in Philadelphia." *New York Times*, June 29.

———. 1997b. "Vacant Philadelphia Tower Casts Shadow." *New York Times*, February 9.

Warner, Sam Bass, Jr. 1972. *The Urban Wilderness*. New York: Harper & Row.

Washburn, Gary. 1998. "Daley Turns a Grabowski into Beauty." *Chicago Tribune*, October 6.

———. 1999. "Compromise Near on Fulton District." *Chicago Tribune*, October 22.

———. 2001a. "City Mulls More Night Games at Wrigley." *Chicago Tribune*. February 23.

———. 2001b. "Zoning Chief out of a Job." *Chicago Tribune*. September 11.

Washburn, Gary, and Ray Long. 2000. "$587 Million Stadium Rehab Will Need Legislative Assist." *Chicago Tribune*, November 16.

———. 2001. "Daley Hedges on Soldier Field." *Chicago Tribune*. September 26.

Washburn, Gary, and Andrew Martin. 1997. "Daley Springs to Defense of City's TIFs." *Chicago Tribune*, November 11.

Washburn, Gary, and Flynn McRoberts. 2000. "Daley Calls Comiskey Area Safe." *Chicago Tribune*, June 14.

Washburn, Gary, and David Mendell. 1999. "Battle of Fulton St. Market Pits Old against Nouveau." *Chicago Tribune*, October 7.

Washington, Harold, and Elizabeth Hollander. 1986. "Keeping the Cubs in Chicago: Business, Community, and Government Working Together," August 8. Neighborhood and Economic Development Policy Papers, 1982–1989, Chicago Historical Society.

Watson, Jerome. 1968. "Wrigley's a Fan of Court for Night Baseball Ruling." *Chicago Sun-Times*, April 27.

Wayne, Leslie. 1996. "Picking Up the Tab for Field of Dreams." *New York Times,* July 27.

Weicher, John C. 1974. *Urban Renewal: National Program for Local Problems.* Washington, D.C.: American Enterprise Institute.

"Welcome to Penn's Landing Online." 2001. Penn's Landing Corporation. Accessed September 27: <http://www.pennslandingcorp.com>.

West Side and Community Development Community Coordinating Committee. 1987. Meeting Minutes, August 13. Neighborhood and Economic Development Policy Papers, 1982–1989, Chicago Historical Society.

White, Byron P. 1996. "Housing Plan May Go Westward." *Chicago Tribune,* April 16.

Whitt, J. Allen. 1987. "Mozart in the Metropolis: The Arts Coalition and the Urban Growth Machine." *Urban Affairs Quarterly* 23 (September):15–36.

Whitt, J. Allen, and John C. Lammers. 1991. "The Art of Growth: Ties between Development Organizations and the Performing Arts." *Urban Affairs Quarterly* 26 (March):376–93.

Williams, Lance. 1997. "Sales Tax Source of Stadium Funding?" *Nando Times News.* Accessed October 18: <http://www.nando.net>.

Wilson, Terry. 1986. "West Siders Fear Home Loss." *Chicago Tribune,* September 26.

———. 1987. "Stadium Opponent's Move Fizzles." *Chicago Tribune,* April 23.

Woodstock Institute. 1996. *1994 Community Lending Fact Book.* Chicago: Woodstock Institute.

———. 1997. *1995 Community Lending Fact Book.* Chicago: Woodstock Institute.

———. 1998. *1996 Community Lending Fact Book.* Chicago: Woodstock Institute.

Working Assets. 1998. "A Moment with Earnest Gates." Newsletter of the Chicago Program of Local Initiatives Support Corporation, Fall. Authors' collection.

———. 2000. "New Homes for the Near West Side." Newsletter of the Chicago Program of Local Initiatives Support Corporation, Spring. Authors' collection.

Wright, Pat. 1989. "Tax Dollars Sacrificed at the Altar of Baseball." *The Neighborhood Works,* April/May, pp. 6–7, 24.

Zukin, Sharon. 1993. *Landscapes of Power: From Detroit to Disney World.* Berkeley: University of California Press.

———. 1995. *The Cultures of Cities.* Cambridge, Mass.: Blackwell.

Index

Addison, Ill., 66–67
Armour Field, 94–101
Austin, Tex., 21

Baade, Robert, 23–24
Bachrach, Peter, 172
Baltimore, Md., 15, 47, 58
Baratz, Morton S., 172
Bauer, Catherine, 37
Beauregard, Robert, 39, 40
Bennett, Marshall, 147
Bess, Philip, 78, 89, 94–101, 175–77
Bridgeport (Chicago), 59, 65, 78–81,
    100, 103, 169, 171, 174–75, 177,
    180, 184
Boston, Mass., 37, 39, 40–41, 44–45, 49,
    53–54, 56–57, 179–80
Boston Celtics, 179
Boston Red Sox, 179–80
Burnett, Walter, 159–60
Bynoe, Peter, 75, 106
Byrne, Jane, 64, 72, 166–67

Caraley, Demetrios, 38
Carter, Marcella, 80, 103
Chapman, James, 103–4
Chicago, Ill., 4–5, 13, 15, 22, 26, 28,
    31–36, 43, 46–47, 49, 51–52, 55–56;
    and the City of Leisure, 166–69; local
    political conditions in, 68–70,
    166–69; neighborhood mobilization
    and sports development projects in,
    172–76; and public support of local
    professional sports franchises,
    180–82; recent sports development

projects in, 5–10, 31–36
Chicago Bears, 5–9, 66, 73–74,
    143–53, 156, 169, 180, 182
Chicago Blackhawks, 153, 155, 184
Chicago Bulls, 153, 156, 180, 183
Chicago Central Area Committee
    (CCAC), 145
Chicago City Council, 115, 119–21,
    124, 128, 170
Chicago Cubs, 108–41; *Chicago Tri-
    bune* commentary on, 123–24;
    and economic impact studies,
    118; and ownership change,
    113; relocation plans of, 117–19
Chicago Stadium, 34, 153
Chicago Tribune, 121–24, 151–52,
    162, 171–72
Chicago White Sox, 59–107;
    Chicago Tribune commentary on,
    69–70; and Near South
    Side/South Loop stadium site,
    73–74; negotiations of, with Ad-
    dison, Ill., 66–67; negotiations
    of, with City of Chicago, 72–75;
    negotiations of, with St. Peters-
    burg, Fla., 67–71; and ownership
    change, 62–66; and State of In-
    diana, 68
Cincinnati, Ohio, 53
Citizens United for Baseball in Sun-
    shine (CUBS), 115, 120–21,
    127–30
City of Leisure, 56–58, 166–69
Clarke, Susan, 44
Cloward, Richard, 172

Comiskey, Charles, 60

Comiskey Park (new), 35, 68, 70, 75–82; local economic impact of, 79–81; reactions to, 77–79; and South Armour Square, 32–33, 173–74, 177, 184–85

Comiskey Park (old), 59–66; history of, 60–62; and national monument proposal, 92–94; as South Side Chicago institution, 91–92

community development corporations, 55–56

Coors Field (Denver, Colo.), 11–13

Corporate community partnerships, 176–79

Crain's Chicago Business, 117

Crosley Field, 110

Cullerton, John, 115, 122–23, 150

culture and urban growth, 14–17

Daley, Richard J., 51, 61, 166, 169

Daley, Richard M., 51–52, 55–56, 154, 157–58, 162–63, 171; pro-growth political regime of, 168–69

Dallas, Tex., 44, 49–50

Daniels, George, 162

Danielson, Michael, 169

Davis, John Emmeus, 53

Davis, Zachary Taylor, 60

deFlon, Rick, 79, 99

Democratic National Convention (1996), 158

Detroit Lions, 28–31

Detroit Pistons, 29

DiGaetano, Alan, 168

Ebbets Field, 11, 97, 180

economic development initiatives by state and local governments, 41–45; enterprise zones, 44; property tax-abatement, 42–43; special taxing districts, 44; support of private investment, 42–43, 45; Tax Increment Financing, 43–44

economic niche strategies, 46–48

Einhorn, Eddie, 62, 64–65, 67, 90

Eisinger, Peter, 42, 43

Euchner, Charles, 71, 169

Fainstein, Susan, 55, 174

Fenway Park, 11, 97, 180

Fishman, Robert, 51

Fleet Center, 19–20

Flint, Mich., 39–40

Flynn, Ray, 56

Fort Worth, Tex., 44

Frieden, Bernard, 57

Fulton County Stadium, 96

Gaile, Gary, 44

Gates, Earnest, 143, 151, 155, 161–64

Gershman, Michael, 78

Goldberger, Paul, 76

Gottdiener, Mark, 139

Green, Dallas, 115

Griffin, Arthur, 150–51

Giuliani, Rudolph, 51

Hanselmann, Sue, 129

Hansen, Bernard, 10, 115

Hellmuth, Obata, and Kassabaum, Inc., Sports Facilities (HOK), 76–77, 79, 97–99, 157

Hirst, Clifford, 174

Holcomb, Briavel, 46

Hudnut, William, 25–26

Hurst, Tex., 45

Illinois Sports Facilities Authority (ISFA), 59, 85, 87–89, 97, 105, 176

Indianapolis, Ind., 25–26

Interfaith Organizing Project, 149–53, 155

Jacobs, Jane, 41, 52

Jordan, Michael, 3, 66, 153, 155, 181

Kahn, Roger, 180

Kass, John, 105

Kendall, Paul, 135–36
Keyes, Langley Carleton, Jr., 53–54
Klemanski, John, 168

Lake View (Chicago), 33, 127–29,
    132–33; impact of nighttime
    baseball on, 133–41
Lake View Citizens Council
    (LVCC), 115, 120, 126–30
Lammers, John, 16–17
Laramore v. *ISFA*, 85, 87–88, 100,
    103–4
Lash, Scott, 17
Las Vegas, Nev., 48
Lefebvre, Henri, 16
Levin, Ellis, 115
Los Angeles, Calif., 21, 27, 47–48,
    50, 52
Louisville, Ky., 16, 44
Lowell, Mass., 47, 93

MacPhail, Andy, 10, 139–40
Masotti, Louis, 147
McCaskey, Michael, 145, 149, 151,
    153, 156, 182
McCuddy's Tavern, 85, 104–7
McDonough, John, 140
McQuade, Walter, 37
Metropolitan Chicago Stadium
    Joint Venture, 154
Mier, Robert, 75, 86, 118, 148, 167,
    170
Mollenkopf, John, 41, 43
Moore, Michael, 39

Nathalie P. Voorhees Neighborhood
    Center, 101
Near West Side (Chicago), 33–35,
    156–61; and proposed Bears Sta-
    dium, 146–49
Near West Side Community Devel-
    opment Corporation
    (NWSCDC), 151, 160–64
Newfeld, Charlotte, 131, 137, 176
New York, N.Y., 42, 45, 47–49, 51,
    139
New York Yankees, 105, 179

nighttime baseball, 110–13
Norfolk, Va., 45

Oakland, Calif., 26
O'Connell, Mary, 86, 90, 94
Orbach, Jerome, 115

Peterson, Paul, 165
Philadelphia, Pa., 15, 21–22, 45, 51
Philadelphia Gateway Project,
    48–49
Phillip, Pate, 67
Piven, Frances Fox, 172
Pizer, Howard, 155, 163, 174
place enhancement strategies,
    48–50
Pontiac (Michigan) Silverdome,
    28–31
professional sports franchises,
    17–28; corporate ownership of,
    18; and community building,
    25–28; as municipal icons,
    179–82; and municipal vitality,
    27–28; relocation threats by, 20

Quigley, Mike, 136

Radford-Hill, Sheila, 85, 103
Rast, Joel, 165
Reinsdorf, Jerry, 62, 64, 66–67, 90,
    153–56, 163
Rendell, Ed, 51
Richmond, Va., 43
Riordan, Richard, 50–52
Riverfront Stadium, 19, 96–97
Royals Stadium, 97
Rush, Bobby, 120, 123, 173
Rush-Presbyterian-St. Luke's Med-
    ical Center, 147
Ruth, Babe, 105–6

St. Louis, Mo., 25, 46, 181
St. Paul, Minn., 47
Sagalyn, Lynne, 57
San Francisco, Calif., 27–28, 41
Save Our Sox (SOS), 84, 86, 90–94
Sawyer, Eugene, 89, 120, 148

Shaw, Robert, 123
Shils, Edward, 21
Shurna, Ed, 149, 151
Sites, William, 45
Soldier Field, 5–9, 143–45, 169
South Armour Square, 32–33,
    84–85
South Armour Square Neighbor-
    hood Coalition (SASNC), 85–89,
    101–3; and Harold Washington,
    89
sports: as a culture industry, 17–18
sports-centered urban economic
    (re)development, 3–4, 50; and
    cultural institutions, 46–48; and
    image positioning, 46; and inner
    cities, 49
sports stadium development,
    18–25; direct and indirect eco-
    nomic benefits of, 21–22; and
    economic multipliers, 22–25; in-
    tangible benefits of, 22; and lo-
    cal economic decline, 29–31; po-
    litical economy of, 18–21; as
    sign of progressive municipal
    leadership, 27–28; and use of
    public funds, 18–21, 28
Suncoast Dome, Fla., 68

Tampa, Fla., 26
Taylor, Julie, 71
Teaford, Jon, 40
Thompson, James, 67–70, 106, 115
Three Rivers Stadium, 19
Tillman, Dorothy, 103

Toia, Sam, 130, 141
Toronto, Ontario, 58
Toronto Raptors, 18
Tribune Company, 113–14, 121–24

Ueberroth, Peter, 116
United Center, 36, 154, 156–61;
    and the Near West Side, 36,
    156–61, 174–75, 177–78, 183–84
urban renewal, 37–38, 40–41,
    52–54
Urry, John, 17

Veeck, Bill, 61, 180
Verdi, Bob, 69–70
Veterans Stadium, 19, 96

Ward, Wilma, 151
Washington, Harold, 68, 87, 89,
    120, 145, 148, 150, 167–68; pro-
    gressive municipal agenda of,
    72–75; and racial politics, 73–74,
    170–71
West Side Development Commit-
    tee, 148
Whitt, J. Allen, 15–17
Wirtz, William, 147, 149, 153–56
Wrigley Field, 9–10, 35–36, 108–41;
    and Lake View, 138–41, 172–74,
    176–77, 183; and Traffic Opera-
    tions Committee, 130–31
Wrigley, Philip K., 112–13, 122
Wrigley, William, 113

Zukin, Sharon, 16, 139